GENERAL THEORY OF THE PRECARIAT

GREAT RECESSION, REVOLUTION, REACTION

ALEX FOTI

Theory on Demand #25
General Theory of the Precariat

Alex Foti

Editorial support: Leonieke van Dipten
Copyediting: Max Hampshire
Cover design: Katja van Stiphout
Figures design: Mirko Bozzato
Design: Inte Gloerich
EPUB development: Inte Gloerich
Publisher: Institute of Network Cultures, Amsterdam, 2017
ISBN: 978-94-92302-18-2

Contact
Institute of Network Cultures
Phone: +31 205951865
Email: info@networkcultures.org
Web: http://www.networkcultures.org

This publication is available through various print on demand services and freely downloadable from http://networkcultures.org/publications

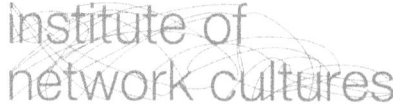

CONTENTS

To Rocco, the only good thing that happened in '16

The ultimate reason for all real crises always remains the poverty and restricted consumption of the masses.

Karl Marx, *Das Kapital*

When the rate of return on capital exceeds the rate of growth of output and income, as it did in the nineteenth century and seems quite likely to do again in the twenty-first, capitalism automatically generates arbitrary and unsustainable inequalities that radically undermine the meritocratic values on which democratic societies are based.

Thomas Piketty, *Capital in the Twenty-First Century*

These systems are failing.

Moby (2016)

ACKNOWLEDGEMENTS

This book has taken three years to complete, and made me painfully aware of my limitations as an intellectual. Trained in political economy and historical sociology, I thought I had it clear from the start. Yet the more I wrote, the more questions were raised by the text, and the more unsure I was as to how to properly answer them. I felt that my ignorance of philosophy, particularly queer theory and critical theory, made (and still makes) this essay woefully incomplete.

Politically, my theory predicts reformist, rather than revolutionary, outcomes of the present capitalist crisis, and this stands at odds with my anti-capitalist beliefs as an activist. However, the reformist way out of the Great Recession also seems fraught with unknowns. In essence, the fight of the precariat against oligarchy must be both expansionary and green. But how to reconcile the egalitarian priority with the ecological imperative? I wonder if I have dealt with this conundrum satisfactorily in the final chapter.

From this conundrum arises the thorniest of issues: class. Is the precariat its own class, or is it just the established working class under a new guise? It isn't a section of the working class, but is what labor has become. If the 21st century precariat is the equivalent of the 20th century proletariat, should it embrace communism as its revolutionary ideology? The short answer to this is: no.

We need to shed communism and go beyond anarchism because they are simply not working as anti-capitalist mass ideals. Much like what is currently happening in Barcelona and Madrid, anarcho-populism and eco-feminism must be fused into a left-populist project, in order to oppose the right-populist politics of Donald Trump and European anti-immigration parties. I call this synthesis social populism. Electoral movements such as Podemos in Spain, as well as Bernie Sanders' campaign in the last American election, evidence the possibility of populist movements of this form. These are themselves germane to anti-systemic movements as diverse as Indignados, Ni Una Menos, Blockupy, UK Uncut, Sciopero Sociale, Nuit Debout, Notre Dame des Landes, Fight for 15, Black Lives Matter, and Standing Rock, to cite only some of the most significant in recent years.

The historical discontinuity of 2016 seemed to make all the chips of the book fall into place. Finally, I had a historical antagonist to test my theory against: nationalist populism. And finally, I had a publisher egging me on to finish the damned thing: Geert Lovink and his Institute of Network Cultures. I got an invitation to MoneyLab #3 and was buzzed by its mix of heretic theorizing on post-crisis capitalism. It's the Institute of Network Cultures which believed this work should be published, and in doing so, has filled the intellectual void that I have felt in my life since the anti-globalization movement ended in the late 2000s. I am forever grateful to Geert, Leonieke, Inte, and Max for putting out, editing, designing, and proofreading *General Theory of the Precariat*.

This work was also made possible by two earlier stages of writing, where various sorts of people provided encouragement, as well as suggestions, to various earlier drafts. In 2014, literary scout Kelly Farber and literary agent Alex Jacobs, two professionals of the New York publishing industry, first believed in this book. They hoped I could get a contract from a U.S. publisher, but the thinking and writing in my proposal was shoddy, in spite of Alex's insightful editorial corrections.

Then in 2015, Marc Monaco and my forever-buddies-in-precarious-struggle in Liège revived the project. Together with feminist activist Emilie Rouchon, bookseller Olivier Verschueren, and his wife, professor Florence Caeymaex, they even tried to set up a publishing house, Pidgin, in order to release my work in both French and English. A heartfelt thanks to all of you, including Eric, Cédric, Marie, Mehdi, and Slim, for this book wouldn't exist without you. Equally important was the intellectual sustenance provided by the Net-Time mailing list, where the sharp minds of those such as Brian Holmes, Felix Stadler, and Keith Hart, always gave me food for thought. I also wish to thank Andrea 'Marvin' Tumietto for his enduring complicity from ChainWorkers until now, Giuseppe 'Peppe' Allegri for generously sharing his culture and knowledge on Europe and the precariat, and Michael Reinsborough for expanding my political horizons from Belfast to London and beyond. Finally, I owe to my friendship with sociologist Paolo Gerbaudo the interpretation of the 2011 revolution and contemporary populism. I strongly recommend you read his latest book, *The Mask and the Flag*, as well any of his future publications.

A sweet thought to my friends in the Comasina hood of Northern Milan: Paolino and Silvano. Unwavering solidarity to the two Milanese social centers that are in my heart: ZAM and Lambretta. A big thank you to the thinkers that have inspired me since I was a teen, Toni Negri and Bifo. A great hug to all those who have been involved in EuroMayDay, in particular Javier Toret, Marcelo Expósito, Vanni Brusadin, Joshua Eichen, Nikolaj Heltoft, Miika Saukkonen, Josip Rotar, Olle Larsson, Ben Trott, Kaz Sakurada, and warm feelings to the San Precario people, many of whom I have parted ways with, for leftist politics is inherently divisive and I am disputatious by nature. A special mention goes to San Precario's co-inventor Stefo Mansi, a great friend and Milan's best union organizer of precarious workers.

Finally, I'd like to thank my lover Eli, my teen daughter Selma and my baby son Rocco for giving me every day a reason to live.

Milan, June 2017

CHAPTER 1. PRECARIOUS TIMES

We live in precarious times, shaken by the long, global economic crisis, and the recent shift to the right of the world's political axis. Our cataclysmic age has many villains and few heroes, and the precarious are amongst them. The precariat is millions-strong in Europe, North America, East Asia, indeed in all the countries existing under contemporary informational capitalism. Who's precarious? A call center operator is precarious. A fast food worker is precarious. A temp coder is precarious. An adjunct professor is precarious. In fact, all youth living and working under informational capitalism are precarious. The precarious are the underpaid, underemployed, underprotected, overeducated, and overexploited.

The *Precariat,* a word that was first introduced in English in 2004 thanks to the EuroMayDay movement, is the class of precarious workers. It contains the mass of people working temporary, part-time, freelance contracts under advanced capitalism. According to the New York Times Crossword Puzzle, 'the precariat is the class of people whose lives are precarious because they have little or no job security'.[1] Thus the precariat includes all those who work short-term contracts, as well as those who are made temporarily or permanently jobless. NEETs,[2] interns, and apprentices also need to be added to this mix. The precariat is a class and it is a generation. It's the new class of workers, and it's the younger cohort of the labor force. But the logic of *precarity* pervades the entirety of society, squeezing the middle class out of decently paid, long-term jobs. Three decades of neoliberal labor market deregulation has swollen the ranks of precariat, and the financial crisis has made the ranks of the precariat further balloon. In fact, this emergent class includes all the casual workers that ensure the life and reproduction of the Western European, North American, and East Asian poles of advanced capitalism. The precariat distrusts the existing political system and remains largely outside traditional unions. Yet its political potential exceeds national boundaries and governments; it is a force that could defeat neoliberalism, nationalism, and engender a radical transformation of capitalism. Simply put, it is the precariat that will topple the oligarchy.

Twentysomethings and thirtysomethings are the bulk of the precariat, mostly composed of urban youth of mixed ethnicity and social provenance. Millennials in contingent employment and the younger Generation Z who are just out of college, and now out of jobs, constitute the *Precarious Generation.* I will discuss how precarious youth stands at the crossroads of history as the (unwilling) protagonist of the wave of political protest brought to life by the crisis of neoliberal capitalism. Insecure, unsafe, abusive, no-future jobs are the hard reality of young people's lives in the late 2010s. Now that total labor market flexibility has become the norm in the so-called 'gig economy', the young find themselves working precarious jobs

---

1   See also 'What the Fuck is the 'Precariat', and Why Should You Care?', *Vice*, 7 May 2017, https://www.vice.com/en_ca/article/what-the-fuck-is-the-precariat-and-why-should-you-care-293. The article opens with the subtitle 'Hint: you're probably in it and it sucks'.

2   'Not in Education, Employment, or Training', according to the bureaucratic acronym which has become widespread in the UK and Europe.

in every region of informational capitalism: America (where they are usually referred to as *temps*), Europe (where they are called *précaires, precari@s, precari/e*), Japan (where they are known as *hiyatoi* and *freeters*) and China (where young office workers mockingly refer to themselves as *diaosi,* losers in dead-end jobs*)*. Due to the decades of neoliberal assaults on organized labor, leading to de-unionization and the aging of surviving union members, the precariat has had to fend off for itself in the worst job market on offer since the end of World War Two. Organizing the self-organization of the precariat is thus crucial to reverse inequality, and redistribute income away from rents and profits towards wages. This would fundamentally rearrange both the political and economic relations of society, thus potentially enabling an economic recovery according to an egalitarian framework.

Precarity afflicts all those generations that have entered the job market after the privileged and spoiled baby-boomers: people aged 18-45 belonging to Generations X, Y, and Z who have seen their lives taken for ransom by precarious employment. Precarity also affects middle-aged people thrown out of permanent jobs, who have a rightful claim to count themselves as precarious. The French distinguish between precarious natives (*jeunes précaires*) and those made redundant who used to have a steady job (*déclassés*, literally translated as 'those who have lost rank'). We are interested in the former, because they are the active members of an increasingly self-conscious precarious class, the precariat, which has already destabilized governments and regimes, and is shaping the kind of economy and polity that will emerge after the Great Recession.[3]

Precarity is the labor, and life, condition marked by unsteady employment and intermittent income afflicting young, immigrant, and female labor. Precarity means not knowing where the next paycheck is going to come from, and that this is the normal condition of living and working under contemporary capitalism. The diffusion of precarious jobs has been mightily accelerated by the crisis. Precarity, also referred to as *precariousness*,[4] is the generalized job insecurity ultimately achieved by thirty years of neoliberal hegemony regarding economic and political affairs. Since the 2008 financial crisis, with its vicious cycle of business closures, lay-offs and cuts in social spending, vast segments of the population have been forced to live in precarious conditions. The Great Recession has made the poor poorer because of auster- ity, and shrunk the middle-class everywhere, as AI and automation create additional labor displacement and exacerbate the inegalitarian bias of the crisis. Due to the social ravages

---

3   There is evidence that Donald Trump won the primaries, and the election, thanks to the vote of white
      people who had been forced by the crisis to shift from salaried positions with benefits to wage jobs paid
      by the hour. Their economic resentment fed the most racist and irrational candidate America has ever
      seen, well exceeding Reagan and Bush Jr. in his lunacy and conservatism. He is politically reactionary,
      something the history of American presidents has never before seen. It's a further sign of how the Great
      Recession has polarized the political landscape between a hard-right, and an embattled center-left.
4   Precariousness has the advantage of not being a neologism, and is increasingly used in the sense of
      labor precarity in academic writing, such as in Emiliana Armano, Arianna Bove, and Annalisa Murgia
      (eds.), *Mapping Precariousness, Labour Insecurity and Uncertain Livelihoods*, London: Routledge,
      2017. However, it has no conceptual traction, and does not convey the social permanence and
      historical relevance of the precarious condition, while precarity (much like modernity, equality, liberty,
      etc.), contains the power of theoretical abstraction. 'A theory of precariousness' sounds awkward, while
      'a theory of precarity' doesn't.

inflicted by the Great Recession, and the disastrous policy responses to the crisis, people are suffering from economic deprivation in record numbers, and precarious work has become the new normal: precarity is the new reality. Mass youth unemployment is the legacy left by neoliberalism after decades of unchallenged rule.

The precarious condition affects all those who have few, or no rights in the workplace, because they are excluded from the job protection and social security traditionally associated with full-time employment. The precarious are the outsiders of the labor market, since they are excluded from the Fordist-era class compromise still providing a modicum of welfare and social security to their forebears. Their role in the information economy is essential, yet they have a say on neither labor relations, nor economic policy. The precarious are subject to flexible exploitation, or *flexploitation*: one day overworked, the following day out of work; one week zero hours, the next thirty on late-night shifts. Not only are their incomes unpredictable, but also their work schedules. One might say the precarious are quantum workers, existing in a superposition of employment states, both temporarily employed and temporarily unemployed. Their social identity is in flux: schizophrenic. A precarious is a worker and a non-worker, a citizen and a non-citizen. The precarious suffer from the indignities of low pay, powerlessness, being blackmailed on the job, and (although this void is being filled in Spain and elsewhere) under-representation in politics and government: it took more than a decade for the reality of precarity to sink in, and shape (inter)national discourse regarding youth unemployment and social exclusion.

The fact is that the precarious are stressed people, constantly fighting for survival, as well as freedom from the steady encroachment into their lives of the capitalist state. The precarious tend to be populist in their aspiration to redistribution, and anarchist in their refusal of authority and their striving for freedom of personal development or expression untainted by government, or corporate, control. Stress and frustration in the workplace inevitably contaminate the home. Thus, labor precarity soon leads to existential precariousness, where young households constantly have to battle the twin demons of psychological depression and social exclusion, and often succumb to them. Personal debt, public service cuts, and rising living costs all translate into an inescapable fact: a precarious person is always a paycheck away from joblessness and homelessness.

Yet precarity is not the same thing as poverty, as contemporary British sociology seems to suggest. Precarity is a labor condition that can lead to poverty, but the precarious are not the same thing as the poor. Poverty is economic destitution, where people are completely dependent on the state, charity networks, and criminal rings for their livelihood. Precarity, however, is the social condition marked by flexible employment and fluctuating income. Whilst precarity usually provides workers with the means of subsistence, it nevertheless puts them in a situation of economic uncertainty and social insecurity. No matter how much money they make today, the precarious are never sure what they'll earn tomorrow. Being precarious means having to jump from temporary job to temporary job in a gig economy that whirs without end on smartphones, for the benefit of consumers, and to the detriment of workers. On-call workers are trying to organize against Uber, Deliveroo, etc. to be recognized as employees rather than independent contractors by the corporations that profit from digital platforms that hire people and deliver services to people. The circus of precarity forces people to become veritable contortionists, juggling jobs and irregular incomes with family duties, as they walk the tightrope of life in precarious balance over the social abyss (and down there safety nets are being removed by austerity-minded politicians!). The sharing economy is expanding fast in all of capitalism's metropoles, but it's certainly not sharing its profits with drivers, cleaners and delivery workers.[5]

The social relevance of the precariat, as well as its potential to impose radical change, remain largely unexplored in mainstream writings on politics and economics. This book contends that the precariat is both the most exploited class, and the one which creates the most social value: the various political insurrections of 2011 were in fact led by the precarious generation. The revolutions of 2011 can be seen as attempts to bring down neoliberal capitalism and state despotism, in order to replace them with democratic, egalitarian, and ecological alternatives. My contention is that today we, the precarious, need revolutionary means to achieve these transformative, progressive, and reformist ends. The current wave of political polarization favors political reaction in various (and often deadly) forms. We need revolution to bring about a social, and environmental, reform of capitalism, since the world's interests are presently stacked in favor of fascist versions thereof. The emergence of national populism as state ideology in America, Russia, Turkey, and elsewhere, poses social-democrats and liberals with an existential choice: either give in to radicals who advance both social and civil rights, or be swept away by the populist right, as happened time and time again in 2016. A titanic clash is taking place in Europe to defend open borders and mixed societies from the continental minions of Vladimir Putin and Donald Trump. Everywhere, the return to the nation-state is evident, even under the banners of left populism. Threatened from the east and the west, the European Union is coming apart at the seams. Liberals, conservatives, and social democrats no longer appeal to the consensus of the European electorate. This threat to the neoliberal establishment is mostly coming from xenophobic movements both old and new. However, a post-socialist, eco-populist alternative can be found and fought for, as the municipal victories of movement forces in Barcelona and Madrid portend. Spain, Portugal, and Greece have shifted towards forms of left populism, albeit forms with a host of political contradictions. But better Syriza in government, and Podemos in parliament, than the shift to the radical right presently seen in the rest of the Eurozone: with Le Front National besieging France, the fascistic right beaten from the threshold of the presidency in Vienna, xenophobic populism dictating foreign policy in the Netherlands, and the islamophobic *Alternative für Deutschland* (AfD) rising in the polls in Germany. Indeed, the AfD's rise appears to be at the expense of ruling Christian-Democrats, who have imposed *Ordoliberismus* at home and austerity on Southern Europe, putting national interest ahead of European solidarity, thus unraveling more than half a century of European integration, as Britain sets sail from the European Union for the uncertain shores of nationalist patriotism.

I am not, however, claiming that the precarious are merely the passive victims of recent political turmoil. In France, Italy, and Spain, they have managed to mount significant challenges to the status quo. In 2006 against the CPE (the first-employment contract proposed

---

5   See Trebor Scholz, *Uberworked and Underpaid: How Workers Are Disrupting the Digital Economy*,
     Cambridge: Polity Press, 2017.

by Chirac and Villepin), then again in 2016 against the Loi Travail (the anti-labor reform passed by François Hollande and Manuel Valls), the precarious youth of France took to the streets and seized the squares for weeks, spooking Gaullist and Socialist governments alike. Italy created the May Day for the precarious at the height of the anti-globalization movement (2001-2008), an experience that evolved into the nation-wide *Sciopero sociale* in 2015 led by social center collectives and student movements. Furthermore, the recent #Lottomarzo on 8 March 2017 saw Italian young women striking in support of the Ni Una Menos global movement, as well as the pink tide in the US, agitating for a #feministrike across the world. Spain's precarious were pivotal in the Indignados' mobilizations of May 2011, animating key groups like Juventud Sin Futuro and Democracia Real Ya, and are the core voters of Podemos and En Comú, the left-populist formations born out of the country's recent period of social turmoil.

Indeed, a new protest culture was incubated by the Italian, Spanish, and French precariat's penchant for creativity and hybridization. Mixing cyber-anarchy with queer self-expression, social mutualism with political solidarity, urban liberation with ecological communes, and no border anti-racism with basic income egalitarianism, they have created a social-populist synthesis. Similarly, the revival of American radicalism is fundamentally predicated on the success of the living wage movement, which from California to New York is fighting for a doubling of the minimum wage. Both the Fight for $15 movement, as well as those calling for the unionization of fast food workers, have significant links with Black Lives Matter. In the space of only a few years, theirs' has become the most important labor conflict in the world, mobilizing hundreds of thousands of service workers in restaurants, supermarkets, schools, and hospitals against anti-union employers. Redistribution within contemporary capitalism begins with victory of the Fight for $15 movement over McDonald's and Starbucks, and unionization of the world's largest private employer: Wal-Mart. In spite of the election of Trump, the American precariat may still prevail in securing a living wage for all in the world's most unequal nation. Blocking the appointment of Andrew Puzder,[6] a fast-food executive, as Labor Secretary, was an early sign that the labor movement would not be easily intimidated by the president. Precarious millennials have 'felt the Bern' since the recent presidential primaries. In reaction to Trump's seizing the White House, and Republicans seizing congress, Bernie Sanders, the socialist senator from Brooklyn, is attempting to push the Democrats towards a form of left populism. He is rallying the popular forces of resistance to discrimination and deportation by saying: 'Despair is not an option.' Long gone are the days of Barack Obama's 'Hope'. The only remaining option is not to give in to dismay and disarray, but to resist and organize against national populism. Resisting chauvinism, xenophobia, racism, class privilege, and rule-by-perjury; this is what is binding movements across

---

6   Who in 2011 had the gall to declare: 'We hire the best of the worst', referring to the fast-food workers employed by his restaurant chain, Carl's Jr., from which allegations of widespread sexual harassment targeting female employees are starting to emerge. Indeed, the fast-food industry has a tradition of treating its workers with contempt; the executives of Yum!, the financial holding controlling KFC, Pizza Hut, and Taco Bell, commented regarding workers' demands for better compensation: '[b]efore they walk, they have to learn how to crawl.' See Eric Schlosser, *Fast Food Nation: The Dark Side of the All-American Meal,* Boston: Houghton Mifflin, 2001.

continents. If liberals and social democrats finally understood that by leaving people exposed to market forces, and pandering to prejudice, they are colluding with the rise of the populist right, the task of the people's resistance would be a lot easier.

Neoliberal capitalism has caused both economic and ecological crises. Ever-growing numbers of riot police are now needed to protect the caste of politicians and financiers from the wrath of the people. Society is polarizing; inequality has escalated since the onset of the Great Recession, and existing liberal democracies have lost evermore political legitimacy, undermined by populism on both the left and right. Political representation and economic management are up for grabs, since liberal power-holders have proved both incapable and incompetent at channeling popular demand into creating a real democracy, and a just economy.

We are living in a multipolar world where the interests of global and regional powers prevail over those of ordinary humans, and inequalities are rising to levels unseen since the 20s. Precarity is not just a labor and welfare issue, it is the fundamental cause of inequality. It is also the source of commonality among social actors seeking political redress and economic retribution. Since the financial crisis of 2008 and the revolutions of 2011, more and more people have been embracing the social values of justice and fairness, and moving against market-enforced values of individualism and competitiveness. The precariat is leading the fight to attain an equal-opportunity economy, and create real democracy, one based on veritable popular sovereignty that can finally redistribute the wealth and power currently appropriated by digital oligopoly as an economic form of exploitation and control, and by government oligarchy as a political form of domination and corruption.

The precariat thus has to defeat both political oligarchy and economic oligopoly, in order to radically improve its collective social standing via creating new institutional arrangements and political technologies. A new social pact must be created, a truce between liberals and radicals, hackers and states, movements and governments, and corporations and society, that will breathe a new life into democracy, and defend open societies. If not, the reactionary forces currently at work will prevail, and plunge the world in an ever-crueler vortex of war and extermination, where all that's human will be lost, and nightmarish autocratic powers will be left to rule the world; an amplification of tendencies already at work that will lead to truly apocalyptic scenarios of global war and ecological destruction.

The Book's Theses and Corollaries

I propose and seek to demonstrate two major theses:

1. A new precarious class has superseded the old working class: the service precariat of the 21st century, the analogue of the industrial proletariat of the 20th century; the precarious are organizing in the workplace, in the streets, and on the net, developing a distinctively anarcho-populist ideology and an eco-queer culture.

2.   The precariat is the revolutionary subject that opposes, and will ultimately overthrow, the (inter)national oligarchs who are replacing the economic and political elites that caused the 2008 financial crisis. Only the precariat has both the energy and necessity needed to dismantle neoliberalism, defeat nationalist-populism, and dispose of fossil-fuel capitalism.

From these theses, the following corollaries follow:

1.   The precariat is at the frontline of political and labor conflict in the aftermath of the Great Recession.

2.   If the precarious radically improve their lot, the resulting jump in effective demand will provide an economic solution to the crisis.

3.   If the precariat is the new proletariat, then the existing parties and unions of the left are obsolete.

4.   The precariat shall lead a social-populist front capable of redistributing power and wealth away from elites, engendering a new form of capitalism based on radical democracy, multi-ethnicity, transgenderism, and drive the transition towards a biosocial economy working for all.

Dawn of the Precariat: the EuroMayDay Network[7]

A decade before Guy Standing wrote *The Precariat*,[8] the precariat had already named itself. In London, during the fall of 2004, anti-globalization activists drafted *The Middlesex Declaration of Europe's Precariat*, a manifesto that sent forth a call for a pan-European May Day, and also comprised of a list of demands. It called for an international May Day across Europe, focusing on precarity and reclaiming those labors, welfare, and social rights denied to precarious youth by neoliberal governments and corporations. As the ChainWorkers Crew had (in)famously written in 2001, the service precariat is to the industrial proletariat what informationalism is to Fordism. From its inception, the EuroMayDay was intended to be for the precariat and by the precariat, the class composed of precarious young, queer, female, and/or migrant workers temping and toiling in the big cities transformed by the transnational flows of capital, knowledge, culture, and information. The precariat was first mobilized by anti-globalization media and union activists in Milan, then in Barcelona, swiftly followed by Hamburg, Berlin, Helsinki, Paris, Liège, Malaga, Seville, Lisbon, Ljubljana, Maribor, Stockholm, and Copenhagen (to name but a few of the EuroMayDay hotspots).

The Milano MayDay Parade was born in 2001, responding to the lack of action from mainstream unions over youth employment issues. By 2003, it had become the city's most important May Day demonstration, surpassing the traditional morning march in participation. By then, the ChainWorkers Crew had started talking of *il precariato sociale* as the key radicalizing

---

7   A different version of this section appeared as contribution to *Mapping Precariousness* (earlier cited).
8   Guy Standing, *The Precariat: The New Dangerous Class*, London: Bloomsbury, 2014.

social subject in the post-industrial economy. Thus, by fighting for their rights, activists turned what was previously a social stigma into a sign of pride and combativeness; *precariato*, in Italy, usually refers to a hopeless condition one has to suffer passively, rather than a subject composed of people capable of self-organization and self-empowerment.

We saw the social precariat as the successor of the industrial proletariat, plain and simple. Unlike social democrats and communists, we harbored no illusions about working class commitment to the left. Furthermore, we were adamant that political and economic arrangements centered around industrial economy were being supplanted by those of the network economy. The factory was no longer the central site for class conflict; the city, the mall, and the web had taken its place. We saw a new class emerging, composed of women, immigrants, working class youth, middle-class youth, cleaners, and hackers, and we imagined it would soon eclipse the political priorities of an aging generation of blue- and white-collars. The precariat was destined to be the gravedigger of neoliberalism.

Online, political media needed to mobilize the precariat were first introduced by a creative collective of Milanese subvertisers. Whilst they began with simply networking Milanese social spaces, in order to combat precarity in the city's workplaces between 2001 and 2003, they soon started to interact with the rest of Italy, and eventually more of Europe. In doing so, they aimed to reinterpret the discourse surrounding both the meaning, and purpose, of International Workers' Day, in the light of the radical transformations in the economy and jobs that had occurred thanks to the combined effects of neoliberal deregulation, and the information revolution. The first ally of the budding precarious workers' movement in Milan was Rome's autonomous student movement, which has since accumulated an interesting string of theoretical reflections on precarity.[9]

It is important to note that the mobilization of precarious workers would have been unthinkable without the hopes and energies raised by the Seattle-Genoa movement. With respect to its successor (the Movement of the Squares of 2011, which inherited some of its characteristics), the anti-globalization movement involved fewer people but greatly extended its reach across borders to create a strongly motivated, transnational community of activists, united by anarcho-autonomous ideology, and willing to create a common style of struggle and set of demands: no borders, no discrimination, minimum wage, and (universal) basic income. All of this occurred on a European scale, in the momentous years when euro bills entered peoples' wallets, and the European Union enlarged to the east. Anti-globalization activists were fewer than those mobilized by Spain's Indignados-style radical populism, but managed to cover a wider range of issues; they never stopped, forever mobilizing onto the next cause. From Zapatismo to veganism, queer rights to bicycle activism, food sovereignty to financial transactions, state repression to climate justice, and finally international solidarity to global precarity, there was no issue that the motley coalition of black, pink, red, and green (h)ac(k) tivists left unturned.

---

9   See: Giuseppe Allegri and Giuseppe Bronzini, *Libertà e lavoro dopo il Jobs Act*, Rome: Derive e Approdi, 2015; Giuseppe Allegri and Roberto Ciccarelli, *Il Quinto Stato*, Milan: Ponte alle Grazie, 2013; Francesco Raparelli, *La lunghezza dell'onda*, Milan: Ponte alle Grazie, 2009.

It was in this heady atmosphere of peer collaboration and social innovation that San Precario and their collective[10] were born on Sunday 29 February 2004, during an action in a Milanese supermarket that had remained open in spite of the then existing prohibition on holiday work. The day was chosen because leap years are intermittent, much like the incomes of precarious workers. At its height between 2004 and 2006, San Precario attracted media and labor collectives from all major Italian cities (Milan, Rome, Turin, Bologna, L'Aquila, Naples, and Palermo), with several of them featuring their own MayDay Parades. What turned San Precario into a social meme was the prayer card that had been designed by a trio of ChainWorkers Crew members. The card became wildly popular, and could be seen on the desks of precarious workers desks throughout Milan, as a symbol of their condition and their complicity in the so-called 'precarious conspiracy'; although they performed the same work of other workers, they had no right to the wages and benefits of permanent employment.

What ultimately projected EuroMayDay, and its accompanying discourse on precarity, onto the international stage was San Precario with their subversive inventiveness.[11] Fantabulous MayDay posters, precarious superheroes trading cards, elaborate fashion hoaxes like that of Serpica Naro, which poked fun at the 2005 Milan Fashion Week (its fictive identity an anagram of San Precario), a Net Parade[12] featuring DIY avatars of social rebellion, full sets of precarity tarots, and much more marked the first few years of the precarious workers movement. However, what was really crucial for the initial Europe-wide projection of the May Day movement was an early collaboration with the Las Agencias and Yo Mango subvertising collective in Barcelona. This cooperation with Valery Alzaga, who was in charge of the Justice for Janitors campaign in Europe, as well as the early attention given to the ferments of the Italian precariat by *Brumaria* and *Greenpepper Magazine* garnered the attentions of *Mute, Adbusters*, and a host of other European publications. It also greatly helped that Michael Hardt and Antonio Negri gave their joint blessing to the EuroMayDay movement, and included precarious labor in their treatment of the multitude in the second volume of their *Empire* trilogy.

In 2004, the entire Italian anti-globalization movement came to Milan in one of the biggest MayDay Parades ever. Over 2004 and 2005, crucial assemblies were held in Paris, Berlin, and Hamburg, giving rise to the EuroMayDay network.[13] It attracted radical European activists working on precarity and migration from across the socio-political spectrum. In France, it was Les Intermittents, in Germany it was Fels in Berlin and no-border networks in Hamburg and Hanau, in Belgium it was Bob le Précaire and Liège's heretic left, in Spain it was Precarias a

---

10 'Their' because 'San Precario is also transgender', quoted in Ilaria Vanni and Marcello Tarì, 'The Life and Deeds of San Precario, Patron Saint of Precarious Workers and Lives', *The Fibreculture Journal*, 2005 http://five.fibreculturejournal.org/fcj-023-on-the-life-and-deeds-of-san-precario-patron-saint-of-precarious-workers-and-lives/. See also Brett Neilson and Ned Rossiter, 'From Precarity to Precariousness and Back Again: Labor, Life, and Unstable Networks', *The Fibreculture Journal*, 2005, http://five.fibreculturejournal.org/fcj-022-from-precarity-to-precariousness-and-back-again-labour-life-and-unstable-networks/.
11 Zoe Romano and Chiara Birattari were the two graphic designers behind much of San Precario's and Serpica Naro's wild creativity, while Marxist economist Andrea Fumagalli emerged as the main thinker of the group. See www.precaria.org.
12 By gaming artist Molleindustria www.molleindustria.org/netparade04.
13 www.euromayday.org.

la Deriva and many other collectives from Malaga to Tarragona (who also created the move-ment's favorite tune, 'Chiki-Chiki Precario'[14]), in Finland it was Prekariaatti, and in Denmark it was Superflex. This list, of course, could go on and on, including Slovenian, Swedish, Austrian, Portuguese, Swiss, as well as Japanese and Canadian collectives.[15] In the years between 2007 and 2009, interest in articulating a set of European demands and in undermining the governance of the European Union grew, after successful anti-Eurocracy exploits in Brussels on Good Friday in 2006, and in Aix-la-Chapelle (Aachen) on May Day 2008. Regarding the latter, that year International Workers' Day coincided with Ascension Day, which since 1950 has stood as the day that the European elite award themselves with the Charlemagne Prize in Aachen, where the Frankish king is buried. EuroMayDay spoiled the public event held in honor of Merkel by Sarkozy, with Barroso and Trichet in attendance. In those same years, thanks to the influence of Northern European movements, Milan's MayDay parade became increasingly queer and eco-active, concentrating more on LGBT rights and climate justice.

The EuroMayDay network no longer exists, although some of its remaining fragments recon-stituted as the Precarious United of Europe movement, who participated in the Climate Justice Action of 2009 in Copenhagen. They have since organized with no-border networks, such as the 2010 Fuck Austerity! demonstration held in Brussels during the European Union Confederation march, in order to protest the summit of European Union finance ministers engineering austerity as the Eurozone's response to the financial crisis. This ended in mass arrests, with union officials helping police officers locate the troublemakers.

When the Arab Spring came and set the world alight for two brief but incredible years, it was clear who the catalysts for the revolutions of Tahrir and Plaza del Sol were. The precarious youth, the vanguard of the precariat, were organizing protests via social media, and managing the logistics for occupations and assemblies asserting the peoples' power to the corrupt elites. What Gerbaudo calls anarcho-populist ideology[16] was the combination of the often anarchist outlook of activists (students, temps, freelancers, and the unemployed) with popular needs: real democracy, and the end of austerity and inequality. To end precarity is synonymous with ending inequality. To end precarity you need to put austerity in reverse: redistribute wealth away from the digital and financial oligarchy, and direct it towards the precariat. The introduction of universal basic income, and the setting of a $/ 15 minimum wage per hour of work, is the beginning of this process of reversal.

---

14   https://youtu.be/TiWTISrgALU.
15   See Marion Hamm, *Media Practices in the Trans-Urban Euromayday Movement of the Precarious*, PhD diss., University of Luzern, 2011, for a more extensive list.
16   Paolo Gerbaudo, *The Mask and the Flag: Populism, Citizenism and Global Protest*, London: Hurst, 2017.

CHAPTER 2. THE ANATOMY OF PRECARITY AND THE PRECARIAT AS HISTORICAL CLASS

For a Notion of the Precariat That Is Coherent With Social Experience

In Italian, *precariato* (precariat) is used to refer to the institution of contingent work, and it is used indifferently along *precarietà* (precarity). Transforming the connotation of *precariato* into a subject, and exporting it to English-speaking lands[17] has worked to a degree, since *the precariat* is now used in academic literature and journalism[18] to refer to the class of semi-employed members of the population. However, these notions have been cause for misinterpretation in academic sociology,[19] which hasn't fully absorbed the debate on precarity developed by movements and intellectuals in Continental Europe, where the concepts of precarity and precariat originate from.

Following the popularity of Guy Standing's book, the precariat was named as the lowest class in the Great British Class Survey released in 2013,[20] which after much elaboration and application of Bourdieu's key insight – the distinction between economic, cultural, and relational capital – has proposed a seven-class model of UK society:

---

17   'Precarity' is a word of everyday usage in Romance languages (*precariedad* in Spanish, *precariedade* in Portuguese, *précarité* in French, and *precarietà* in Italian), that has become increasingly common in media and popular discourse in a number of countries in the European Union over the last two decades. Its transfer to the English language as *precarity* occurred at the start of millennium, and began to appear across the board, from European Union documents to pan-European, anti-globalization marches and protests. The EuroMayDay movement, which had a strong German component, also fostered the use of *Prekariat* in political and theoretical pamphlets in Germany, Austria, and German-speaking Switzerland. As for France, *précariat* has not really caught on, but *précaires* and *précarité* have been objects of academic investigation, journalistic discussion, and activism, for at least twenty years.

18   'The American Precariat', *New York Times*, 10 February 2014, https://www.nytimes.com/2014/02/11/opinion/brooks-the-american-precariat.html?_r=1.

19   Stephven Shukaitis, 'Recomposing precarity: Notes on the laboured politics of class composition', *Ephemera*, http://www.ephemerajournal.org/contribution/recomposing-precarity-notes-laboured-politics-class-composition.

20   'Huge survey reveals seven social classes in UK', *BBC News*, 13 April 2013, http://www.bbc.com/news/uk-22007058; 'Social Class in the 21st Century by Mike Savage review', *The Guardian*, https://www.theguardian.com/books/2015/nov/13/social-class-21st-century-mike-savage-review.

Elite - the most privileged group, distinct from the other six classes through its wealth. This group has the highest levels of all three capitals.

Established middle class - the second wealthiest, scoring highly on all three capitals. The largest and most gregarious group, scoring second highest for cultural capital.

Technical middle class - a small, distinctive new class group which is prosperous but scores low for social and cultural capital. Distinguished by its social isolation and cultural apathy.

New affluent workers - a young class group which is socially and culturally active, with middling levels of economic capital.

Emergent service workers - this new class has low economic capital but has high levels of cultural capital and high social capital. This group are young and often found in urban areas.

Traditional working class - this class scores low on all forms of the three capitals although they are not the poorest group. The average age of this class is older than the others.

Precariat - this is the most deprived class of all with low levels of economic, cultural and social capital. The everyday lives of members of this class are precarious.

Table 1: The Great British Class Survey

Note how the classification uses the term *precariat* in a distorted fashion, essentially referring only to the unemployed, and the working poor; this classification, for example, includes miners in the ranks of the precariat. However, few in Britain would argue this, instead claiming that miners should be instead classified as belonging to the traditional working class; few have a better claim than them! Conversely, my notion of the precariat, which is arguably what people in Continental Europe have in mind when they think of people in a precarious condition, refers to both emergent service workers and the low-wage precariat in commerce, government and industry. Thus, in the classificatory terms of this misleading framework, my notion of the precariat actually stands as an umbrella term incorporating all those in Classes 5 and 7.

Again differently from what the Great British Class Survey says, I understand the precariat as not being the poorest of social classes (the residents of *banlieues* and *favelas,* for instance, are not represented by it). The precariat has considerable relational and cultural capital, due both to social media, and its comparatively high education. With respect to this latter element, it stands in stark contrast with the traditional working class.[21] From the point of view

---

21   In fact, the precariat is an ill-defined concept and this book intends to pay remedy to that. Standing includes all those who are underpaid and/or economically insecure, and thus at risk of downward social mobility. The precariat is dangerous, he argues, not because it's composed of an underclass ready to loot and riot, but because the precariat could veer to the right by becoming nativistic. His notion seems more an analogue of the right-leaning petty bourgeoisie in Marx (18 *Brumaire*) and Poulantzas (*Fascism and Dictatorship*), than a description of the normally left-leaning generation of Millennials and Generation Z. He has written that the precariat is both a major resource for the renewal of the left,

of the *technical* division of labor, the precariat mostly contains young people working in the information, culture, knowledge, and service industries, who have unstable jobs and suffer from the twin evils of oligopoly and oligarchy.[22] In terms of the *social* composition of labor, the precariat are young, women, and immigrants working in multi-cultural, and multi-gendered (generally) urban environments.

This book argues that the precariat (temp workers, working poor, migrant laborers, etc.) stands below the salariat (middle managers, office clerks, factory workers, etc.) and the elite (millionaires), and above the underclass (ghetto youth, refugees, etc.).

Thus, my basic class model is stands as such:

I. Elite (high political, high economic, and high cultural power)

II. Salariat (high political, middling economic, and low cultural power)

III. Precariat (low political, low economic, and high cultural power)

IV. Underclass (low political, low economic, and high cultural power)

Table 2: Basic Class Stratification in Contemporary Capitalism

The political strategy I advocate is essentially an alliance between the two lower classes against the top two, for most of the salariat is becoming increasingly xenophobic, and lost to any leftist cause, overwhelming choosing the most evil sections of the global elite as their rulers. Pace Slavoj Žižek,[23] there is no anti-neoliberal silver lining in Trump and Brexit, it is a reactionary shift occurring in response to the crisis in Anglo-America. Yet the left, including Žižek, has no real alternatives to neoliberalism. By defending narrow sections of the Salariat, while selling out to neoliberalism and leaving the precariat hang to dry, social and Christian democrats have undermined their key bases of support. Contrary to what was argued at the 2017 World Economic Forum at Davos, it's certainly not the precariat (young, female, black, yellow, and brown) that's behind the rise of right-wing populism. Rather, it's the fear felt by the working class and petty bourgeoisie at the prospect of losing welfare guarantees, social standing, and

but also that it is feeding reactionary populism. The *New Left Review* has dismissed the concept out of hand, quoting the remarks I made in a video interview: 'The precariat: is it a social subject, a social stratum, a class, a category, a cohort, a generational concept—who cares?' In that context, I simply meant that loose theory didn't prevent the precariat from acting out its grievances: definition could wait, activism could not. Even if this work takes a different route to the precarious question, Standing's book does not deserve haughty rebuff, because the notion of the precariat as a class-in-the-making is to be welcomed and should be widely embraced by social research. Standing is right, however, in arguing that only by building a practical utopia for the precariat can democracy recover and thrive again.

22   Franco Berardi (aka 'Bifo') and other autonomous writers speak of *precari* and *cognitari*: of average precarious workers and cognitive precarious workers. See Franco Berardi, *La fabbrica dell'infelicità: New economy e movimento del cognitariato*, Rome: Derive Approdi, 2002.

23   'Zizek: Electing Trump 'Will Shake Up' the System', *Al Jazeera*, 16 November 2016, http://www. aljazeera.com/programmes/upfront/2016/11/zizek-electing-trump-shake-system-161116062713933. html. See also his BBC interview on YouTube: https://youtu.be/2ZUCemb2plE.

cultural identity that is feeding the dragon of nationalist populism. Populist demagogues play on the sentiments of anomie and displacement characterizing societies that have polarized and changed beyond recognition under neoliberalism due to unprecedented migration and technological advancement. The precarious don't fear precarity because they know no other way of living. They are ready to fight for their rights, and when it comes to fighting, acting in conjunction with the riotous force of the underclass leads to an uprising that will be hard to subdue. The social alliance between the mass civil disobedience of the precariat and the insurgent underclass can block anti-egalitarian and repressive measures, thus defeat the xenophobic right currently striving for world power.

The alliance between the precariat and the underclass could also be unmade by a recrudescence of Islamic terrorism in Europe and America, alongside other forms of sectarian conflict, polarizing society in accordance with ethnic, rather than class, divides. After the Trumpian turn, we are not witnessing a classic head-on capital-labor conflict, but rather the clash between two versions of modernity: one open and liberal, the other closed and illiberal. Combining the traditional left-right political axis with the new open-closed ideological divide that contrasts national and cosmopolitan versions of capitalism yields the following ideal types of contemporary forms of political mobilization. Note how social democracy is still strongly rooted in the nation-state. This is reflected by the fact that in its heartland, Europe, social democracy's greatest achievement – the welfare state – still remains outside the reach of European Union treaties, since national governments consider it their preserve.

	Left	Right
Open	Social Populism	Liberal Democracy
Closed	Social Democracy	National Populism

Table 3: The Quadrant of Contemporary Politics

The clear polarity in the table is the one between social populism and national populism, the two political ideologies that are on the rise since the crisis of liberal democracy. Between Pablo Iglesias and Donald Trump there is a wide gulf, filled by intermediate positions. In simple terms, social populists care about equality like the left nominally does and liberalism doesn't. But liberals care about open borders, more for economic than political reasons, so this is an area where the interests of liberals might converge with the ideals of social populism against the hard right who oppose immigration. On the other hand, there are two strong areas of disagreement and potential conflict: the disagreement between populists and liberals regarding resource distribution, and the disagreement between the multiethnic precariat represented by left populist forces, and the domestic working class usually championed by social democracy.

A contemporary case from France reveals some of the complexities at hand in the interplay between social mobilization and political outcomes. In the spring of 2016, the student and labor movements rose against the *Loi Travail* (i.e. the Labor Law, which allowed lengthening of hours and cutting of wages in defiance of industry-wide union agreements), occupying the main squares of French cities large and small, in open defiance of the socialist government proposing it. The political dynamics were not driven by the red union officially calling the strikes, the Confédération Générale du Travail (CGT), but by high school and university students balking at their precarious future and fighting for their rights, one night after the other for a month in Place de la République. In spite of the increasing radicalization of the French youth of *lycées* and *facs* in the Nuit Debout movement, the protests were not successful in blocking the law, but merely added to the trademark image of the Hollande-Valls government: a government marred by incompetence and political betrayal. The French youth precariat was inspired by the autonomous revolutionary theory of the Invisible Committee,[24] expressed in a series of powerful pamphlets, *The Coming Insurrection, To Our Friends,* and, in time for the French presidential elections, the even more simply titled *Maintenant* (Now).

In the recent presidential elections, the liberal Emmanuel Macron ended up squarely defeating nationalist leader Marine Le Pen, after both socialists and gaullists failed to make it to the second round of voting for the first time in the history of the Fifth Republic. Benoît Hamon, a socialist who ran on a platform of basic income, 'tax-the-robots', and anti-racism, was betrayed by his own party. The conservative candidate, the *républican* François Fillon, squandered his early chances to be elected as allegations emerged he had put his entire whole family on the government payroll. The 2016 protests were a major factor in securing 7 million votes to Jean-Luc Mélenchon a leftist firebrand who ran on anti-elite, and anti-Europe platform. His positions on Putin and Aleppo during the campaign bordered on red-brown, as the French and the Italians refer to those who mix bolshevism with nationalism; were I French, I wouldn't have voted for him. Personal preferences aside, the sum of Mélenchon and Hamon's votes would have been enough to send a candidate of the left to the second round. But with the left divided, the road to the Elysée was wide open for Emmanuel Macron, a young banker and former economic minister supported by the financial and political establishment, who managed to easily defeat champion of reaction Marine Le Pen by campaigning on a pro-Europe position, asserting the value of France's multicultural liberalism. Before founding his centrist movement and seizing control the Elysée Palace and the Assemblée Nationale, he had become famous for deregulating shopping hours with the eponymous Loi Macron. In fact, the candidate most in favor of Loi Travail – due to the flexibility it grants the French labor market – won the elections, a paradox of unintended consequences[25] for a mass movement denouncing flexibility as exploitation. Since the French Socialists have now disappeared from Parliament, Macron and his government, headed by former right-wing mayor Édouard Philippe, are ruling the country with little opposition. It will be the French people in the streets that will bring Macron to account. A so-called Social Front has been

---

24 The Invisible Committee, *The Coming Insurrection,* Cambridge: MIT Press, 2009; *To Our Friends,* Cambridge: MIT Press, 2015.
25 *Mutatis mutandis,* this also occurred in 1968, with Pompidou in France and Nixon in the US ending up being the main short-term political beneficiaries of seismic student protests.

constituted by radical unions and the autonomist left[26] to oppose the man they call 'the CEO of France'. As they say in their protests, *liberté* should never rhyme with *précarité*.

The Precariat: A Salmagundi of Lower Classes

I propose an alternative description of the precariat in the following table, condensing many categories that have been used to describe the new actors emerging out of Jobsian and Walmartian production relations. The ordering differentiates the various sections of the precariat in terms of income received.

i) *Creative Class* (artists, coders, squatters, engineers, designers, etc., in internships, apprenticeships, or in freelance and/or temporary employment)

ii) *New Working Class* (subcontracted employment as unskilled workers or technicians in warehousing, logistics, industrial manufacturing, food processing, construction, etc.)

iii) *Service Class* (waiters, baristas, busboys, cashiers, cleaners, fast-food workers, or employed as education, welfare, health care, child care, or home care workers in part-time and/or temporary employment)

iv) *Unemployed Class* (NEETs, short- and long-term unemployed, labor force dropouts, welfare recipients on workfare, illegal migrants, and refugees)

Table 4: The Precariat: Its Internal Segmentation

Considering the unemployed class, one has to note that the proportion of the adult population not in employment is huge, ranging from about 45% in Italy, to 35% in France, 30% in the US, and 25% in Germany and Japan.[27] In fact, the employment rate – the percentage of people within a given country that are employed – has shrunk dramatically since the onset of the Great Recession in 2008.

The service class is the second largest section of the precariat. The following are the frequent occupations in the United States, according to BLS data for May 2015 (see table 4 below). Note that retail workers make up the largest single category of working people. The service class includes all pink-collar jobs: store workers, supermarket cashiers, food workers, nurses, waiters and waitresses, and janitors and cleaners. It amounts to almost 19 million people working precarious service jobs in the US alone.

---

26   A record number of people didn't vote (12 million) or voted blank (4 million) in the second round, a position expressed in the streets by the slogan: '*Ni Le Pen, Ni Macron, Ni Nation, Ni Patron*' (*Neither Le Pen nor Macron, neither Nation nor Boss*).

27   Comparative data from Organization for Economic Cooperation and Development (OECD), https://data. oecd.org/emp/employment-rate.htm.

Retail Salespersons	4,612,510
Cashiers	3,478,420
Combined Food Preparation and Serving Workers, Including Fast Food	3,216,460
Office Clerks, General	2,944,420
Registered Nurses	2,745,910
Customer Service Representatives	2,595,990
Waiters and Waitresses	2,505,630
Laborers and Freight, Stock, and Material Movers, Hand	2,487,680
Secretaries and Administrative Assistants, Except Legal, Medical, and Executive	2,281,120
Janitors and Cleaners, Except Maids and Housekeeping Cleaners	2,146,880

Table 5: Largest U.S. occupations in 2015. Source: Bureau of Labor Statistics

The creative and/or 'boring' office class, either temporary (most assistants and most customer representatives) or not (most clerks), are over 7.5 million. By comparison, the new working class is fairly small, comprised of merely 2.5 million people.

Radical political scientists like Andrew Ross prefer to consider the global precariat,[28] and emphasize the commonalities between exploited service labor (located in the core of the capitalist world-system), and sweatshop industrial labor (located on the semi-periphery of the capitalist world-system). Other social researchers even include the kind of informal labor common in developing countries in their definition of the precariat. I suggest we limit ourselves to informational capitalism (i.e. the advanced capitalist core in the Global North), and take a different tactic. We should start by considering who actually is precarious, in order to arrive at what the precariat is, and what it might be. First and foremost, it is youth who are precarious, and who overwhelmingly constitute the precariat today.

The precariat and the creative class are the two conflicting signifiers of class positioning in contemporary capitalism. While the first evokes social exclusion and political resentment, the second bespeaks of prosperous bohos enjoying the so-called sharing economy. In reality, the precarious are both excluded from political power yet central to economic innovation. The precariat is a generation in the process of becoming a general class in the Marxian sense;

---

28 Andrew Ross, *Nice Work If You Can Get It: Life and Labor in Precarious Times*, New York: NYU Press, 2009.

capitalist corporations and state administrations could not function without their labor. This puts them in a league very close to that of the 20th century working class: disposable as individuals, but indispensable as an aggregate. Unlike the working class, the precarious class owns the means of production (networked personal computers and smartphones), however juridical and political domination still grants the elite the means to appropriate social surplus. Capitalist command operates through blackmail (the livelihood threat) or coercion (the repressive threat), to mask the fact that capitalists are no longer needed to organize production. Increasingly, contemporary capitalism appears parasitic to social relations, now that wealth has become more concentrated than ever before in human history, with a handful of digital and media corporations controlling the entirety of society's cultural production and reproduction.

There has been some discussion on whether the precariat is the new proletariat, or whether the precarious are just the children of downwardly mobile middle classes. They are both. It's a class of people working today, but it's also a generation: the generation of twentysomethings and thirtysomethings whose exploitation and mobilization affects the society as a whole.

Matrix of Precarious Labor

In order to better illustrate the various forms of precarious labor in the current economic environment, I have compiled the following matrix. This provides a viewpoint from which we can analyze precarity from the perspective of the kind of labor market prevalent in contemporary information economies around the world.

Those employees who have allowed worktime to colonize their lives are in the best position in regard to the labor market. Their minds belong to their employers. In exchange for their loyalty, they are granted access to the salariat, the safe island of guaranteed long-term employment. The benefits of this group, however, do not extend to paid leisure. Every day, weekends included, must be sacrificed on the altar of the employer's superior need. The permanently employed might be overworked and overstretched, but they are the only insiders of today's labor market.

The *Sarariman* is a perfect example of this kind of worker. It is the Japanese name given to office workers who, in exchange for a lifetime of employment, slavishly devote themselves to serving their company. They are an overworked, male figure that is fast disappearing from Japanese society. Their profits swallowed by two decades of stubborn deflation (so much so that the Nikkei has yet to recover from its 1990 peak), *keiretsus* (business groups) are shedding them by the thousands. Yet in spite of this, salaried middle-managers are what the media portray as typical, contemporary employment; they are smartly dressed, travel abroad on business, and the lucky among them may eventually join the upper echelons of company management. These upper levels are still overwhelmingly male, as corporations frown upon motherhood, obviously negatively affecting women's careers (it is important to note here that paid maternity leave doesn't yet exist in many parts of the global economy).

	Paid	Unpaid	In Labor Force	Not in Labor Force
Short-Term Relation	Temp	Intern	Precarious, Laid Off	NEET
Long-Term Relation	Employee	Volunteer	Unemployed, Permatemp	Outcast

	Part-Time	Full-Time	Under-the-Counter	Illegal
Short-Term Relation	Retail Chain Worker	Clerical Temp, Construction Worker	Daily Laborer	Mule, Pusher, Prostitute
Long-Term Relation	Pink-Collar	White-Collar, Blue-Collar	Squatter, Indentured Worker	Hooligan, Gambler, Gangster

Table 6: The Precarity Matrix: Precarious and Outcasts in the Labor Market Today

At the opposite end of the spectrum are the outcasts of the labor market, a descending segmentation of hidden layers of workplace exploitation and forced precarity. No matter how educated, the precarious are considered as inferior, second-class employees.

Below full-time workers in terms of job guarantees are part-time workers, who are similarly regarded as having a lower status within the company. Alongside them sit temporary workers (temps), who usually work full-time, and are either directly recruited by a company or rented from a temp agency. Temps and part-timers might be granted some pocket-sized benefits (some paid holidays and minimal health care packages), but both are frequently cut loose during lulls in business, and conversely must work extended hours when business picks up.

I consider the temp the ideal type of precarious worker. Younger generations initially thought they could be temporarily flexible under neoliberalism, but in fact became stuck in seemingly permanent precarity, or 'temp hell', to quote the name of one of earliest fanzines devoted to the phenomenon. No matter the industry in which they are employed, due to the strictures of their short-term contract, a temp's leverage on their superior is far lower than that of their permanent colleagues'. The demand for permanent workers suddenly dropped thirty years ago, when neoliberalism became the dominant form of economic logic within information economies. Neoliberalism hired temps whilst shedding perms, thus precarious workers are legion today. Just over 15% of all employees in the Eurozone work on temporary contracts. According to Eurostat data and definitions, temporary employees made up 15% of dependent employment in France and Germany in 2013. These same figures hold in Finland and, outside of the Eurozone, Sweden as well. In North America, the share of temporary employment had climbed to 14.5% of the total working population by the end of 2012, according to the OECD's *Employment Outlook*. Focusing on this data according to a generational cross-section is yet more worrying. In Europe, short-term and temporary employees account for roughly 25% of people in dependent employment aged 15-39. In Mediterranean Europe specifically, these numbers are even higher: almost a third of workers under 40 in Spain and Portugal work short-term jobs, while in France and Italy, 23% and 21% respectively of young workers are permatemps without hope of long-term employment. In the Netherlands, the corresponding percentage stands at a high 31%. However, unlike most Eurozone countries, this is matched by high, rather than low, employment rates for people under 40. Focusing only on people under 25 years of age, the OECD reported that in Europe more than 39% of employees were temps (up from 36% in 2000).[29]

I call the proportion of workers in temporary employment the *precarity rate*. It is essentially a proxy for total precarity amongst a given population, since it refers only to a subset of the precariat (this will be explained fully later in this text). Temporary workers *are* precarious workers. The precarity rate within the Eurozone is around 15% (early 2013 figures), the total number of employees is in excess of 115,000,000, thus there are currently more than 17 million precarious workers in Europe. These statistics signify a harsh reality: informational capitalism depends on precarious labor for its extended reproduction. Crucially, when we talk about the gig economy, we're really discussing labor performed by the precariat (and the precariat alone). The profits of the sharing economy and social media empires would be unthinkable without the flexibility, and knowledge, of the precariat.

Although temps work the same number of hours (if not more) than permanent employees, as well as do the same kind of work, they are paid less by the hour. Their permanent colleagues tend to overlook this patent discrimination, and thus tacitly collude with employers as they work alongside temps at meetings, or converse with them casually by the coffee machine without worrying about their predicament. They extend no solidarity to their temp colleagues when employment contracts expire and are not renewed. Their precarious status is usually knowledge private to them, and permanent employees don't want to hear about it. One day precarious workers will simply vanish from the office, perhaps preceded by a tearful little ceremony in a cheap restaurant. It is only after they are terminated that long-term employees are confronted with the fact that their able and smart colleagues were in fact temps, existing with an invisible expiration date floating over their heads. In general, the surviving employees merely count themselves lucky, and disregard the destiny of the hapless temps, as if there were some kind of superstition that precarity might rub off them and soon become their destiny as well.

If temporary labor is neglected, internships (i.e. the free labor provided by young college graduates to build up their CVs), barely register in the eyes of permanent and temporary employees alike. Interns (in French and Italian they are called *stagiares* and *stagisti*, respectively) constantly rotate every three to six months. The rest of the office doesn't even remember their names; one young face after another passes them by. Interns start their jobs in a bright mood initially; their expectations progressively dim as the nature of gratuitously imposed free labor becomes apparent even to the most ardent believers in careerism. Young people are

---

29   OECD, *Employment Outlook*, Labor Force Statistics and Standardized Unemployment Rates.

often conscripted into internships, because they are educational credits required for gradua-tion, and because they have become stepping-stones to a paid precarious job. The hardened temp was once a hopeful intern.

Sometimes interns work longer hours than everyone else; sometimes to extremes. Merrill Lynch intern Moritz Erhardt died from an epileptic fit in November 2013, at the end of his third night spent in the office. The coroner said overwork (what the Japanese call *karoshi*) was the cause, yet corporate lawyers tried to make him revoke this: the Wall Street company feared a lawsuit. His young colleagues simply went on working, despite the fact that the bank (embroiled in the financial crisis) had given employees the opportunity to time off to mourning the loss of one of their peers. The living seemed more preoccupied with holding onto their jobs, no matter how precarious, than commemorating the death of an unknown intern.

Employment as an agency worker entails being hired by a temp agency that periodically rents your services out to a company for the duration of a temporary employment contract (typically less than a year). The company has only limited responsibility for a temp's fate after their contract with the temporary work agency ends. The fee paid by the employer to the agency is indirectly a cut on the temp's wage, since companies pay temps less by the hour than employees they themselves hire. Originally used solely for office work, temporary labor has penetrated every economic sector, even the manufacturing sector. In fact, blue-collar jobs in the early 10s accounted for 47% of all temporary labor, up from 30% in 1993.

Temporary workers were initially used as substitutes for permanent employees during an interim period where they were otherwise unavailable. In fact, in France, they are still referred to as *intérimaires*. Whilst temps are still commonly used to replace female employees on maternity leave, for the most, temps do not in fact 'replace' anyone. Their temporary work is carefully planned, and managed, by firms on a regular basis in relation to foreseeable business events, rather than to cope with temporary labor shortage. A temp's contract is with Adecco, Randstad, Manpower, or Kelly Services (once Kelly Girls, when temporary employment was still predominantly feminine), to name but a few temporary employment companies. Their contract is not with the employer that actually manages their labor. These three corporations are among the largest US employers today, and are creating a disproportionate number of jobs as the economy recovers. It is no wonder that *The New York Times* wrote about the rise of the permatemp economy in relation to the precarious nature of jobs created since the Great Recession.[30]

Temporary labor agencies have only been legal in Europe since the 1990s, due to the entrenched hostility of unions and the left towards private labor intermediation, reminiscent of indignities inflicted on industrial and rural laborers in the 19th and early 20th centuries.

---

30   Erin Hatton, 'The Rise of the Permanent Temp Economy', *New York Times,* 26 June 2013, https://opinionator.blogs.nytimes.com/2013/01/26/the-rise-of-the-permanent-temp-economy/?_r=0. See also "Feeling the 'Pressure All the Time' on Europe's Treadmill of Temporary Work", *New York Times,* 9 February 2017. https://www.nytimes.com/2017/02/09/business/europe-jobs-economy-youth-unemployment-millenials.html.

It's revealing that, during the 70s, the first American temp agencies mostly managed female employees, and referred in private to their workers as 'warm bodies', or 'skins'. Whilst the European left forestalled what it saw as a trade in human beings, the battle was finally won by the likes of Adecco, and Manpower. Worse yet, informal labor markets have recently made a comeback in both the European agriculture sector (in the form of migrant pickers), as well as American industry wholesale (in the guise of the *raitero* system). While emblematic of the new age of flexibility, agency labor is not yet the dominant form of temporary employment in Europe. The standard temp is a young, educated individual who signs a temporary contract with an all-powerful employer, unassisted by a union, and likely unable to find alternative forms of gainful employment if dismissed.

Neoliberalism aims to turn every worker into a free agent, an independent contractor. This tendency is most evident in platform capitalism, which profits from on-demand labor. Drivers, riders, and home workers are considered entrepreneurs-of-themselves by corporations operating service apps, in a travesty of the capital-labor relationship. Uber drivers in Seattle, helped by the City Council and the Teamsters, are making the first serious unionization drive against the most funded company in history (one which has yet to turn a profit). As Trebor Scholz argues, under the platform capitalism that sells itself as the sharing economy, workers are *uberexploited*.[31] They are self-employed, and have neither sick leave nor insurance against accidents. Gig workers can fight back in two ways, either by unionizing and gaining recognition of their de facto employee status, or by forming online co-ops; thus counterposing platform cooperativism to platform capitalism. Since I'm rather a believer in platform syndicalism (for a contemporary expression of this originally Latin American anarchist tendency, the Workers' Solidarity Movement in Ireland is a good example), I believe that precarious workers exploited by the likes of Travis Kalanick have to organize against the power of digital capital. In the United Kingdom, Uber drivers and Deliveroo riders are fighting via the courts for their employee status, minimum wage, and sick pay.[32] In London, Uber is appealing a decision that ruled against the company for its unfair treatment of drivers. After protests across the USA, most notably in New York and Texas, Obama's National Labor Relations Board sided with drivers in a class-action suit seeking federal recognition of their status as statutory employees. Considering Uber's Trumpian slant, this is unlikely to continue. That's why the Seattle unionization drive is so important, in the city that was among the first to introduce living wage laws, and where a major portion of the central nervous system of contemporary capitalism (Microsoft, Amazon, and Starbucks) resides. Uber is, via their app, sending messages and podcasts to its drivers, attempting to persuade them to remain as 'partners', and vote for the company

31   Scholz, *Uberworked and Underpaid*.
32   Kirsty Major, 'Uber's happy go lucky drivers never existed - it was exploitation from the start', 28 October 2016, *The Independent*, http://www.independent.co.uk/voices/uber-drivers-employment-tribunal-never-existed-a7385691.html; Homa Khaleeli, 'The Truth about Working for Deliveroo and the On-Demand Economy', 15 June 2016, *The Guardian*, https://www.theguardian.com/money/2016/jun/15/he-truth-about-working-for-deliveroo-uber-and-the-on-demand-economy; Cara McGoogan 'Tribunal to rule on Deliveroo riders' employment status', 6 March 2017, *The Telegraph*, http://www.telegraph.co.uk/technology/2017/03/06/tribunal-rule-deliveroo-riders-employment-status/.

in the unionization election.[33] Uber cannot afford to lose this battle. Yet neither can its 1.5 million precarious drivers, whose incomes are currently at the mercy of customer ratings, and exploitative algorithms.

The digital and the service components of the precariat have converged, creating the sharing economy. Lyft drivers and Foodora cyclists (to cite the two major competitors of the Uber and Deliveroo) feel they are employees with shared, collective interests, rather than the self-employed individuals that the corporations dominating the online service economy want them to be. These workers are the latest addition to the Pangea of precarious labor. Although their legal status is still uncertain, what is certain is that these precarious workers have started to rebel. In doing so, they have destroyed the veil of complacency surrounding abusive labor practices in the sharing economy, a completely deregulated sector where the value created is not shared with the workers creating it.

The Precarious' Universe: Temps, Part-Timers, Freelancers, and Interns

Now that we have in mind how people are variously affected by precarious labor, we can provide an accurate definition of the precariat, via set theory. All things considered, the precariat counts among its members those who: work in temporary and/or part-time private or public employment; are self-employed as freelancers (often for a single employer); work in poorly paid apprenticeships; work in unpaid internships; do not work because they are unemployed; officially do nothing (NEETs) and/or perform under-the-counter, black-market labor.

Essentially, the precarious perform contingent labor for substandard (or even no) wages in an individualized, casualized work environment. Alternatively, they are officially unemployed, meaning they live off a subsidy (if there is one), at times supplemented by jobs paid in cash. This is often a necessity for undocumented migrant workers, tellingly referred to as *sin papeles* or *sans-papiers* (those without papers), in Spanish and French respectively.

I played with Euler-Venn sets to draw the borders of the precarious' universe, and break it down in subsets and overlapping sets of precarious workers, so as to arrive at a precise representation of the precariat. Fundamentally, the precariat set is constituted of the two intersecting subsets of temps (short-term employees and agency workers) and part-timers (who can be either short-time or full-time – the latter are predominately concerned with wage precarity, rather than employment per se). These subsets are united by the legions of (always belatedly) paid freelancers and unofficial workers, and further supplemented by the universe of unpaid labor and idle human capital: internships, unemployment, and inactivity. It is now time to finally draw the contours of the growing reserve army of labor in the wake of the Great Recession: the burgeoning mass of the precariat.

---

33 Greg Bensinger, 'Uber Gears Up to Block Bid to Form a Union in Seattle', 11 March 2017, *Wall Street Journal*, https://www.wsj.com/articles/uber-gears-up-to-block-bid-to-form-a-union-in-seattle-1489237201.

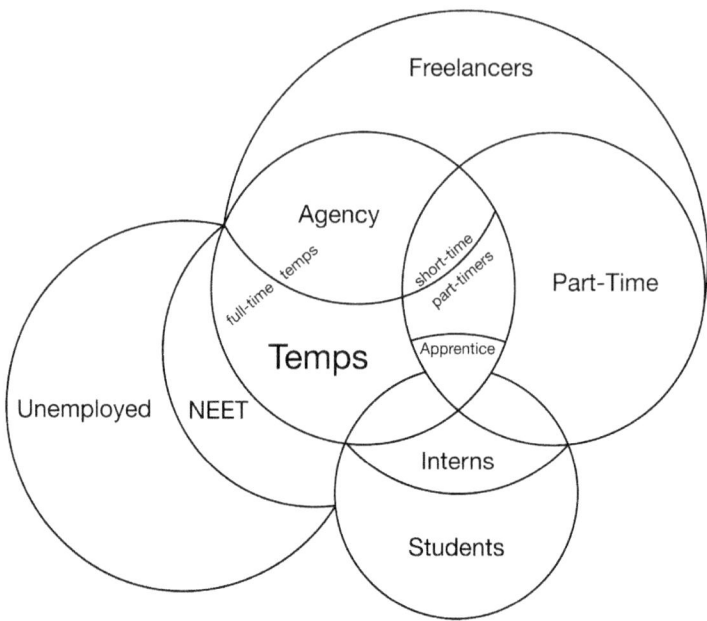

Fig. 1. The Precariat Set

Temps, part-timers, and freelancers make up the subset of paid precarious work. Workers that temp agencies outsource to companies are a significant portion of the total of
temporary workers (it is perhaps of interest this portion is larger in regards to America
than within the European Union). They can either work full-time or part-time, depending on the job profile they allegedly substitute. It should therefore be noted that the
agency labor subset partially overlaps with the set comprised of part-time workers. Paid
apprentices are instead a subset of part-timers intersecting temps, since apprenticeships always entail less than a full workweek (since apprentices need time off to study),
and have a fixed duration. Interns, a sizable subset of the student population, are the
missing link between the world of the precarious at work and the precarious at home:
the unemployed, and NEETs. Students are not precarious insofar as they don't have to
work; their precarity is potential, not actual. They will become precarious in the majority
of cases, but their non-work is of a different order than the refusal to work of NEETs,
(very) young people who do not care to study or seek work so as to obtain additional
benefits, as those officially registered as unemployed do. They may live off welfare if they
are in a country civilized enough to pay anti-poverty subsidies, or are dependent on their
families. Mostly they perform black labor and possibly criminal activities. Conversely,
the unemployed are usually subjected to re-training and workfare requirements in order
to be entitled to receive social transfers. The NEET rate is counted as a percentage of
the young population, while the unemployment rate is counted as a percentage of the
active population, i.e. young unemployed people divided by young people in the labor
force (the sum of people in employment and unemployment).

Using formal notation with we can thus summarize the basic coordinates of the precariat set:

Paid Precarious

TEMP U PART-TIME U FREELANCE with TEMP ∩ PART-TIME ≠ ∅

Unpaid Precarious

INTERN U UNEMPLOYED with INTERN ∩ STUDENT and NEET ∩ UNEMPLOYED

College and high-school students are of course an endless reservoir of temporary and part-time labor. But the oversupply of educated labor has brought the entry wage down to zero, so that corporations can now hire young people for nothing, as shown by the inexorable rise of internships.[34] Only very few internship programs pay something like the minimum wage – the lucky ones only get food and transport – and this also applies to interns working for prestigious companies and financial institutions. Some parents in Europe are actually ready to *pay* a company to get their daughter or son taken on as an intern. Furthermore, the institutionalization of internship in Western universities as a preliminary requirement for degrees has created a vast pool of officially sanctioned, unpaid precarious work. Consequently, the majority of final-year students are now unpaid interns for Fortune 500 companies, corporate foundations, and high-flying independent professionals such as lawyers and architects. Others are old-fashioned working students, who toil because they cannot afford not to earn money during their studies, since they have incurred high levels of debt to pay for increasingly expensive tuition.

The luckier students, usually in the less noble but more established trades, where craftsmanship and dexterity still pay a market premium in spite of automation and 3D printing, get apprenticeships via the state in Europe, and through unions in America. An apprentice gets paid considerably less by the hour than a hired employee and works part-time. Outside the apprenticeship, they attend technical classes in a university or union center. In countries such Germany and America, there has long been a tradition of individuals gaining decent, blue-collar jobs through apprenticeship schemes. Whilst countries such as France and Italy want to introduce them in order to improve the performance of their manufacturing industries, to young locals, the schemes feel like yet another way to defer a guaranteed job paying a full wage.

Some exclude formal part-time employment from the precariat. Conversely, I argue that its marked feminization and/or juvenilization, and the fact that much of it is involuntary, on-call, and non-unionized labor, make the inclusion of part-timers into the precariat a matter of course. What could be more symbolic of precarious labor than a McJob?[35] What's more

---

34 'Generation i', *Economist*, 26 September 2014, http://www.economist.com/news/
international/21615612-temporary-unregulated-and-often-unpaid-internship-has-become-route.
35 The term McJob was first popularized by Douglas Coupland in *Generation X*, his first novel, published in
1991 and set in L.A.

emblematic of the struggle of the precariat than the Fight for 15's struggle against US retail chains? McDonald's employees, just like Starbucks baristas and Wal-Mart associates, earn the minimum wage and have next to zero benefits. If they try to form a union, they are harassed, intimidated, and subsequently fired. Fast-food workers were long seen as unable to form a union and strike; however, the recent drive for service unionization all across the United States has perhaps proved otherwise. Finally, labor boards are beginning to rule against corporations exploiting precarious labor through their franchises, like fast-food chains do. McDonald's was among the first corporate franchises to force retail workers to all dress alike. Just like army recruits (and prison inmates), chain store workers must wear uniforms; big-box stores (also known as supercenters, or megastores) and fast-food restaurants are totalizing institutions where uniformity and discipline must be strictly enforced, in order to prevent any attempt at organization that would drive up wages. However, history is on the side of the precariat, and the eventual raise of minimum wages to a decent level is likely to (finally) be won across America, Europe, and East Asia.

Precarity Rankings

I have included below a 10-category precarity ranking, identifying various umbrella categories of precarious people, in order to highlight those most in danger (as well as what they are in danger of). The logic of this ranking is based upon the idea that being a migrant worker (especially if undocumented) is the worst condition possible; they are exposed to discrimination, abuse, and arbitrary detention. The condition of an unemployed person is slightly better, even those who are unemployed long-term, and/or not being eligible for unemployment benefits. If decent subsidies for the unemployed existed, not having to report to work wouldn't be so bad. Yet the callousness of western governments is such that, nowadays, the unemployed are forced to work for free (or next to nothing) as part of a workfare program (known as *mini-Jobs* in Germany) in order to retain this subsidy. Workfare is for those that governments believe can be reintegrated into the active labor force. Being an unpaid intern (and possibly also having substantial student debt) is one level higher, though still firmly within, precariat hell. After interns come those who are laid off. Being laid off is distinct from becoming unemployed; the term usually refers to full-time workers who are only temporarily made redundant by a large-scale employer, live off a decent wage-based subsidy, can work on the side for cash, and are likely to be rehired by the company when business recovers.

In the middle of the precarity ranking stand contractors: independent workers, or 'bosses of themselves'. While they usually have a fair amount of income security, they are disproportionately likely to fall victim to occupational hazards (such as those that affect workers in the construction industry).

Similar to contractors, freelancers are self-employed, and as such are worse off than temps, who gain some safeguards from being considered employees, albeit of a non-standard, atypical sort (a regular paycheck, and paid sick leave, for instance). Unless contractors associate for insurance purposes, like the Freelancers' Union has done in the US, and SMart is doing in

Belgium and the rest of the EU,[36] they are on their own if their employers refuse to pay them, or cease hiring them (it bears mentioning the almost certain termination of their contract if a freelancer falls seriously ill). Contract workers cannot rely on any sort of unemployment or sickness compensation, although this is offset by the fact they make (on average) higher incomes than those workers with a regular wage. They often have a higher mean salary, but also a higher variance in labor income compared respect to temps, who are wage-earning employees and thus at least know in advance what their net pay will be, and usually have the right to unemployment compensation. As already noted, temporary workers can be bought by firms from temporary labor companies, who manage their labor in conjunction with the client firm, leaving temps exposed to a weird form of double exploitation. Short-term part-time workers are practically indistinguishable from temporary workers, save for the fact that being hired directly by the firm grants them a little more leverage in the workplace. Part-time workers who are long-term employees are among the least precarious. Their precarity is due mostly to insufficient income; working part-time usually translates into half the wages of a full-time employee. Furthermore, most part-time jobs are paid only the minimum hourly wage, and the real value of the minimum wage has been steadily falling for three decades.

1. Migrant

2. Unemployed

3. On workfare

4. Intern

5. Laid Off

6. Contractor

7. Freelance

8. Temp

9. Short-Term Part-Time

10. Long-Term Full-Time

Table 7: Precarity Rankings (1 = Max. Precarity, 10 = Min. Precarity)

Thus, we move to examine the final category. Category 10 has long meant living without precarity; it is about being a permanent employee, one who considers it a privilege to receive a 40-to-life work sentence. The employees most secure in their jobs are usual-

---

36 SMart is a non-profit organization based in Belgium. It helps those who are self-employed and work in creative industries across several EU countries with potentially problematic issues such as getting paid, and various other occupational pitfalls, like invoicing.

ly government workers, since not even the largest companies can now guarantee their employees permanent employment. Times of fierce international competition, as well as accelerating technical change, require increasing productivity from an ever-reducing workforce, in order to merely stay afloat. If you can't keep the pace, you can pack your personal belongings before being kindly escorted out by security; you're on the street, and out of work.

Only in Scandinavia are welfare provisions generous enough to enable workers to give the boss the finger when their patience expires. In fact, it's in Finland that universal basic income (UBI) is being tested for all people that are officially classed as unemployed or precarious (the money is paid even if you later find a job). The introduction of a basic income would complement the existing employment model called *flexicurity*, which has become a typical feature of Nordic capitalism, characterized by the social-democratic bent of its politics. Although it is not without faults (such as persistent youth unemployment, as well as punitive workfare), it reduces the market's power over the lives of the precariat (in more academic terms, it *decommodifies* precarious labor).

However, Scandinavia aside, within the rest of the world of informational capitalism, those in precarious positions are constantly blackmailed by businesses and administrations. It's either kowtowing, or facing the harrowing prospect of joblessness and financial distress. Unemployment benefits are usually not enough to cope with basic economic needs (such as food, housing, and transportation), especially if you have a family. Furthermore, they are consistently being scaled back. That's why a fundamental demand of the politicized sections of the precariat has always been UBI, in order to provide some stability independent from the instability of the economy, and secure fundamental rights for all.

The working poor are starting to go hungry even in Europe, whose indifference to the plight of the weakest strata of society is beginning to rival America's (and also Japan's, where casual workers and destitute people are treated with contempt). In Britain and Germany there has been serious pressure from governments to push people into workfare programs, thus linking the payment of unemployment benefits to accepting jobs in the private sector at below-minimum wage rates. The disciplining function of workfare is not lost on young people, who resent being subjected to considerable government intrusion into their lives, forced usually into jobs of no social value, and benefit only the companies who are permitted to pay them meager wages. There is a growing call for UBI from the public, not least because of the vast numbers of people forced into precarity by the Great Recession. UBI would mean the end of workfare and all forms of means-tested welfare designed to regulate and stigmatize the poor. It would also make it far easier to enforce a higher minimum wage. It would limit the necessity for workers to accept less than the statutory minimum wage in grey and black markets, since they have some economic stability, in the form of basic income. UBI, therefore, is both a key welfare provision to properly address social insecurity, and also a form of empowerment, one which will unleash social creativity in non-economic activities.

Precarious Work: Damnation vs. Liberation

Although I have sketched the circles of the precarious inferno, yet I am not sure which is the worst; temporary work, or permanent? In general, leftist writings on precarity portray precarious employment as a negative condition, known as the oppressive model of precarity. On the other hand, there is also a wealth of literature that highlights the liberating energies unleashed by precarity which lead to solidarity with others; one's identity is not defined by one's work, but rather in relation to one's activities, and relationships with other precarious people sharing a common condition.[37] While there is little doubt that no longer having a job for life is positive, being jobless is not an ideal condition. Both are social life sentences. One must consider that, due to the financial crisis, creativity and solidarity have been undermined by lack of jobs (any job), and surviving the ensuing rat race means undercutting your fellow precarious beings. Texts written by the precarious authors underscore the overcommitted, albeit unstable, nature of precarious jobs, but also their unwillingness to return to the regimentation of the office or factory. Most precarious workers wish to attain employee status and benefit from introduction of a basic income and the setting of a high hourly wage, so that precarity can be a way of life, rather than a daily fight for survival. Considering the looming threat of technological unemployment, due to automation and machine learning, worktime reduction also needs to be taken into account.

This book thus proposes a combination of the 4-day workweek, a $/ 15 minimum wage, and a $/ 1,000 basic income for all adults, starting with people aged between 18 and 30. These basic measures will to bring precarity under control, and reverse the growing economic inequality of the post-crisis world. These reforms are significant, substantial, achievable and also necessary to restarting the economy. The book concludes with an open strategy for the emancipation of the precariat, which will hopefully be subjected to both discussion and criticism. It will be the precariat that will collectively decide its own organizational forms, as well as its social and political program. Since the year 2000, I have been dreaming of founding the revolutionary union of the precarious of the world, starting from within the European Union. What is clear is that there must be a decisive step forward in labor organization, advocacy, and conflict, for and by the precariat, for general social emancipation to take place, beginning with precarious youth.

Immigration and Discrimination

Immigrants are by definition precarious. Like the young, they are easy to hire and easy to fire. In a country like France, young *beurs* (French citizens of Algerian, Tunisian, or Moroccan descent) are treated as second-class citizens, experiencing levels of unemployment and discrimination matched only by that historically experienced in American by young black men. France holds to the principle of *ius soli* (right of the soil): if you are born there, you are a citizen (much like in Canada and Australia). Its opposite principle, *ius sanguinis* (right of blood) – the fact that one needs native parents in order to be a citizen, a principle with clear

---

37   See the elegantly written and argued Patrick Cingolani, *Révolutions précaires,* Paris: La
      Découverte, 2015.

ethno-fascist connotations – rules over much of Europe. An Italian born in Buenos Aires stands a better chance of getting Italian citizenship than a young Eritrean born and bred in Milan. By the same token, French-speaking African immigrants are better off if they live in Montréal rather than in Paris. Especially if they're middle-class, they are respected and treated as equal citizens, and typically acquire nationality in the space of a few years.

During the neoliberal era, Europe trailed behind North America in regard to integration. Poor, immigration-dense *banlieues* are to blame for the worst nightmares of the European elites: fantasies ranging from class war to apocalyptic jihadism. However, fundamentalism is still very much a minority currency, even in places like Saint-Denis and Molenbeek. Nowadays, Antifa and Antira movements rallying anarcho-autonomist youth, local people, and the hooligan supporters of certain soccer teams, are some of the few remaining antidotes to national populism. Mirroring this, they also stand against the dangerous lure of nihilism embraced by the tiny minority of young, European Arabs, tempted by the extreme nature of Salafi jihadism.

Social movements must find a way to connect with immigrant neighborhoods, or reactionary politics will prevail in Europe, and groups such as Le Front National will gain enough power to fracture it irreparably. Younger generations within the *banlieues* are rightly enraged at mounting police violence, catalyzed by the state of emergency put in place after the Charlie Hebdo and Friday the 13th attacks. Hollande caused the rebellion of half of the socialist party when he threatened to abolish *ius soli* for Daesh supporters having double nationality. On the issue of citizenship, as on the issue of labor, the socialist administration betrayed its voters. Thus, Macron has emerged as the champion of openness and change, standing against the National Front, leaving fractured, warring camps of the anti-racist behind.

In the summer of 2015, when Germany and Austria opened their borders to the flow of Syrian refugees crossing the Balkans, as well as fascistic Hungary, a potent image was captured. The migrants on the highway carried a European flag at their head. The symbolism was powerful: Europe was a continent of human rights, and of peace. The good people of Vienna and Munich welcomed the migrants arriving at railway stations, the same migrants who had been blocked by Hungary's barbed wire fences. It was one of the few moments in recent history that made me proud to be European. Europe will be made or destroyed on the issue of migration, the veritable dividing line between progressive and reactionary populism. The Trump administration, by decreeing a Muslim ban and planning to build a wall on the US-Mexico border, is honoring its racist campaign promises. Migrants are fleeing the East Coast of America and pouring into Canada, which, under liberal Justin Trudeau, is maintaining the open-door policy on which the country's fortunes were built. America is instead freewheeling backwards, adopting policies reminiscent of the period between 1920 and 1965, when immigration was seriously curtailed in the name of 'American' values. In Europe, if the Eurozone were to collapse, the continent would be set to revert to the kind of nationalism that caused the most murderous wars in its history. The precariat must thus continue to stand for the rights of migrants, and for freedom of movement within the European Union, across the Mediterranean, and the Balkans. The precariat must take heed of the actions performed by activists in Ventimiglia and the Brenner helping African and Syrian migrants cross the border.

Precarious Labor and Autonomous Marxism

In a literal sense, the precariousness of labor has existed since the dawn of steam-powered, industrial capitalism. Karl Marx addresses the issue in the first volume of *Das Kapital*,[38] when he discusses the reserve army of labor. He described how the wage demands of the factory-bound proletariat were kept in check by the precariousness of labor demand, due to the irregular, crisis-prone process of capital accumulation (i.e. investment). If laborers didn't organize, unchecked exploitation and misery would befall those working in the mills and fields. However, below the proletariat in the socio-economic hierarchy was the *lumpenproletariat*, whom Marx wrongly despised (and Bakunin eulogized): thieves and other petty criminals, prostitutes, tramps, vagrants, etc. The lumpenproletariat made up a reserve army of potential replacement laborers, keeping those in the factories in line, and keeping wages low.

A temporary workforce is a permanent feature of certain industries, exemplified by seasonal workers in sweatshops, and laborers in commercial agriculture. In this respect, things have not changed much since the 19th century. Informal labor remains the norm in emergent and developing economies. However, the recent swelling of the precariat is a symptom of a troubling return to informal labor markets inside the relatively wealthy societies of advanced capitalism.

While contingent labor has always existed in capitalist societies, Italian Autonomous Marxism was the first to argue that precarious labor had moved from the peripheral position it occupied under keynesian, industrial capitalism, to a core position in neoliberal, informational capitalism. Negri and others argue that informational capitalism – the current technological and social paradigm, according to Manuel Castells' seminal work of social theory *The Information Age*[39] – is based on casual, affective, creative, immaterial, and precarious labor.

However, a theory of the precariat is not immediately able to slot into the world as understood by Autonomous Marxism. The precariat comprises of two categories of workers with very different levels of skill and education: pink-collars working in retail and low-end services (cashiers, cleaners, janitors, cooks, waiters, etc.) under constrictive but standardized employment norms, and the digital creative class (editors, graphic artists, programmers, etc.) who are temping, sometimes at high wage rates, in the information economy connecting the world's major cities. Furthermore, the precariat is also a plurality of young people of different genders, different classes, and different ethnicities.

Aside from Autonomous Marxism, contemporary Marxist thought tends to discount the notion that this precarious plurality constitutes an analogue of the 20th century working class; there might be precarity, but there's no precariat. At most, they make up a section of the working class. I deny this. The precariat is the successor of the working class, emerging from the new form of informational neoliberalism expanded and radicalized in the crucible of the Great

---

38   Karl Marx, *Capital: A Critique of Political Economy. Volume I: The Process of Capitalist Production*, 1867.
39   Manuel Castells, *The Rise of the Network Society: The Information Age: Economy, Society, and Culture Volume 1*, Oxford: Wiley-Blackwell, 2010.

Recession. The precariat is a generation becoming a class. It has become a new historical subject, and is the only subject capable of progressive collective agency; it's the precariat that both performs general labor, and constitutes the general intellect (to use Marx's terms). The precarious have their identity based on exclusion from social status, rather than on nationalist, or cultural norms. The centrality of the service precariat for 21st century capitalist accumulation is equivalent to the role played by the industrial proletariat in determining the fortunes of 20th century capitalism.

Autonomous Marxism, as elaborated by Antonio Negri, Mario Tronti, Paolo Virno and others, places the revolutionary agency of the exploited subject at the center of philosophical analysis. After the defeat of the 1968-1979 insurgency of the western working class,[40] the theorists of *operaismo* (*workerism*) turned to focus on urban movements, as well as emerging forms of service and intellectual labor, as a new Post-Fordist, digital economy was consolidating out of the ashes of industrial Fordism. In the work of Negri especially, this position is made clear: the precariat must be radicalized, in order for the multitude to cast off the dominating weight of imperial structures. It is within the relative obscurity of this intellectual tradition that the radical theory of precarity was forged in the 00s, centered around Milan, Rome, Barcelona, Madrid, Paris, Berlin, Helsinki, and Liège.

To summarize my previous point differently: the new digital capitalist class is confronted by a multitude of young precarious workers. It is the precariat's labor, communication, and distribution that is making internet billionaires rich beyond imagination. The oligopolists have long acted jointly to protect their class interests (low taxes, low wages, etc.). However, the time has come for the precarious to act as class, and work with their collective interest in mind. It is time to cut into profits and end income insecurity. Just as Henry Ford needed to be buried for Fordism to rise, not only Steve Jobs, but also his free-market ideology, needs to die for *Jobsism* to rise. Although in vastly different technosocial paradigms (industrialism and informationalism, respectively), the implications of the Fordist and Jobsian compromises are the same regarding regulation: let workers share the bounty of productivity, either individually in the form of wages, or socially in the form of welfare, else risk economic crisis and class warfare. If an egalitarian solution to capitalist crisis was found against National Socialism in the last century, it can also be found against national populism in this century. Capitalism can be reformed. It has been reformed before, during the Belle Époque, and again after World War Two. However, today we need a simultaneous revision of both social and ecological regulation of capitalism. Social regulation has been experimented before with success, yet ecological regulation has not. If we consider Piketty's laws of capitalist motion valid, and I think any thinking left-leaning individual should, then growth must be restarted, so that it can jump above the profit rate, and reduce capital-labor disparity. However, this 'red' (social) objective is posed to clash with the 'green' (environmental) objective, since additional growth would lead to even greater carbon emissions, pushing the planet further towards environmental chaos.[41]

---

40   An insurgency that Autonomists had predicted would occur (much to the surprise of traditional communist and socialist parties), and came in the form of an extensive wildcat strike coupled with union demands, rendering factories unmanageable for a decade.

41   This is what climate activist George Monbiot argues in his dismissal of a Keynesian way out of the

Of course, anti-capitalists of all tendencies will just question why we don't simply ditch capitalism instead. My answer to them is that capitalism makes innovation and material progress possible in ways that state communism has been unable to deliver at any latitude, even under well-meaning leaderships like those of the Soviet Union's Mikhail Gorbachev, and Tanzania's Julius Nyerere. Communism simply doesn't work as an economic system; look at what China accomplished when it switched from Mao Zedong's communism to Deng Xiaoping's capitalism. Immediately following the fall of the Soviet Union, Russia's GDP was still larger than China's, at exchange rates reflecting purchasing power parities. By 2016, China's GDP was more than five times larger that Russia's (536% larger), making the country the workshop of the world, pulling hundreds of millions out of poverty. It is hard to argue with these facts. Although the Communist party officially retained power in spite of the Tiananmen Square student rebellion, the lives of over one billion people were drastically improved by market reform: the rate of extreme poverty in China went from almost 90% in 1980, to less than 2% in 2013 (World Bank data). China's might be state-controlled capitalism, but it's capitalism nonetheless. In light of this, I do not see a viable economic alternative that can replace firms and markets. To adopt an effective, populist strategy, the instinctive anti-capitalism of the precariat must be of the transformative kind: changing both the state, and market institutions, in order to achieve social and ecological regulation of capital, abolishing the dictatorship of global finance, and expanding the domain of commons-based peer production, as an alternative to both state and market production.

The Precariat is the New Proletariat

I have argued that the core of the precariat includes the emerging social class composed of young, urban temps, of both middle-class and proletarian origins, living and working in the global north. Furthermore, the precariat is disproportionately female and immigrant. In terms of its technical class composition, the precariat performs service labor in low-tech retail industries, and high-tech information industries.[42]

This internal variety is problematic. A social alliance is needed amongst the constituents of the precariat, to further their common cause. Yet this alliance is by no means a foregone conclusion, but a matter of labor agitation, and populist politics. When Oakland residents threw rocks at the Google bus, they were protesting the fact that residents – generally of African-American and Latino descent – had to pay more than double the fare than coders – generally Caucasian – traveling to the Googleplex on buses provided by the city. The city was subsidizing a corporation while simultaneously cutting essential welfare and housing services. The residents' rage was mainly directed at Google as a company, although its employees were still resented as agents of gentrification. Yet

---

current crisis of capitalism. Theoretically, a carbon-neutral form of capitalist accumulation can exist, mitigating this issue, and will be discussed in the final chapter of this text.

42   Although this divide is being bridged by the app economy, that mixes geo-location technology with personal services performed by digital labor. When everybody owns a smartphone, everybody is a digital worker, independent from their occupation or education.

how many of those on the Google bus were interns, or temps? Surely many; a long-term employee at Google does not take the bus, but instead drives a Tesla, or bikes to Mountain View on a $2000 fixie.

From a political perspective, the precariat is the social subject at the vanguard of the political constitution of those opposing both financial and political elites. People are angry because bankers are bailed out while ordinary citizens are left to suffer job losses and welfare cuts. The precariat is a culmination of different grievances, and different constituencies, in the common fight against inequality, and for the reassertion of social and political rights. The precariat might not be the 99% (it stands at around 15-25% of the working population), but it gives voice to the people's majority. Similarly, the industrial working class was not the majority of the people (it never grew beyond 33% of the population), yet the social and political logic of its unions and parties permeated the whole of society, its emancipation opening the gates of equality for all. If austerity and inequality are to be defeated, the precariat must achieve full emancipation from social and political inferiority.

The industrial proletariat has been replaced by the service precariat, as the class that is at the spearhead of social movements opposing domestic racism and global inequality. Marx famously distinguished between class *ex se* (*in itself*) and class *per se* (*for itself*). The precariat is a class in itself, in the process of becoming a class for itself. Although Standing[43] didn't acknowledge his intellectual debt to the movement, he was right in arguing that the precariat was making the leap from class in itself to class for itself. These are clearly Marxian categories, yet Marxists have in general been critical of furthering their usage (don't touch the centrality of the working class!). Marxists aside, the fact of the matter is that, post-Great Recession, the increasing precarization of the middle class, as well as the pauperization of the service class, have both made precarity a mainstream concern. The precariat has stopped being merely the jargon of the moment, and instead is discussed by major media outlets across the globe. Never has the word 'precarious' has been used with more frequency, and applied to a larger variety of contexts (see for instance, Judith Butler[44]).

Standing, contradicting his own thesis, envisages the precariat veering to the right. Conversely, I think it is already veering to the left, and is in fact behind the grassroots political revival occurring in Spain, Greece, Portugal, and France. It's the petty bourgeoisie and the native working class – not the precariat – that are voting in large numbers for Marine Le Pen in France, Norbert Hofer in Austria, and Geert Wilders in the Netherlands, to name but a few of the despicable xenophobes threatening European unity today.

---

43   Standing, *The Precariat*.
44   Judith Butler, *Precarious Life: The Power of Mourning and Violence*, London: Verso, 2004. See also Isabell Lorie, *State of Insecurity: Governing the Precarious*, London: Verso, 2015.

Western Middle Classes: Marx vs. Weber[45]

Class theory comes in two large sets: Marxian and Weberian. For Marx (particularly in sociological works such as *18 Brumaire or Civil Wars in France*) society can be segmented downwards, from the top of the socio-economic hierarchy, into: the industrial, financial and commercial bourgeoisie, the petty bourgeoisie (shopkeepers, middlemen, government employees, etc.), the industrial proletariat, farmers and the peasantry, and finally the lumpenproletariat (the unemployed / illegally employed). Marx always thought in terms of class polarization, his theory forcing a final showdown between industrialists and industrial workers, organized by vanguard socialist parties and workers' unions. In stark contrast, Max Weber[46] instead argued that nationalism was going to lure workers away from the appeal of socialism (as both a liberal and a nationalist, he was well placed as to understand why), and capitalism was bound to integrate the growing middle class, so as to form a political counterbalance to the volatile mass of the proletariat. Similarly, Weber contended, while the bourgeoisie was tiny and stood to lose against mass parties in the emerging sphere of democratic politics, it could either ally itself with old traditional elites,[47] or with the newly emerging bureaucratic and clerical classes, in order to achieve cultural and political hegemony, to borrow the terminology of Antonio Gramsci.[48]

National warfare would end up trumping class struggle in the senseless carnage of the World War One. Peasants and workers from neighboring European countries slaughtered each other over four years of ceaseless trench warfare, disavowing the pacifism declared by both French socialists and German social democrats during the Second International. However, by toppling the Russian, Prussian and Habsburg Empires, World War One actually contributed to the worldwide spread of socialism, and not only in Bolshevik Russia, but also across Europe, Asia, Africa, and Latin America, greatly contributing to early anti-colonial movements.[49]

According to Weber, there were two countervailing trends opposing the spread of socialist ideology: the cross-class appeal of nationalism, brazenly evident at Verdun or Gallipoli, and the growth of the middle class. He was the first observing that the modern state was creating an intermediate stratum of bureaucrats, and the modern corporation was creating an intermediate stratum of employees between workers and management (clerks, technicians, secretaries, etc.). These people usually professed conservative values, and were faithful to the party of order and authority. They could be counted on to stave off the socialist threat if workers' councils attempted to seize factories and government buildings, attempting to replicate in Berlin and Turin what the soviets of Petrograd and Moscow had successfully accomplished in November 1917.

---

45 Like anyone with an interest in social science, I am indebted to Michael Mann's fundamental quadrilogy *The Sources of Social Power*, Cambridge: Cambridge University Press, 1986-2013.

46 Max Weber, *Economy and Society*, Vol. 2, University of California Press, 1928.

47 Something which Joseph Schumpeter abhorred – it attributed the war-mongering bent of German capitalism to its unholy alliance with Prussian and later Nazi elites; liberalism had to eschew any intermingling with nationalism for capitalism to be peaceful, and the international economy unperturbed.

48 Antonio Gramsci, *Quaderni del carcere*, Torino: Einaudi, 2014.

49 See Michael Mann, *Sources of Social Power: Volume 2, The Rise of Classes and Nation States*, Cambridge: Cambridge University Press, 1986.

In fact, the defeat of the 1919-20 revolution in Germany and Italy can be attributed to the effective mobilization of the middle classes by the bourgeoisie against bolshevism in defense of the liberal order. This mobilization subsequently degenerated into open fascism, as well as repression of the working class wholesale. The fascist dictatorships of Italy and Germany, as well as their many imitators on the Continent, enjoyed mass appeal amongst the lower layer of the middle class: the petty bourgeoisie, comprised of state officials, shopkeepers, farm owners, and tradesmen.

Conversely, in France, Great Britain and America, what came to be known as the educated middle class stayed centrist and mostly clear of fascism, both before and after World War Two. During the Great Depression, the middle class of the few surviving liberal democracies veered to the left, as vast numbers of artists, intellectuals, and engineers joined the Popular Front in Europe, and the progressive New Deal in America. Similarly, in the 60s and 70s arose a general discontent with constrictive social structures and hierarchies, as well as large-scale protests against western military intervention against guerrilla armies. The radicalization of the children of the middle class in the universities of America and Europe was a symptom of this, evidenced by the meteoric rise of the Students for a Democratic Society movement, and the proliferation of Marxist and anti-imperialist groups (some even embracing armed struggle), respectively. Revolutionary Marxism exerted considerable influence on the Western middle classes until neoliberalism defeated it, both from inside and outside.

The catastrophic (but also radically reformist) 30s and 40s are much closer to today's experience than the revolutionary 60s and 70s. A political radicalization of the middle class, as well as a renewed wave of labor conflict similar to that of the Great Depression, is occurring today in the aftermath of Great Recession. Arguably, the middle class has been a major force for social change since 1945. The peace movement, the international student movement, the women's movement, the anti-nuclear movement; these were all middle-class movements. Now that the Great Recession has severely squeezed its living standards and made its children precarious, will the middle class ditch neoliberalism and become progressive, by allying itself with the radicalized precariat, to stand against national-populist reaction?

Certainly, the Occupy movement of 2011-2012 in America was an early sign of this. It was a left-populist movement mainly composed of young people, born into the middle class. Students, interns, and the newly-unemployed constituted the vanguard of an ostensibly anarchist movement, making socialist demands, by virtue of an *a priori* popular investiture ('We are the People, We are the 99%!'). The political legacy of Occupy is nurturing the current mass resistance to the Trump administration. Under Franklin D. Roosevelt, it was workers, intellectuals, artists moving to the left of the political spectrum, and since Obama it's been the precarious young who have become impatiently radical, evidenced in the popularity of the Bernie Sanders' campaign, and the incredible growth of the Black Lives Matter and Pink Tide movements. With Trump attacking immigrants and women, the issue of the radicalization of the middle class has a renewed political urgency, if resistance to fascist national populism is to prevail in the land of Thomas Jefferson and Abraham Lincoln.

Of Generation and Class

The worldwide protests of 1968 was, in my opinion, a case of generation against class.[50] In France, it was the anarchist and Maoist students pushing for revolution, while the working class pushed for reform under the aegis of the French communist party (PCF); in America, it was SDS, hippies, and Black Panthers seeking to overthrow the system and stop war, while an overwhelmingly patriotic, unionized working class defended American capitalism because it brought them economic prosperity (it would stop doing so shortly after). In both cases, it was 'working-class friendly' reform that prevailed in the short-term, bringing wage increases, and more generous welfare provisions. In the long term, however, it was the generational aspect of 1968 that won; the baby boomers soon discarded leftism to embrace the market, create new digital industries, impose new sex and gender norms, and in doing so, ended up replacing previous paternalistic elites.

The 68ers themselves didn't lose much sleep at witnessing the defeat of the socialist-leaning working class. Neoliberalism provided plenty of room to fulfill their personal and generational aspirations. Some of them, of the ilk of Steve Jobs and Bill Gates, went on to become billionaires, or join the ranks of the political class (countless former 1968 revolutionaries are now party officials and Eurocrats). Anti-Vietnam protesters morphed into upwardly mobile yuppies, as baby boomers started entering the establishment. They rode the wave of the information and media revolution they had created, and became rich and influential in the process. The precariat is made up of those that came after them, and weren't nearly as lucky.

The Making of the Precarious Class

Following E.P. Thompson and Stuart Hall,[51] we have to ask where the precariat derives from, how its associated subculture(s) counters domination, and how this counterculture potentially creates a new space for radical hegemony. The precariat is an urban, multicultural, rebellious class. It is strongly influenced by pop subcultures (punk, techno, reggae, and hip-hop, essentially), the cyberpunk culture of the 90s, and the free media and hacker movements of the 00s. A whole generation of uprooted cosmopolitans came together in squats, raves, and street parades, determined to change the world by reclaiming the streets and producing political art. Instinctively, the early precariat detested racism and forged multicultural bonds of friendship and solidarity, prescient examples being the SOS Racisme movement, and Le Mouvement de l'Immigration et des Banlieues (MIB), which were active in France during the 80s and 90s.

The politicization of the precariat has occurred over three seminal issues: the politics of partying, the fight against fascism and racism, and more recently, youth unemployment and the accompanying protests against corrupt elites engendering this.

---

50 See Herbert Marcuse, *One-Dimensional Man,* Boston: Beacon Press, 1964.
51 See E.P. Thompson, *The Making of the English Working-class,* London: Penguin 2013, and Stuart Hall, *Resistance Through Rituals: Youth Subcultures in Post-War Britain,* London: Routledge, 2006.

Spain is a test case for considering reactions to these three issues. The country traditionally has a higher rate of youth unemployment than the rest of the Eurozone. In the 80s, the *la movida* in Barcelona and Madrid attracted youngsters from all over Europe. In the 90s, Valencia and Ibiza became the world capitals of euphoric house music. In the 00s, as Spain's youth dispatched the pro-Bush Aznar government by sending millions of text messages denouncing him as a liar, the country boomed. Floating on a real estate bubble, the mid-00s saw Socialist Prime Minister José Luis Rodríguez Zapatero legalizing gay marriage, as well as legislation protecting women from domestic abuse: it seemed as if Almodovar had gone to power.

Unfortunately, this wave of progress didn't last. When the global credit crunch started hitting the Spanish economy, young Spaniards felt doubly betrayed. Their aging country seemed to only offer joblessness and evictions, while bankers were still getting fat off corrupt practices. In 2011-2012, precarious Spanish youth led millions to occupy the central squares of cities across the country. The Indignados were Europe's most powerful movement in 2011, the year of global revolution. Although Zapatero's nemesis, the current Prime Minister – conservative catholic Mariano Rajoy – was not thrown out of power; the political legitimacy of the post-Franco establishment was gone forever. The precariat in charge of organizing the *acampadas*, however, succeeded in reclaiming democratic sovereignty for the people of Spain. The movement against mortgage evictions became more powerful than labor unions under the charismatic leadership of Ada Colau, who was then elected mayor of Barcelona in 2015. Her election was, to date, the most significant political victory of any achieved by the anarcho-populist movements that shook the world in the 10s. Since then, Spain's major political developments have centered around the actions of Podemos, a political party born just before the European elections of 2014 under the leadership of former *tuta bianca* (*white overall*)[52] Pablo Iglesias, and Laclauian ideologue Inigo Errejon. This party, comprised of former Indignados, could soon become the second largest in Spain, dethroning the socialist party of their majority.

The proletariat that developed over the course of first two industrial revolutions built tight, mostly male, communities centered around working class solidarity in industrial towns and cities. These communities, which successfully existed as lived acts of resistance for most of the 20th century, were shattered by the deindustrialization engineered by monetarist policies in the early 80s. From the aftermath of this shattering, the precariat coalesced amidst the relentless drive of neoliberalism toward individualization. The trend toward singlehood in urban and suburban environments, or uneasy communal living among underpaid temps, made community much harder to achieve for young precarious workers. However, the internet (chat rooms, mailing lists, social media platforms, etc.) acted as a substitute for traditional working class milieux (the factory, the bar, the sport stadium, etc.) in the age of postindustrial labor. Dilapidated neighborhoods in neglected areas of cities connected to the global network of financial and informational transactions acted as a magnet for the multicultural precariat. Rich in ideas and short on cash, they have flocked to major world cities, their only capital a university degree and a PC with internet access. In urban areas on the verge of gentrification

---

52   Term referring to Negrian anti-globalization protesters, who wore white overalls in Genoa and other early
       00s counter-summits.

(where, during good economic times, the so-called creative class of affluent bohos was to be found), young knowledge, culture, and service workers have coalesced informally, often around localized non-market or anti-market economies. Pertinent examples of these informal economies include squats, social centers, communal spaces with free-wifi, food and clothing exchanges, freegan food distribution networks, civil rights associations, and environmental activism initiatives. Bushwick, Hackney, Kreuzberg, Ixelles, and Isola: these are the hubs in which the precariat lives and acts in New York, London, Berlin, Brussels, and Milan.

These multiethnic neighborhoods are spaces of interaction and aggregation, often catalyzing protest movements against precarity, evictions, urban speculation, and ecological degradation, acting in solidarity with migrants, and in opposition to fascists and xenophobes, whose influence has been steadily growing since the Great Recession. The precariat acts as the general intellect in the social factory of information, goods, and needs, brought about by the recent transition from Fordism to Jobsism. It raises claims, and formulates demands to improve its own welfare, as well as that of society in general. It is at the forefront of anti-racist movements, present at the front of demonstrations fighting austerity and corrupt politicians, and does not shy away from rioting when police are too many, and the unemployed too angry. Clashes with the police always garner media attention and keep pressure on established power, but what is really at hand is something under-reported: the emergence of a social economy based on peer production and open technology; software, services, culture, and entertainment. Of course, just like the dot-org activism of yore, the contemporary sharing economy has already been colonized by a digital oligarchy. Whilst the realm of non-profit platforms is steadily expanding (both online and offline), the ubiquity of smartphones maintains the dominance of market logic with regards to online interactions. Nevertheless, a new social economy based on mutuality and reciprocity, respect for all genders, and the environment is clearly emerging, and municipalities and corporations are grappling with both citizens and consumers beginning to assert their power.

Postcapitalism and Anticapitalism

Journalist Paul Mason[53] sees this burgeoning third sector as evidence that the transition toward postcapitalism has already begun. He envisages the world of postcapitalism as a not-too-distant situation in which the current abundance of both informational and financial wealth is distributed more equally across the whole of society. Capitalist corporations, in this world, have gone the way of feudal castles, and are simply relics of a distant past. Although Mason doesn't explicitly say it, it is the sharing economy – which is supported by the post-working-class precariat alone – that will dissolve the exploitative capitalist power relations present in contemporary labor and goods markets. Giuseppe Allegri and Roberto Ciccarelli label this new class as the *Fifth Estate* (succeeding the bourgeoisie and the proletariat), but reduce it unconvincingly to the world of self-employed professionals and freelancers. What

---

53   Paul Mason, *PostCapitalism: A Guide to Our Future*, London: Penguin, 2016. Although I hereby highlight my differences with Mason, I was so struck in 2012 by his book proposal read on his agent's Kindle at the Frankfurt Book Fair, that I immediately pre-empted the Italian translation rights. When the book was finally published in Italian in 2016, my job was no longer there.

Standing and Mason treat too broadly, they treat too narrowly. All these authors seem to hint at an organic growth in the size and reach of the social economy, thinking that a solidaristic polity will emerge, built around mutuality. However, this growth (and the polity that comes with it) is not something that we can take for granted now the precariat has been put on the defensive by the Trumpian turn.

Mason, in spite of his Trotskyist politics (suggesting a penchant for permanent revolution), implies that capitalism will die of natural causes. However, that seems unlikely at best: capital is about power over people, and only struggle and counter-hegemonic actions can begin to dislodge its current economic, political, and social stranglehold. Both the reversal of neoliberal inequality, and the defeat of nationalist populism, require huge conflicts to take place involving massive, populist mobilization in order to be achieved. Bear in mind that these are necessary merely to abolish neoliberalism, not capitalism wholesale. Unfortunately for my anti-capitalist persuasion, I don't think postcapitalism is on the cards in the post-Great Recession bifurcation. Those alternatives currently available consist of a choice between reform and reaction, not between reform and revolution. What the precariat can achieve, via its struggles and revolutions, is the final defeat of neoliberalism and petro-capitalism, and a return to progressive social and economic policy making. It cannot overthrow capitalism itself. It can bury neoliberalism, and it will. In order to do that, precariat-led resistance will have to win against the reactionary forces currently spreading across Europe and America, forces which stand an equal chance of prevailing in the chaos created by the crisis of neoliberalism. In a historical bifurcation, ideology is what determines which version of regulation (of capitalism) will emerge out of global strife and war. After World War Two, the welfare state and social democracy emerged as responses to the devastating memories of Great Depression and war. Now, in the wake of the Great Recession and in the face of climate change, informational democracy and ecological populism should be used to redefine the boundaries between the individual and the market, as well as those between the social economy, private enterprises, and the public sector.

CHAPTER 3. THE ECONOMICS OF PRECARITY AND THE GREAT RECESSION

Neoliberals and Neoclassicals: Only Markets Count

Neoliberalism refers to the ideology first championed by conservative economists like Friedrich Hayek and Milton Friedman. Reacting to the growth in the role of the state after World War Two, Hayek and Friedman advocated free markets, monetarism, deregulation, and privatization as alternatives to the tactics of Keynesian demand management, indicative planning, and the welfare state favored by social democracies.[54] Neoliberalism started as a rearguard battle against Keynesianism in the decades following World War Two, but became increasingly influential as the Cold War progressed, particularly after the inflationary shocks caused by the 1973 and 1979 oil crises. Its status as a global hegemonic ideology was sealed in the 90s after the fall of the Berlin Wall, and the subsequent breakdown of Soviet communism. The combination of these two events led to a widespread discrediting of central planning strategies, as well as all forms of government intervention in the economy, seemingly proving Hayek's point that the market was superior to the plan in terms of informational efficiency and innovation.

Neoliberalism was born to be global. It liberalized information and communication networks and dismembered monopolies. However, its precepts were applicable to illiberal regimes, too. In the western world, particularly after 1989, neoliberalism chimed with freedom, human rights, and democracy. It was in equal measures economically conservative, morally libertarian, and socially multicultural. Yet the tone of western neoliberalism radically changed following the September 11th attacks in 2001, and mildly tolerant neoliberalism yielded to intolerant neoconservativism. Following this, the Great Recession struck, and neoliberalism unraveled in less than a decade between 2008 and 2016. With his Keynesian fiscal stimulus, Obama saved both America and the world from economic meltdown, yet his embattled progressivism created a reactionary backlash so strong that neoliberalism was rejected for something far worse: Trumpian national populism. The winds of closed borders and racism are now blowing strong through the western world, threatening European unity. The two mainstays of post-1945 liberalism, America and Great Britain, have turned their backs on both Europe and globalization, favoring instead nationalist alternatives bound to breed geopolitical rivalry, and macroeconomic chaos. A social-populist alternative must emerge; one that is sufficiently powerful to counter the reactionary malaise that is currently seizing Europe, America, and Asia.

Neoclassical economics provides the basic philosophical tenets to neoliberalism – complete faith in the invisible hand of the market and total mistrust in the visible hand of the state, the axiom of methodological individualism and the assumption of the rationality of investors and all economic agents, combined with a complete indifference toward inequality. It has dominated the academic teaching of economics in American and European university departments until

---

54   Daniel Stedman Jones, *Masters of the Universe: Hayek, Friedman, and the Birth of Neoliberal Politics*, Princeton: Princeton University Press, 2012.

very recently, when its hold over theory and policy became weakened by the financial crisis. Neoclassical economics provides a scientific foundation to the neoliberal fixation on the liberalization of markets and the privatization of public goods. In particular, neoclassical economists justified the excessive risk-taking that led to the financial crisis by professing a blind faith in the efficiency of financial markets. This is the main reason why mainstream economists were unable to see the crisis coming, and have similarly been completely incapable of solving it. If anything, their policy recommendations (based on the assumption that austerity measures increase growth) have made the recession even worse, creating the perfect breeding ground for right-wing, populist sentiments.

The Great Recession and the End of Neoliberalism

Just as the 1929 financial crash brought an end to laissez-faire economics, the economic meltdown of 2008 punctured the neoliberal illusion that markets were always right, a dogma invariably taught in universities around the world. Following the pattern that runs through capitalism's history, a long cycle of financial exuberance ended in a sudden, major depression. This trend should serve to remind even its most ardent believers that capitalism cannot regulate itself, as Keynes pointed out in *The General Theory*; a work that revolutionized economics during the Great Depression. Also prescient about our current crisis is Karl Polanyi, whose work *The Great Transformation*[55] (written in the ideological chaos of the 30s) outlined how early industrial capitalism destroyed pre-existing social relations in order to impose market forces on a recalcitrant population, and described the countervailing institutional and political forces that could arise in response.

Thirty years of unchallenged neoliberal rule has shattered the economy and diminished the middle class, ultimately bringing a demagogue to power for the first time in American history. Precarious jobs have become the norm. Precarious millennials, who played a pivotal role during Obama's two terms in office, deserted the polls in 2016 and let the enraged proletariat elect Trump on racist, populist grounds, rather than mobilizing in support of Hillary Clinton, the baby-boomer candidate of the neoliberal elite.

Free-market liberalism didn't survive the Great Depression. Neoliberalism hasn't survived the Great Recession. Brexit and Trump have destroyed the international foundations on which both the post-1945 liberal order, and the post-1989 neoliberal disorder, were erected. The Trans-Atlantic alliance is withering, and nationalism is spreading across Europe abetted by Putin's authoritarian control of Russia. As a result of this, neoliberalism, although enshrined in international institutions like the IMF, World Bank, WTO, and NATO, is being contested as transnational doctrine, in favor of unilateralism, which makes for an uncertain world where racist fear and civil wars proliferate. Free-trade agreements are worth only the paper on which they were signed, and both TTP and TTIP have been shelved amidst popular reject of globalization and immigration. For the first time since 1945, Europe is going alone, its path set by Angela Merkel's Germany, who faces elections in the fall of 2017 after twelve years in

---

55   Karl Polanyi, *The Great Transformation: The Political and Economic Origins of Our Time*. Boston: Beacon Press, 1957.

power. It is worth noting that France is now rising to the rescue of European centrism after Macron's stunning victory against Le Pen's nationalism; Macron has managed the dubious feat of outclassing France's political establishment while simultaneously underwriting the continuity of France's financial establishment.

Yet from Moscow to Ankara, and Manila to Delhi, nationalist, xenophobic, and homophobic regimes cling to power. Illiberal regimes are presently in the majority at the UN Security Council. In the Middle East, three strong men, Putin, Erdogan, and Trump, are now calling the shots, constituting a new axis of evil that spells doom for Aleppo and the Syrian opposition, and seriously endangers Kurdish aspirations for autonomy both in Rojava and elsewhere. Europe is on the defensive; NATO, the military alliance that was the bedrock of the alliance Anglo-Saxon and European liberalism during the Cold War, has been seriously weakened by Trump's hostility to Germany and the EU, as well as his murky relationship with Russia's regime. Recent political developments at the White House, namely the consolidation of a paranoid regime that practices protectionism and selective isolationism, have destroyed multilateral neoliberalism. The 'West' as we used to know it, no longer exists. Its core, the Anglosphere, is no longer synonymous with openness and freedom.

In economic terms, Trumpism is a mix of restrictive monetary policy and expansionary fiscal policy, the latter in the form of massive tax cuts. Trump wishes to put America 'back to work' with tariffs and infrastructural investment, as the Federal Reserve brings the long stretch of zero interest rates to a close. The return to positive interest rates would be a macroeconomic shock to a global economy still ailing from the 2008 crisis. Unemployment could yet again begin to rise across the world as capital flows back to American shores. However, in order to maintain domestic consensus, national populism must keep its election promise and give people jobs. A program of public works is likely to be launched, which would serve to give economic substance to Trump's 'Buy American' philosophy – a philosophy which was key to his victory in the Great Lakes states of the Rust Belt. This logic does, of course, create trade tensions with China, Europe, and even Mexico and Canada. America's early confrontation with China seems to have given way to a mutual understanding between Trump and Xi Jinping, although this is in no way stable: the North Korean crisis is ongoing, and Trump is supporting Japan against China's claims over the South Sea islands. The tycoon enthusiastically endorses the nationalist government of Shinzo Abe. He got a long handshake from Trump, while Angie Merkel got none. Gone are the days of John Kennedy's declaration: 'Ich bin ein Berliner'. Today brings private meetings in the Oval Office with the Russian ambassador and foreign minister. The hitherto unimaginable closeness to Russia, and the subsequent thawing of relations between Europe and America could have permanent geopolitical consequences: for Eastern Europe, it means to be left vulnerable in case of Russian expansion. Western Europe, on the other hand, must now deal with threats to its economic prowess and political stability, posed by the close relationship between the White House and the Kremlin. Reliance upon America's nuclear umbrella is no longer unconditional, as Germany and South Korea are painfully discovering.

Although capitalism is being appropriated by populist nationalism and authoritarian regimes, is also pressed from below by movements for a radically democratic, more egalitarian, and less carbonized alternative to neoliberalism. I term this movement eco-feminist populism, or more simply *social populism*, which stands in opposition to mounting national populism. Since the Great Recession started in 2008, neoliberalism has entered a critical phase which has now ended with the death of the patient: the liberal west. The electoral defeats of David Cameron in England and Hillary Clinton in America (the candidates of the City and Wall Street, respectively) signals the end of Anglo-Saxon neoliberalism.

Expansionary monetary policy, such as quantitative easing at both the Federal Reserve and the European Central Bank, has cushioned the effects of the crisis on banks and financial markets, and ultimately kept the economy alive. However, due to restrictive fiscal policy, particularly in the Eurozone given the adoption of German-backed austerity, its effects on growth have been modest. The net result of post-crisis economic policy across advanced capitalism has been to further enrich the financial elite, while barely making a dent in unemployment levels (particularly youth unemployment). Worse yet, the quality of jobs and levels of pay, not to mention employment rates, have nowhere climbed back to the levels of the pre-crisis world.

Insiders, Outsiders, and Biased Economists

There are two basic drivers of precarity. One stems from neoliberal economic policy and free market ideology, the other from the dual structure of labor markets. In the 80s, a two-tiered job market came into being, initially only in Europe and Japan, although it soon spread elsewhere. This new job market discriminated against newcomers, and economists soon took notice.[56] On the upper tier of the market there were the insiders, aging, unionized, full-time employees who worked for either the government or large companies, and had guarantees of safe employment, as well as a clear career advancement trajectory. On the lower tier of the labor market were the outsiders, the newcomers to the labor force: mostly women, young people, and immigrants. These outsiders weren't warranted the kind of employment rights enjoyed by the insiders, and only worked short-term contracts that allowed employers to terminate their jobs with ease if they complained or went on strike. The two markets for labor, that of incumbents and that of new entrants, operated under two different regimes, as if belonging to two different economies. Insiders could tie their wage to productivity, profitability, or seniority through collective bargaining, while outsiders could not. Whereas in the insiders' market, wages and hours were jointly set by oligopolists and oligopsonists,[57] such as big companies and major unions, in the outsiders' market wages were set by competition in a labor market where expanding supply was unmatched by a corresponding growth in the labor demand

---

56   Assar Lindbeck and Dennis J. Snower, *The Insider-Outsider Theory of Employment and Unemployment*, Cambridge, Massachusetts: MIT Press, 1988.
57   Oligopsony means control of supply by few sellers (unions in this case) just as oligopoly means control of the market by few firms.

coming from firms. Since the early 90s, real wages for the outsiders have irreversibly declined. The outsiders of the job market are none other than the precarious workers at the center of this book.

In the conventional microeconomics of the labor market, the neoclassical model posits a decreasing returns production function, from which a demand of labor by firms can be derived. The equilibrium wage level is at the point where a positively sloped supply of labor (peoples' decisions about whether to work, and for how many hours) intersects the negatively sloped labor demand curve. An increase of the minimum wage depresses labor demand and causes unemployment. In a depression, since there is unemployment, neoclassical economists recommend wage cuts, a contemporary example of this being the dramatic wage deflation experienced by Greek citizens in the wake of the euro crisis. The policy decisions of the neoclassical labor market model depend crucially on the shape of the labor supply and demand curves: a rigid labor supply and a decreasing labor demand. However, this does not fit the stylized facts of the post-depression labor market, namely a flat supply curve, which means that, at a given minimum wage, there will always be people ready to fill positions – a reserve army of labor, if you will. On the other hand, empirically, labor demand has not been negatively but *positively* sloped since the crisis,[58] which is consistent with the fact that the technology prevalent in the economy exhibits increasing returns to scale. The prevalence of oligopoly in information industries is an indirect proof of this, since this particular market form tends to emerge when unit costs fall, as production increases and the network expands. If that holds, a positive labor demand emerges as the one supported by American data. In this situation, the upward shift in the labor supply causes by a jump in the minimum wage, *increases* (rather than decreases) employment, and enlarges the share of income going to labor. The theoretical relevance of increasing returns was underscored by Adam Smith, Allyn Young, Nicholas Kaldor, Paul Romer, and other classical and Keynesian economists. Furthermore, it appears that labor demand is influenced by product demand, as John Maynard Keynes and Michal Kalecki showed in their pioneering macroeconomic writings,[59] for a decrease in the nominal wage further shrinks an economy already mired in depression. So, if wages are not only a cost, but also the main driver of demand, in a depression, when capacity utilization is low and inventories high, an exogenous increase in the minimum wage could in fact shift labor demand upwards, thus further enhancing the positive employment effect of raising the wage.

---

58   Alan de Brauw and Joseph Russell, 'The Labor Demand Curve Is… Upward Sloping? The Wage Effects of Immigration and Women's Entry into the US Labor Force, 1960-2010', *SSRN*, October 2014, https://papers.ssrn.com/sol3/papers.cfm?abstract_id=2509372.

59   John M. Keynes, *The End of Laissez-Faire: The Economic Consequences of Peace*, London Prometheus, 2004; *The General Theory of Employment, Interest, and Money*, New York, Harcourt, 1964. Michal Kalecki, *Theory of Economic Dynamics: An Essay on Cyclical and Long-Run Changes in the Capitalist* Economy, New York: Monthly Review Press, 2004; *The Last Phase in the Transformation of Capitalism*, New York: Monthly Review Press, 2011.

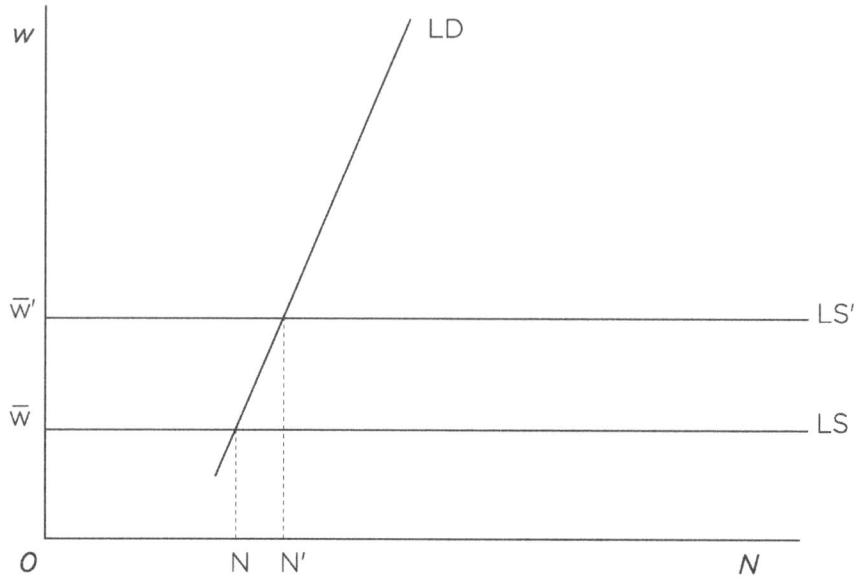

Fig. 2. Doubling the minimum wage under alternative economic assumptions

Neoclassical economics, already hard-pressed to explain the return of mass unemployment its models rule out as a possibility, also has troubles explaining the yawning gap in wage differentials seen since the 90s. They typically justify widening pay disparity with the so-called theory of skill-biased technological progress. The reason that so many are paid little, and so few a lot, they argue, is that technical progress has been biased against uneducated, low-skilled workers, and in favor of educated, high-skilled workers since the advent of computer technology. Faced with the task of justifying widening wage disparity in a pitiless, winner-take-all world, neoclassical economists typically blame disadvantaged workers for rising inequality. Demand for highly educated workers has risen, the reasoning goes, and consequently so have their salaries, while demand for low-skilled workers has decreased or stagnated, and therefore so have their wages. Thus, inequality is due to the normal functioning of the labor market in times of accelerated technological growth; if workers want to earn more money, they should get a better education. This, however, is utterly disingenuous, since job security is independent from skills, and is under attack across the spectrum of labor. An alternative interpretation of growing wage discrepancies is instead centered on precarity and the balance of power in the neoliberal job market. Levels of education have gone up, but wages have gone down. The reason for this is precarity and the enfeeblement of collective bargaining. Young people have plenty of degrees, for which they have paid dearly and often sunk into debt, but can't find paying jobs. When they do, they discover their graduate degrees do not command high salaries. Furthermore, no unions protect temps, adjuncts, indebted students, or the unemployed (although this is changing, especially in American universities).[60]

---

60   An important example is the Graduate Employees and Students Organization (GESO) that has agitated
     for change on American campuses since the 1990s. See Danielle Douglas-Gabriel, 'Yale graduate
     students look to unionize after labor board ruling', *Washington Post*, 30 August 2016.

In order to provide a more accurate view of contemporary work as mutated by the pre-carization process, I examined job security in relation to working skills, and arrived at the following table:

	Low-Skilled	High-Skilled
High Job Security	Public employees, unionized industrial working class – standard workweek, overtime labor.	Bankers, managerial elites, top-level professionals – most hours worked, overtime used as a status symbol.
Low Job Security (Precarious)	Chain workers, service labor-ers – fewest hours worked per job (involuntary part-time), irregular work hours and moonlighting.	Freelancers, creative class, knowledge / cognitive workers (cognitarians) – highly variable work hours.

Table 8: Job Security, Skills and Hours Worked in Today's Segmented Labor Market

The major cause of widening wage and salary differentials is thus not skill-biased technol-ogy (technological changes that are disadvantageous for insufficiently trained or educated workers), but an on-going process of the precarization of employment, which has depressed wages for incomers with respect to incumbents. In other words, the reasons for low wages and underemployment are not technological (with workers lagging behind technical innovation) but political, namely the consequences of policies that have diminished workers' rights, and depressed demand.

Skill-biased progress and meritocracy are baseless myths of contemporary capitalism; a good education is no escape from precarity. On the contrary, the increasing cost of higher education is depressing youth engagement via student debt and unaffordable rents. The 'brain drain' of college-educated youth across both Southern and Northern Europe, North America, and Australia is a tale of thwarted ambitions and burning delusions. Capitalism is not rewarding the brightest. It's those with connections, wealth, or fame (financiers, rentiers, pop stars, pro athletes, corporate lawyers, etc.) that pocket income growth at the expense of all else. Cronyism and nepotism are rampant.

Precarious work does not lead to overall economic improvement. In fact, the opposite is true. It pushes families to the brink of working poverty, and demoralizes workers. It shrinks the share of the pie going to labor, which has fallen steeply since 1990 from about 2/3 to little more than 1/2 of the wealth produced by the business sector.[61] Shortchanging workers drives

---

61   OECD, 'The Labour Share in G20 Economies', https://www.oecd.org/g20/topics/employment-and-social-policy/The-Labour-Share-in-G20-Economies.pdf.

down productivity, and thus growth. Conversely, empowering the precariat would increase wages, jumpstarting economic growth. Fighting for a major increase in the minimum wage is one of the most effective ways of doing so; an increase to $/€15 across America and Europe would boost labor demand, economic growth, and decrease wage inequality.

The Birth of Precarity: The Defeat of Keynesian Rigidity and the Rise of Neoliberal Flexibility

In the name of flexibility and individual freedom, precarious employment relations first became common in the 80s, after Margaret Thatcher and Ronald Reagan came to office in Britain and America. Between them, they successfully imposed a new, transatlantic ideological template: neoliberal economics. This was a watershed moment in the history of capitalism. Before the conservative free-market revolution of the 80s, progressive Keynesianism was the hegemonic economic order. In order to defend labor from financial dislocations, the monetary order which emerged after the defeat of Axis powers severely restricted international capital movements, and tied the war-ravaged economies of Western Europe and Japan to a monetary system built around fixed parity with the dollar. Neoliberal doctrine abruptly changed this. Neoliberals explicitly pursued financial deregulation, floating exchange rates, labor flexibility, and wealth concentration, in order to undermine the power of unions, restore profitability to corporations, and impose stricter labor discipline in the workplace.

Friedman-centric neoliberalism prevailed over Keynesian liberalism; the compresence of high inflation and high unemployment in the 70s (called *stagflation*) was something the *General Theory* had not contemplated, but which Milton Friedman's monetarism could explain and redress, by defeating inflation at the cost of even higher unemployment. Neoliberalism emerged as a viable economic alternative to Keynesianism, overseeing the then-burgeoning technological turn of capitalism, which was based on a deindustrialization of capitalism's old heartlands, as well as the digitization of information, knowledge, and culture. In other words, neoliberalism fostered the information revolution, and the birth of the network society. It provided the institutional framework of the new economy. However, unlike Keynesianism in the 50s and 60s, neoliberalism did not distribute the fruits of increased productivity to wage-earners. The neoliberal economy almost exclusively rewarded top managers, corporate bankers, and all kinds of international rentiers.

Therefore neoliberalism, unlike Keynesianism, lacked a solid demand base, for the new informational products and services that corporations sold to consumers. Since flexible jobs lead to precarious workers with uncertain incomes, a huge consumer credit bubble was needed to keep the population buying. Another way of sustaining customer demand was by decreasing prices; although this applied particularly to electronic devices, this price suppression was applied to all kinds of manufactured goods and packaged commodities. The combination of Moore's Law in electronics, and Wal-Mart's ruthless efficiency in retail, brought ever-lower prices to consumers. These low prices came, however, at the cost of lower wages.

The issue of the distribution of productivity is crucial. The structural cause of the Great Recession lies in the failure of neoliberalism to distribute the growth in productivity, afforded by the digital revolution, to working people. Because of this, they had to burden themselves with debt, in order to finance constant consumption of novel informational goods and services. The crisis will really end when what Negri and Hardt call 'common wealth'[62] is finally re-appropriated by the precariat, whose members vitally contribute to the social media, e-commerce, and platform economies that have emerged from the Great Recession. Neoliberalism is based on the assumption that flexible, self-regulating markets for money, goods, and labor are the model of economic organization. Between democracy and the market, it is the latter that must prevail, in the name of freedom; this is what neoliberalism ultimately preaches. It is a form of economic fundamentalism (or 'market theology' as Marxist historian E.J. Hobsbawm once quipped during class at the New School) which harks back to 19th century laissez-faire liberalism, and has nothing to do with the 20th century liberalism of The New Deal or The Great Society. In fact, the liberals that introduced social security and fought poverty, are the arch enemies of any self-respecting Chicago boy. However, Thatcher and Reagan were not alone in enforcing neoliberal ideals; also regimes as different as those of Deng Xiaoping and Augusto Pinochet, enforced neoliberal economic policies, as David Harvey has rightly noted.[63]

The ideological hubris of free-market capitalism became unassailable after it vanquished state-planned communism. Throughout the 90s and the 00s, neoliberalism and monetarism ruled unchallenged; apologetic economists call the period between 1989 and 2007 the age of Great Moderation, but it was in fact a sharp turn to the right in economic governance after the socialist and Christian democratic consensus of the postwar years. Reagan and Thatcher had imposed conservatism at home and struck a deal with Deng abroad, giving rise to the globalization of trade, finance, technology, and labor that has reshaped the world. Swiftly, Keynes was replaced by Friedman: deficit spending, inflation, and fixed currencies were replaced by balanced budgets, high interest rates, and flexible exchange rates. Attendance of the Washington Consensus on free trade and financial deregulation became an obligation for all governments in the world; access to money from the International Monetary Fund, as well as inclusion in lucrative international loans, were conditional on the appropriate amount of international kowtowing.

The Roaring 90s brought prosperity, but only for the upper middle class. The Asian crisis of 1997-98, and the dot-com crash of 2000, were the first cracks in the facade of neoliberalism. Yet business continued as usual, thanks to the moves made by Alan Greenspan at the Federal Reserve Bank, and George Bush at the White House. They propped up financial interests, allowing the housing and asset bubble to continue to grow to immense proportions all across America and Europe. When the subprime crisis destroyed the US mortgage market in the summer of 2007, it soon led to the complete unraveling of the American financial industry. In September 2008, Lehman Brothers, along with a score of other international banks, began irreparably hemorrhaging money. A panic that lasted well into 2009 seized the financial markets, puncturing the illusion of ever-rising asset prices, and paralyzing world trade. Finance

---

62 This means the flow and backlog of collective inventions, creations, relations and desires appropriated
    by Mark Zuckerberg, Jeff Bezos, Evan Spiegel, Howard Schultz, Travis Kalanick, and the like.
63 David Harvey, *A Brief History of Neoliberalism*, Oxford: Oxford University Press, 2005.

had frozen, thus trade stopped too, leading to thousands of container ships laying idle in Asian ports. With the Great Recession, neoliberalism finally met its nemesis, and capitalism fell into its second historic depression. Unbridled greed and deregulation had again destabilized the economy, much like in 1929.

Neoliberal Globalization and Labor Defeat

The period between 1989 and 2008 was marked by an exceptional expansion in international trade and global finance, commonly labelled as *neoliberal globalization*. The City and Wall Street were accumulating huge financial wealth by speculating on currencies, commodities, mergers, and acquisitions. The Dow Jones Industrial Index skyrocketed from 4,000 points at the worst of the 1987 stock market crisis, to 16,000 points on the eve of the 2007 subprime crisis. As of 2017, it is above 20,000 points. As America and Britain became financial casinos, China entered the international market, and soon became the leading global export hub. Since communist China turned progressively towards capitalism after 1978, its manufacturing exports have grown at astonishing rates; worth just $27 billion in 1985, China's exports grew to about $2.3 trillion in 2015.

As the Cold War yielded to neoliberal globalization, a huge number of internationally mobile workers flooded the market. Just as Western Europe and America were deindustrializing, shedding millions of well-paid blue-collar jobs, millions of economic and political migrants from not only Eastern Europe, Russia, China, but also Latin America, India, the Maghreb, and Sub-Saharan Africa started to fill positions in menial, dangerous, and poorly paid jobs, or start small businesses of their own. Along their families, they also began to take residence in global metropolises of the Global North. In the late 20th century, population movements across continents grew in size, reaching proportions comparable to the mass migration of poor and persecuted Europeans towards the Americas in the first age of globalization at the end of the 19th century.[64] The ensuing wave of redundancies due to downsizing and offshoring, combined with an influx of migrants, exerted a downward pressure on wages across the capitalist world, even during the boom years of the 90s and early 00s.

When the labor supply exceeds labor demand, and there is no counterbalancing pressure (in the form of unions, for instance), companies can easily bend the rules in order to profit from individual laborers. Flexible, non-standard precarious forms of work, such as part-time employment and internships, began being tested on women and young people; typical newcomers to the expanding service industries of the 80s. These were new industries in which there was no union culture, and the uncouth male chauvinism of many labor unions held little appeal to women and modish young people. What's more, Thatcher and Reagan had squarely defeated unions and crushed their power. This was particularly evident in the 70s, when wage hikes and oil shocks had caused an upsurge in inflation. Thatcher – also known

---

64   In America, for instance, the percentage of the population who are of foreign birth was similar in 2010 as it was in 1900. However, the proportion of American residents that are immigrants went from 1 in 21 in 1970, to 1 in 8 in 2015. For more, see: Robert J Gordon, *The Rise and Fall of American Growth*, Princeton: Princeton University Pres, 2016.

as 'the Iron Lady' – managed to erase one of strongest, and oldest, working-class cultures of the world. She overcame the resistance of striking coal miners in Yorkshire and Wales, disbanding the National Union of Miners (NUM), the most radical, and historically powerful, union in the country. Following both this, a slew of similar defeats followed. Organized labor was defeated time and time again, in pitched battles with business and government; another key example of this is the fiasco of 1980, when a sit-down strike called by Italian unions at Mirafiori, FIAT's main car plant in Turin, was defeated. Unions became undesirable and unfashionable, and utterly lost the respect and admiration they had commanded amongst working people since 1968.

The following waves of automation and delocalization that transformed manufacturing greatly damaged the power of organized labor, so much so that union membership fell dramatically all the world in the 90s and 00s. In Australia, for example, unionization levels dropped from a peak of 48.5% in 1980, to a trough 15.5% in 2014, a class defeat of historical proportions. This was mirrored in Britain, where trade unions took a similar beating: unionization levels fell from 51.7% to merely 18.7% between 1980 and 2014. Across the same period, in America, unionization rates dropped from 22.1% to 10.7%, and today in the private sector only 6.4% of employees are members of a union. All in all, union membership was halved in OECD countries in years between 1980 and 2014. It now stands, on average, at 16.7%, down from 34.1% in 1980. Even in the labor bastions of Germany (down from 34.9% in 1980 to merely 18.1% in 2013) and, to a lesser extent, Scandinavia (Sweden saw a decline from 78% membership in 1980, to a still hefty 67.3% in 2014), unions lost members, and social democrat parties lost votes. As their blue-collar constituencies were disappearing, socialists in Southern Europe and social democrats in Northern Europe were swayed by the neoliberal consensus, and stopped furthering the interests of working people as they had done until the final days of Fordism. No longer facing friendly governments, American and European labor unions were unable to overcome the challenge represented by the shift from the old industrial manufacturing economy, to the new informational service economy.[65] Old industrial unions largely proved incapable of reforming their ranks, policies, and communication styles to deal with the tertiarization of the economy, and a feminized and multicultural workforce. In the majority of cases, women, immigrants, and the young, were excluded from traditional union representation, and thus from collective bargaining with enterprises and governments.

The weakening of trade unions on both sides of the Atlantic coincided with rise of the Pacific in world trade. First Japanese, then Korean, and finally Chinese exports redesigned the industrial landscape of American and European economies. The highly competitive goods coming from the Orient altered the structure of a global marketplace that had not changed since the Second Industrial Revolution. Japanese and Korean cars, Japanese and Taiwanese electronics, and Korean and Chinese steel (to name but a few), flooded world markets at the expense of Western European and North American producers. East Asia emerged as a formidable industrial competitor in international trade; prior to Trump, the United States and the European Union opposed economic protectionism, and allowed their steel industries to wither

---

65   With a few notable exceptions, like SEIU (Service Employees International Union) in America and Ver.di
      (Vereinte Dienstleistungsgewerkschaft) in Germany.

away (think, for instance, of Pittsburgh or Liège). European car manufacturers fared better with respect to Asian competitors, while the American car industry was drastically downsized as a result of Pacific exports: cities like Detroit soon became ghosts of their former selves.

The Precariat During High Neoliberalism: from McJobs to Permatemps

It was Generation X who brought down the Berlin Wall and invented the internet. They did it to the benefit of all, but for the profit of very few (who were usually older than them already). GenXers were the first to experience precarity in their office cubicles, working as temporary employees for downsizing corporations throughout the 90s. Due to their resistance to 'careers for life' and reluctance to define their lives according their professions, they ended up striking a Faustian bargain. They accepted labor flexibility and a degradation of workers' rights, because this allowed for the number of flexible jobs to increase. These jobs allowed GenXers to accommodate the increasing diversity of roles the individual had come to experience in society; working by day to pay the bills, but producing an underground movie by night; waiting tables or working as a bike messenger, while simultaneously pursuing a career as a graffiti artist. Today, it is known as the gig economy. Smartphone apps and smart aggregators did not exist back then, but the roots of the platform economy were present from the beginning of neoliberal flexibility, and the free-agent model of the worker it projected.

Aided by pro-business governments, corporate and financial elites popularized the idea that flexibility was the only possible solution to rising unemployment. Since neoliberals believed in free markets, prices had to be flexible, free to move up and down depending on the supply and demand of goods, assets, currencies, and, crucially, workers. Central banks were not blamed for the sudden unemployment spike that wreaked havoc in Northern England and the American Midwest in the early 80s, a spike caused by their drastically increasing real interest rates. It was in fact the unions who were blamed, for resisting technological change, and its Schumpeterian 'creative destruction'. Their imposition of wage rigidity (labor agreements according to which union members' wages would not fall in real value) as well as restrictive employment norms (thus limiting market freedom and innovation) got to be blamed for unemployment. In the neoliberal model, wages had to become flexible, thus labor markets were deregulated just as the financial markets had already been. To achieve this, the unions had to be thoroughly undermined, and the minimum wage cut in real terms. Republican and Conservative governments thus took a rabid anti-labor stance, passing laws and policies that gave employers a free rein, and seriously weakened the unions' ability to organize and strike back. These policies were not reversed when Tony Blair and Bill Clinton, financial deregulators themselves, took office in the 90s. Critics pointed out that, for all the growth of the mid-80s and early 90s, many of the employment positions created were unstable McJobs, a fact ardently denied by the business press; these jobs were not unstable, but flexible, temporary jobs, perfectly suited to a neoliberal lifestyle.

In 1985, the *New York Times* hailed the early spread of temporary work as befitting the lifestyles of young artists, former housewives, and laid-off managers. Neoliberalism promised freedom, and young people eagerly embraced it. They were finally free to be what they wanted to be: single, gay, African-American, alternative, yuppie, etc. Neoliberalism won the day because it promised the liberation of individual identities held in check by the constrictive institutions of the Fordist deal: powerful bureaucracies, and the idea of the nuclear family. Neoliberalism offered this individual freedom in exchange for labor flexibility. Each individual would be left free to seek their own fortune, rather than being member of a faceless workforce. Free markets fostered free networks, and decreasing prices for computer power, communication, and travel, empowering individual lives (and enabling labor mobility) in ways that had not seemed hitherto possible. Until the economy crashed, the freedom to sell and the freedom to hack went hand in hand: market freedom and digital liberty didn't appear mutually exclusive.

Precarity, dressed as flexibility, was accepted by governments and unions as a short-term solution to the difficulties that young people faced trying to get entry-level jobs in the 80s and 90s. Companies, of course, knew better. They used flexibility as a way to break the rigidity of existing labor norms, to manage cheaper workers as they pleased with minimal union or government interference. Full-time workers began to be portrayed as sluggish, contentious, ungrateful, and inefficient. As large employers replaced difficult to please permanent workers with docile temporary workers, precarity began to permeate to all industries, and all forms of labor. New entrants to the job market were easy to discriminate against and be denied equal opportunities in terms of civil, labor and welfare rights; the balance of power was always favorable to employers. Following the defeat of organized labor, transformations in the organization of work and management of personnel (Human Resources Management, in today's bizspeak) cemented the transition to an economy increasingly based on short-term employment.

The temporary help industry was born in the 70s, by providing overstretched companies with female office workers (*temporaries*) on an irregular basis. The industry bloomed in the 80s, as temporary help was renamed *temporary employment* in official jargon, and temporary labor agencies became big business. As the president of Manpower revealingly wrote in 1988:

> Our objective is to take what is viewed as a commodity (an unskilled worker), bring sophistication to the selection process, and deliver a premium product. In the process we will be able to deliver more value for cost.[66]

Management theorists soon started selling flexibility as the new corporate gospel, and temporary labor as a panacea for excessive overhead labor costs. Flexible companies meant lean corporations, and lean meant mean, to employees and competitors alike. Firms offered flexibility when there was an increasing demand for it, because post-Cold War freedom increasingly meant freedom to do as one desired, to be unconstrained in individual choices by any form of communal shackle or social bonding: freedom of expression, yes, but also market freedom as consumers, and freedom to work when one chose to. Single mothers could now work while their kids attended day care, and university students of modest backgrounds could work their way through college by moonlighting many part-time jobs, both on- and off-campus. Of course, employers always tended to gloss over the hidden, degrading

---

66   Quoted in Vicki Smith and Esther Neuwirth, *The Good Temp*, Ithaca: Cornell University Press, 2008.

aspects of temporary and part-time employment, but a largely obedient workforce decided to wear blinders and buy into the mantra of flexibility as an enabler of social progress and individual advancement.

The fact was that flexible jobs paid less – even by the hour for comparable job positions – and largely were not unionized. Flexibility gave staff managers the ability to organize the workforce so as to optimize business activity across the economic cycle, hiring temps and part-time employees during peaks, and laying them off in troughs. This, however, meant that flexibility quickly became unilateral, undermining the promise of flexible hours that had lured people into precarious employment. At the end of this process emerged zero-hour contracts, guaranteeing no minimum compensation, with work schedules completely dictated by market demand. It is now common for employers to impose variable hours upon employees, rather than delegate predictable shifts. Part-timers often clock in more than a full-time workweek; being ready to work non-traditional hours and holidays has become a job requirement, inversely mirroring the diffusion of the 24/7 culture of the finance and media spheres. Gradually but irreversibly, the 40-hour workweek has been supplanted by intermittent worktime, also aided by the spread of mobile technologies, which have given managers the opportunity to keep potential workers always on the alert so to have a just-in-time workforce at their disposal. This has most worryingly led to the recent emergence of platform capitalism, wherein most labor hiring and supervision is attended to by algorithms.

Organized labor mostly didn't care that the young were getting short-term, low-wage contracts with no benefits, as long as the entitlements of long-term employees and pensioners remained largely untouched. During the zenith of neoliberal hegemony at the turn of the millennium, the precariat was neither seen as a social problem nor listened to as a political constituency. It was then that the anti-globalization movement started agitating against the worsening conditions of flexible workers (or 'flexworkers'). For instance, in 2005, the precariat in Helsinki collective staged a coordinated performance of precarious aerobics. Dressed in red gym outfits, they picketed a Lidl supermarket (a company notorious for its anti-labor practices across Europe). This picketing also served as a clear allegory of the fitness and flexibility companies demand from young workers, provided they want to keep their job. This kind of creative picketing was replicated in Italy, Spain, Germany, and elsewhere. Uniformed employees inside chain stores reacted with a mix of sympathy and indifference.

The fact was that the precarious did not take pride in their jobs. They dreamt of professional success while they carried out low-payed, demeaning jobs. They mostly cared for themselves, and found nothing wrong in stabbing colleagues in the back, or selling themselves at a lower price than their peers (even their friends). At first, the precarious thought they were the flexible workers of the digital future, on the road to become powerful managers or rich entrepreneurs. However, they eventually found themselves heavily indebted, with their jobs and livelihoods constantly at risk. When the financial crisis hit, the truth was finally exposed: flexibility had been *precarity* all along, and talk of a work-life balance was nothing more than corporate propaganda.

The Great Recession and the Wasting of a Whole Generation

Even in periods when the economy was booming (particularly the periods between 1993 and 2000, and 2003 and 2007), the precarious were not able to cash in on this, save for the lucky few who had been paid with valuable stock options by successful technology companies. The lives of precarious young people were far more irregular than those of their parents, who had attained economic security and gained access to property in their thirties, after starting families in their twenties. The precarious rented, they didn't own. They didn't form family households, they shared an apartment with their peers like the characters of the sitcom *Friends*. Their lives, however, were much less amusing; bills came faster than checks, and credit card and banking debt inevitably rose. A health mishap or a spell of psychological illness (an increasingly frequent occurrence) threw young people out of jobs and housing arrangements. Irregular income fed anxiety and fear; good ways to keep temporary employees tame, and pliable. The office became a schizophrenic environment of superficial cordiality and friendliness, hiding unprecedented levels of psychological abuse and wage inequality under the veneer of sociability. The hard truth was that that the precarious existed at the mercy of their superiors. When kept out of jobs, many precarious started businesses to survive, giving life to what has come to be called the *entreprecariat*,[67] meaning ridiculously undercapitalized firms which struggle to stay afloat in a depressed economy.

Precarious workers neither went on strike nor complained, since they could lose their jobs for the slightest act of insubordination. When the financial crisis hit, the young, saddled with student debt and unemployment, returned to their parental households in droves. They are commonly referred to in America as the *boomerang generation*, and in France as *génération Tanguy* (named after a movie in which a man lives with his parents well into his thirties). In mom-loving Italy, male youngsters have become increasingly reluctant to leave the family nest, and only begin living alone in their thirties, a decade later than their Northern European counterparts. The Great Recession has further exacerbated this trend, so much so that almost 14% of Italian adults have gone back to live with their parents since the crisis. In a nation of pensioners, the parents' social security checks are the welfare of last resort for adults who have lost their jobs and / or seen their sentimental unions fall apart.

In 2009, it was shocking to see the children of the American middle class return home, their Masters and PhDs made useless by the financial crisis. Leaving for college had traditionally meant leaving the family home behind forever, joining society as an adult, and forming a new household. The Great Recession has in fact made the younger generations jobless, and thus caused a tremendous waste of human capital, with lasting effects on long-term growth. It is the young and highly skilled, the educated, the workforce with up-to-date talents and knowledge, that are being left to rot in forced inactivity or imposed precarity, left unemployed, or coerced into jobs that are inferior in terms of pay and security to their qualifications and possibilities. The working conditions of today's youth are fundamentally worse than those experienced by people over the age of 50, be they industrial workers or office employees. Across the world

---

67   The term, fusion of entrepreneurship and precariat, was coined by Silvio Lorusso, *Entreprecariat* http:// networkcultures.org/entreprecariat/.

of advanced capitalism, the precarious' lot is typically worse than the pensioners'. While the former contribute to national wealth, the latter only detract from it. The wasting of America and Europe's younger generations will not be without economic consequences. This wasting signals the start of a long-term decline, since the youngest generations are endowed with state-of-the-art knowledge, the input that enables, as Nobel economist Paul Romer has shown,[68] the increasing returns and productivity dynamism first observed by Adam Smith in *The Wealth of Nations*.

The most worrying indicator of youth precarity – and its attendant waste of knowledge and skills – is the rate of youth unemployment, which has skyrocketed in Europe since 2009. Whilst the European Union has devoted more than a few summits to the issue, youth unemployment remains high; over 40% across Mediterranean Europe. This appalling state of affairs has led to major riots and protests in Greece and Spain. Mass youth unemployment undermines both social reproduction (by depressing birth rates) and democratic cohesion (by increasing inequality). An entire generation has been made precarious by a deadly combination of restrictive fiscal and welfare policies – respectively, austerity and workfare.[69]

Due to the lasting effects of the Great Recession, the younger, better educated, better-equipped generations of neoliberal societies are seeing their lives wither on the vine. Sometimes they cannot take it anymore. Michele was a graphic artist who could not find a job in his native Udine, in Italy's North-East severely struck by the crisis. After a string of humiliations due to failed job interviews and unpaid jobs, he committed suicide, aged 30, on 5 February 2017, leaving behind a poignant letter accusing Italian society as a whole of finding a place for neither him, nor his generation.[70] Michele's parents told the press that it was precarity that had killed him. With ghastly appropriateness, the Deutsche bank calculates a 'youth sacrifice ratio', quantifying the amount of economic pain inflicted on Europe's youth since the onset of the Great Recession. It is highest in the PIGS countries (Portugal, Italy, Greece, and Spain), particularly Greece and Italy. Analysis shows that those who lived in the time of the Great Depression never completely closed the income gap with those generations working during the post-World War Two economic boom. This could mean – extrapolating this trend outwards, and speculatively applying it to future generations – that precarious generations will never bridge the economic distance separating them from their forebears, the prosperous and increasingly resented baby-boomers. If there are no decisive

---

68   Paul Romer, 'Endogenous Technical Change', *Journal of Political Economy*, 98(5), 1990; 'The Origins of Endogenous Growth', *Journal of Economic Perspectives*, 8(1), 1994. See also: David Marsh, *Knowledge and the Wealth of Nations*, New York: Norton, 2007.

69   By workfare, we mean welfare systems like those currently in place in Germany, Britain, amongst others, which require some work or attendance for training from the recipients of unemployment benefits, a considerable precarious constituency. In fact, precarious individuals on workfare schemes have staged protests against what they see as a constrictive system, which is not only undermining individual freedom, but also implicitly subsidizing low-wage industries.

70   'From this reality you cannot expect anything. You can't expect a job, you can't expect to be loved, you can't expect to be acknowledged, you can't expect security and a stable environment.' You can read the whole of his letter here: http://www.huffingtonpost.it/2017/02/07/lettera-precario-suicida_n_14634010.html.

interventions, such as the introduction of a basic income, or free university tuition, jettisoning the economic potential of the young could have lasting repercussions for the long-term prospects of western societies. Indeed, talk of a Transatlantic 'lost generation' is everywhere in mainstream media.[71]

At the height of the Eurocrisis, youth unemployment exploded across Southern Europe. Between 2011 and 2012, the unemployment rate skyrocketed to 55.3% in Greece in 2012, to 53.2% in Spain, and 35.2% in Italy (according to OECD standardized unemployment rates). In fact, many young people have dropped out of the labor market altogether, meaning that the inactivity rate is in fact much higher than official unemployment rates, as a recent study of the ECB has observed.[72] They are the NEETs, bearers of the nasty new acronym that defines a growing portion of today's youth: *Not in Employment, Education or Training*. In late 2013, over 13% of young people in the European Union existed in this condition, according to the OECD. In Italy, there were 4,310,000 young people aged between 15 and 24 who were neither in education, nor in employment (22% of the entire age bracket). Spain fared even worse, with a 23% NEET rate (over 3,500,000 people), about the same proportion as Ireland. Even in Germany, NEETs make up almost 12% of people under 25 (compared to about 17% in France and Britain). In essence, these are young people doing nothing (or at least not working legally). The term 'NEET' originates from the British employment bureaucracy, when it began to register the peak in the number of idle youth caused by the financial crisis. In Spanish-speaking countries they are referred to as *ni-ni*, while in lusophone countries as *nem-nem*, meaning 'neither-nor'; they are young people who neither study nor work. When youth unemployment was not improving in spite of the recovery, the then-Prime Minister of Britain, David Cameron, sprightly told the English youth their choice was either 'earn or learn', or face the termination of unemployment benefits. This is the tough love that neoliberals have for the generation they betrayed. Consider the case of the rich and privileged Macron, the young banker who triumphed over Marine Le Pen to become France's youngest president. He caused an uproar when he said: 'If I were unemployed, I would not sit there and wait for handouts.' Easy for him to say as graduate of a top school. He's likely to encounter the stiff resistance of French leftist movements, which present themselves as either *insoumis* (*unbowed*), or *ingouvernables* (*ungovernable*). Organized, insurgent members of the precariat make up the latter of these groups.

The fact is that Generation Z is made to feel as it has no future, in a hopeless world. Hence its anti-system anger, and street-bound rage in countless black blocs. 'Welcome to Hell' declared the poster calling legions of anarcho-autonomists to protest at the G20 summit in July of 2017, in order to fight both the police in Hamburg and the legitimacy of global rulers, and especially national-populist strongmen in power in America, Russia, Turkey.

---

71 'Generation jobless', *Economist*, 27 April 2013. Catherine Rampell, 'Great Recession's Lost Generation? Older Millennials.', *Washington Post*, 2 February 2015, https://www.washingtonpost.com/opinions/catherine-rampell-older-millennials-are-paying-the-price-for-bad-timing/2015/02/02/4ef644c8-ab1c-11e4-ad71-7b9eba0f87d6_story.html?utm_term=.6ef5d9d663c8.

72 Claire Jones, 'Plight of Eurozone Jobless Found to Be Worse Than the Data Show', *Financial Times*, 2 May 2017, https://www.ft.com/content/6dbe2196-34d1-11e7-bce4-9023f8c0fd2e.

Much like Japan's reclusive *Hikikomori,* who never leave their bedrooms to venture in the outside world, late teens and young people who could be in college lack the resources, and energy, to leave their parental homes. They instead find social support by assembling online, and creating rich online cultures that are shielded from adult interference (partially because they are hard to decipher: suits just don't get it). They might run with street gangs in the blighted cities where the British and French underclasses live. They might be squatting, and waiting the crisis out, as autonomists and anarchists are doing in Brussels and Berlin. They might be chatting with far-away peers, sharing their specialty interests and tech passions, snapping their nude selves, or commenting on politics and celebrity culture. No matter whether they are hoodies or nerds, the young are full of resentment, for they know there is no future in store for them. As the Great Recession finally subsides, they are unlikely to find anything other than unpaid internships and precarious employment.

Generation Z has no present and no future, thus cannot but express anger at still-rising uncertainty, and ever-worsening prospects. When rage mounts, as in Paris in 2005, London in 2011, or Ferguson in 2014, unemployed and precarious youth are liable to riot, and set entire neighborhoods alight. Their fury is blind, their hatred compounded by their daily experiences of residential segregation, and exclusion from legal sources of income. The NEETs are a multiethnic underclass. Whilst they are the nightmare of governments and xenophobes alike, their underground culture is what makes people dance across Europe, and America (global hip-hop, grime, the dubstep invasion, and the continuation of rave culture, stand as notable examples that have crossed into mainstream culture). In place of anything else, NEETs are also the newest cohort of soccer hooligans and / or black blocs, standing off with the riot police, who are increasingly the last line of defense for politically discredited institutions.

If Generation X struggles to balance increasingly insecure jobs and mortgage payments (provided banks haven't yet repossessed their homes), and Generation Y is experiencing either heightened precarity (as periods of inactivity get longer, and the incidence of on-demand labor grows) or outright joblessness, Generation Z have become a generation of NEETs whose existence is outside of work, possibly permanently.

The following table provides an illustration of the evolution of unemployment rates for people under 25 (the labor cohort that was worst affected by the crisis) across advanced, capitalist countries. Note how rates overshot after the 2008 financial crash, and have yet to properly recover. Note also the trough of the depression between 2010 and 2011, forcing youth unemployment to record levels in the PIGS economies. Greece was worst hit, with 50% of under-25s out of jobs due to the Troika's austerity package. Italy's youth unemployment remains stubbornly high at 40%, undoubtedly a factor in former Prime Minister Matteo Renzi's defeat in the December 2016 referendum, while the Spanish unemployment rate climbed yet higher to 50% at the height of the crisis (although it now shows a decreasing trend). Portugal has held a fairly steady rate of around 30% since 2011.

Table 9: Youth Unemployment Since the Great Recession, Various OECD Countries (%).

Country	2007	2008	2009	2010	2011	2012	2013	2014	2015	2016
Australia	9.36	8.80	11.45	11.54	11.36	11.72	12.21	13.31	13.13	12.67
Austria	9.38	8.47	10.65	9.47	8.95	9.40	9.68	10.28	10.57	
Belgium	18.88	17.82	21.90	22.40	18.68	19.68	23.68	23.30	22.10	
Brazil	21.20	18.00	18.47	16.04	14.47	13.48	14.02	13.38		
Canada	11.20	11.62	15.30	14.91	14.27	14.41	13.72	13.45	13.18	13.08
Chile	17.84	19.73	22.60	18.54	17.54	16.26	16.05	16.44	15.50	15.66
Czech Republic	10.72	9.85	16.57	18.35	18.07	19.52	18.98	15.82	12.55	
Denmark	7.50	8.03	11.85	13.97	14.22	14.15	13.03	12.63	10.85	11.97
Estonia		11.75	27.40	32.80	22.38	20.80	18.75	14.97	13.20	
Euro area	15.00	15.53	20.00	20.90	21.20	23.43	24.23	23.75	22.35	
Finland	16.45	16.18	21.00	21.13	19.75	18.77	19.55	20.35	22.02	
France	18.85	18.30	22.98	22.57	21.98	23.63	24.07	24.23	24.68	24.57
Germany	11.93	10.57	11.25	9.82	8.53	8.05	7.80	7.75	7.25	
Greece	22.68	21.88	25.73	33.00	44.70	55.30	58.25	52.42	49.80	
Hungary	18.00	19.50	26.38	26.43	25.95	28.23	26.60	20.40	17.30	
Iceland	6.95	8.22	15.60	16.07	14.38	13.50	10.53	9.75	8.75	6.50
Ireland	9.05	13.30	24.02	27.63	29.05	30.38	26.75	23.93	20.88	
Israel	16.02	12.61	14.55	13.60	11.57	12.09	10.50	10.52	9.24	8.59
Italy	20.38	21.23	25.32	27.88	29.07	35.30	40.00	42.67	40.33	
Japan	7.72	7.28	9.17	9.32	8.29	8.13	6.81	6.20	5.58	5.16

Korea	8.79	9.27	9.84	9.77	9.61	8.99	9.34	10.03	10.52	10.68
Latvia	10.55	13.82	33.35	36.05	31.00	28.52	23.07	19.63	16.30	
Mexico	7.21	7.70	10.09	9.76	9.84	9.44	9.48	9.47	8.61	7.73
Netherlands	5.97	5.30	6.60	8.72	10.00	11.72	13.20	12.75	11.25	
New Zealand	9.88	10.94	15.87	16.39	15.95	16.72	15.05	13.89	13.70	13.20
Norway	7.42	7.50	9.18	9.25	8.68	8.45	9.13	7.85	9.88	11.13
OECD	11.86	12.71	16.51	16.74	16.28	16.29	16.16	15.11	13.89	
Poland	21.65	17.30	20.65	23.68	25.77	26.50	27.27	23.85	20.75	
Portugal	16.70	16.68	20.32	22.75	30.23	37.92	38.10	34.83	31.95	27.93
Slovak Republic	20.32	19.02	27.18	33.50	33.42	33.98	33.67	29.70	26.45	
Slovenia	10.15	10.53	13.65	14.70	15.75	20.52	21.65	20.30	16.43	
South Africa		45.61	48.35	51.19	50.28	51.69	51.42	51.27	50.13	53.34
Spain	18.10	24.48	37.75	41.50	46.23	52.88	55.48	53.20	48.35	44.45
Sweden	19.32	20.15	24.90	24.77	22.75	23.60	23.52	22.88	20.32	
Switzerland	7.10	7.00	8.50	7.85	7.63	8.43	8.50	8.55	8.57	8.40
Turkey	17.27	18.48	22.85	19.77	16.73	15.70	16.95	17.82	18.52	
UK	14.25	14.9	19.10	19.88	21.25	21.20	20.65	16.95	14.63	
USA	10.53	12.82	17.57	18.42	17.28	16.18	15.52	13.37	11.60	10.42

Source: OECD, *Employment Outlook.*

European youth are similarly disadvantaged elsewhere. In Finland, 20% of people under 25 are unemployed, a figure so worrying that the country has recently launched a pilot basic income scheme aimed specifically at idle young people. All across Scandinavia (particularly in Denmark and Norway), youth unemployment has increased, putting pressure on the social-democratic welfare state. In France and Belgium, youth unemployment is over 25%. In Europe, only Germany has benefited from the crisis, and this is also evident from examination of its youth unemployment rates, which have decreased from about 12% at the start of the crisis and to around 7% today. In East Asia, South Korea displays the strongest tendency toward an increase in the number of young people out of work. In Japan, however, fiscal and monetary expansion under nationalist Abe has led to a reduction in the proportion of youth seeking jobs from 9% to 5%. In America, from a peak in 2010 where more than 18% of young people were unable to find jobs, the youth unemployment rate has decreased to little over 10%. Conversely, in Canada and Australia youth unemployment rates remain as high as they were during the worst of the crisis.

Precarionomics

Neoliberal deregulation produced major financial instability, which in turn made the global economy nose-dive in 2008-2012. Yet it was not the financial elite who took the plunge, but everybody else – namely, the precarious youth, as the data above shows. In the creative industries that had employed Millennials in droves, the comedown was especially harsh. Creatives were suddenly no longer a hot commodity, and countless advertisers and graphic designers, journalists and editors, and even engineers lost their jobs, possibly forever. The weak economy, coupled with increased digitization and disintermediation, made them quickly redundant, the same fate that had befallen the resilient steelworkers of Pennsylvania and Ohio thirty years before.

Technological unemployment is always a looming possibility under capitalism. Machines displace workers: the power loom put weavers out of work, as today robots are set to replace service workers, while artificial intelligence promises to abolish many well-paid professions, including medical technicians, and legal analysts.[73] However, just like past disruptions brought by labor-saving technical progress, the net effect on total employment depends on economic, rather technological, factors. If the economy stagnates, output growth will be less than productivity growth, and unemployment will rise. If the economy accelerates, the opposite occurs. So, while it might well happen that I, a professional translator, will be made redundant by Google's machine learning, much like McWorkers are being replaced by monitors upon which customers take their own order, my ability to find a job in another industry is really dependent on growth conditions. A Keynesian-Schumpeterian state would have both the macroeconomic, and microeconom-

---

73   Martin Ford, *Rise of the Robots: Technology and the Threat of a Jobless Future*, New York: Basic Books, 2015. See also Daron Acemoglu and Pascual Restrepo, 'Robots and Jobs: Evidence from the US', http://voxeu.org/article/robots-and-jobs-evidence-us. They show that unemployment is caused by automation, rather than globalization.

ic, tools to counter technological unemployment through public investment, re-training, basic income, demo-grants, and free, science-oriented higher education. Only social conflict, however, can erect such a state.

In the worst years of the Great Recession (2008-2010), everybody seemed to be going bankrupt: the recently unemployed, long-established firms and businesses, and even governments. Portugal, Ireland, and (of course) Greece, were put under international tutelage: financial markets would no longer buy their debt. Italy and Spain were massively targeted by international speculation. Rating agencies – the same agencies that previously claimed toxic assets to be first-rate, before these were sold to gullible investors – were now declaring that Greek and Portuguese bonds were to be avoided. Investors, unfortunately, still heeded their advice. As markets stagnated, businesses and governments became insolvent, and unemployment, particularly youth unemployment, immediately soared. It has not really dropped since.

Austerity was the disastrous policy response to the onset of the Great Recession. Austerity just made precarity worse. As business was plummeting and unemployment soaring, governments cut spending and raised taxes, unnecessarily inflicting additional economic pain on a population already tried by the crisis. The number of evictions and repossessions went through the roof, and entire industrial districts disappeared in the space of a few months. The Great Recession was reshaping the economic landscape. Austerity was remaking society, by creating more poverty and precarity. Instead of spending cuts to balance budgets, governments should have taken the opposite approach to the crisis, accepting the necessity of temporarily widening deficits, and funding environmental investment, alongside social spending, in order to speed up economic recovery. Faced with the sharp rise in unemployment claims, rather than making the jobless pay for the system's inadequacies, they should have accepted the reality of chronic precarity and unemployment, and from this design an alternative welfare system. This system should be based on different sources of funding and recipients of transfers, to replace the existing one, still based on the surreal assumption of full-time, permanent employment for the vast majority of the population.

Deflation in the Eurozone and the structural-adjustment punishment meted out on the Greek people[74] have destroyed the traditional principles of European integration, namely prosperity, and economic solidarity of better-off member states. A rift has opened between Northern and Southern Europe: between creditor and debtor countries. Europe is no longer a union of equals. The European Central Bank (ECB) prevented sovereign debt from sinking beyond repair in 2009, and again in 2010-2012. Then in 2015, it started a massive program of quantitative easing, buying government bonds to defeat deflation. In spite of this belatedly pro-active stance, it has been unable to persuade banks to return to lending to people and firms. Not even negative interest rates have done the job: banks are drowning in a sea of bad loans and have little appetite for risk. Radical movements should force Frankfurt to place money directly in the pockets of consumers, who would spend

---

74   Yanis Varoufakis, *And the Weak Suffer What They Must? Europe's Crisis and America's Economic Future*, New York: Nation Books, 2016.

it, rather than give it to banks who hoard it. However, the days of quantitative easing are numbered; the Federal Reserve is tightening monetary policy, and the ECB might have to follow suit in order to prevent capital flight.

Quantitative easing (QE) was inaugurated by Bernanke immediately after the crisis struck in 2008, with the Fed buying off banks' toxic assets. The ECB only adopted quantitative easing as a permanent policy seven years later, and has almost solely purchased government debt, rather than corporate debt. The effect of QE was anyway similar in the two currency areas. It propped up the monetary values of equities, bonds, and real estate, but did little to address unemployment, and nothing to address inequality. Europe has given trillions to banks to fund this move, all the while slashing essential services, and destroying the economic future of its youth. The ECB burns €80 billion every month buying bonds. That same money could be used to grant every adult in the Eurozone €400 per month. Thus, it appears that the target of many universal income schemes – a monthly sum of €1,000 – is perhaps more a matter of conflicting political priorities, than of financial sustainability.

Precarity in the labor market deepened after the financial crisis. The crisis sapped demand by decreasing the share of output going to workers, who tend to spend all they have, while enabling a crippling increase in the share going to capitalists, who tend to accumulate wealth, rather than spend. The rich and privileged didn't suffer from fiscal austerity. On the contrary, austerity safeguarded asset prices and the value of capital investments, and thus allowed a continuation of rentier capitalism, with its stellar salaries of top managers and high-ranking officials – an insult to people existing in economic precarity. Europe seems to be mired in permanent stagnation, while America and Japan, having been less affected by austerity measures, are stumbling into a precarious recovery. However, this could easily revert to crisis again, as protectionist and monetarist tendencies grow stronger after the recent wave of national populism in American politics.

Trump's economic policy is similar to Reagan's in two fundamental respects: military spending, and tax cuts. The effect of Trump's rise to power has been to galvanize the stock market, similarly to what happened after Reagan's election. If the supply-side economic program of Trump succeeds in increasing growth, this economic surge should normally translate into higher trade deficits. However Trump's instinctive economic nationalism calls for protectionist measures to be adopted, in order to prevent large trade deficits accumulating with Europe and Asia. This is Trump's fundamental difference from Reagan, who was fundamentally a free-trader, in spite of his occasional anti-Japanese jibes. Trumpism breaks decisively with neoliberal orthodoxy and its apology of free trade and sound government finance, by advocating protectionism and fiscal deficits, a classic Keynesian recipe embraced by both left- and right-wing governments across modern history. Whether this will be enough to boost America's economy and create jobs, only history will tell. However, the alliance with the worst of both Wall Street and corporate America is a guarantee that labor income will not rise as much as is needed to spur growth.

We are witnessing the end of the international system created after 1945, and it is unclear what kind of international political economy will emerge. Those on the left who wish to see a return to protectionism are wrong, because trade promotes the diffusion of technology and prosperity, and (more importantly) prevents war, as Giovanni Arrighi reminds us in his masterpiece on China and the future of capitalism.[75]

To sum up: in the 90s, labor flexibility slowly gave way to workers' precarity. In the 00s, as the economy slowed down, the precarious became millions-strong. Close to 300 million young people around the world are unemployed, according to the *Economist*. In the aftermath of the Great Recession, those languishing in unemployment, as well as those harried by under-employment, have become multitude. They are the precariat, resolved to rise in defense of their livelihood against the onslaught of austerity and craven privilege, and now confronted with the dual peril of European *and* American fascism. Only by defeating national populism can they hope to defeat precarity, restore equality, and salvage democracy across the world.

Fordism vs. Walmartism: From Blue-collar to Pink-collar Work

The narrative of the industrial postwar age revolves around two job roles, the middle-class office worker (the 'white-collar' worker), and the proletarian industrial worker (the 'blue-collar' worker). We owe these distinctions to Claude Wright Mills, the great Columbia sociologist who wrote *White Collar* and *The Power Elite*, and was a keen observer of the transformation of the American workplace in the 50s and 60s. Wright Mills also coined the term 'pink collar', to refer to the feminized sections of the economy that commanded inferior status and lower pay: waitresses, nurses, hotel employees, care and domestic workers, and kindergarten and elementary teachers. If the Fordist era saw blue- and white-collar workers as its protagonists, the unfolding story of informational capitalism in the 21st century should revolve around the legions of service temps, particularly pink-collar and green-collar workers. 'Green collar' is a term coined by environmental advocate Van Jones, referring to the growing proportion of the labor force involved in solar and wind energy production, as well as in gardening, forestry, and other forms of environmental management or remediation. This form of worker currently stands at around 3% of employment (about 4 million jobs) in America, according to the Bureau of Labor of Statistics.

As the curtain fell on the 20th century, the blue-collars of the working class had been numer-ically overtaken by the pink-collars of the service class. The industrial proletariat has given way to the service precariat. Today, Ford is no longer the representative enterprise of capitalist rationalization that it was a century ago. Under neoliberalism, it is Wal-Mart that has taken Ford's mantle as the iconic corporation, especially in terms of organizational efficiency, and labor management. Today Wal-Mart, the first supermarket chain in the world, is the largest employer in America. It employs over 2 million people, mostly part-time workers on minimum wages. In America, there are today 64 million people that work minimum wage jobs, spread across the fast food, restaurant, and hotel industries, as well as janitorial and cleaning ser-vices, personal care, and social welfare services. McDonald's and the Yum! brands (which include KFC, Pizza Hut, and Taco Bell) are the third and second largest employers in America respectively. McDonald's currently employees 400,000 precarious workers in America alone. The fact the Wal-Mart, McDonald's, and Yum! are America's three largest private employers is

75   Giovanni Arrighi, *Adam Smith in Beijing*, London: Verso, 2007.

a sign of the hold that brand retail chains have over the labor market. By paying substandard wages, they keep the general pay level depressed. Real median wages have never returned to the heights reached in the 70s, when strong unions made sure that incomes rose as the economy grew. Industrial unions had emerged from the crucible of the Great Depression, and global war, as powerful social actors. In America, out of the sitdown strikes of the 30s, the United Auto Workers (UAW), under the leadership of socialist Walter Reuther, emerged as the most powerful union of the postwar period, securing wage increases and cost-of-living adjustments that were replicated after 1947 in other American industries, as well as in other western economies.

Since the neoliberal age (1980-2008), it has been the Service Employees International Union (SEIU), which has spearheaded the labor counteroffensive against the flexibilization and individualization of employment relations. From the 'Bread and Roses' Justice for Janitors campaign of the mid-90s, to the ongoing national labor drive to double the minimum wage, and unionize retail chains, this innovative labor organization has been among the few American unions countering the anti-union neoliberal trend, practicing a form of social unionism that heavily relies on community organizing and local institutions. This has enabled the union, currently led by Andrew 'Andy' Stern, to attract historically non-unionized African-American and Latino members, to become intensely multiethnic. The more moderate United Food and Commercial Workers (UFCW), representing supermarket workers, has yet to succeed in unionizing Wal-Mart. Of course, retail chains like McDonald's are generally anti-union, both in America and across the world (even in Europe).

Starbucks, the Seattle-based coffee chain founded by Howard Schultz, has experienced tremendous global expansion thanks to its espressos, lattes, and frappuccinos. It prides itself on caring for consumers and employees alike. Baristas, however, have a different opinion. In May 2004, the Starbucks Workers Union was born in New York City. Affiliated to the Industrial Workers of the World (IWW) and led by Daniel Gross, it managed to organize five stores in Manhattan, and gain union certification. On 17 May 2007, workers at a Starbucks in Grand Rapids, Michigan went on strike, and asked the IWW to represent them in successful negotiations with the company. Although temporarily defeated via a mixture of police repression and appeal to legal technicalities, the neo-wobblies dissolved the aura of warmth and social responsibility surrounding the mermaid brand. In 2013, it was over the issue of tipping at Starbucks that a national debate ensued regarding whether waiters and waitresses should be paid by their employers, rather than out of customers' tips (the prevalent source of income for those waiting tables in bars, diners, and restaurants; tipping fast food workers, however, is prohibited). More recently, Brandworkers has started a crowdfunding project to the support all striking retail workers in New York City.

It was the Supreme Court that provisionally let Wal-Mart off the hook in 2014, in a major class action lawsuit undertaken by Betty Dukes in the name of all the chain's female empoyees, regarding widespread abuse against women, as well as demeaning work practices. A single family – the Waltons – own Wal-Mart. They are one of the richest families in the world, and deserve the Scrooge Award for their grotesque tight-fistedness. They pay wages so low that workers are encouraged to apply for food stamps to supplement their meager part-time incomes, to the effect that tax-payers are subsidizing the wages of one of the most profitable companies in the world. Wal-Mart has since rechristened its employees as 'associates', to make them feel they are part of the family, and therefore do not need a union to vent their problems to, or represent them in court. The company has a long record of intimidating employees into submission, and spreading fear among personnel in order to curb attempted unionization. Similarly, Amazons' recent moves to defeat unionization drives in Washington State is a clear sign that Amazon CEO, Jeff Bezos, considers maintaining the union-free nature of the e-commerce giant a serious priority. Both companies have repeatedly come under the scrutiny of the National Labor Relations Board for unfair labor practices. Our Wal-Mart, a network of workers who want to unionize the chain and end the scandal of poverty wages subsidized by states and the federal government, filed for discrimination and intimidation during the 2012 Black Friday protests at various supermarkets across America. A national fast-food strike campaign, Fight for 15, is currently unfolding, aiming to double the wage paid to McWorkers from $7.25 (the current level of the Federal Minimum Wage, although many cities and states enforce higher hourly compensation) to $15 an hour. They are also suing the multinational for wage theft in three states: the highly profitable multinational corporation, headquartered in Oak Park, turned a blind eye to the fact that in many (read: the majority) of franchises, employees are forced to put in free hours simply to keep their jobs.

One could debate whether Amazon, one of the Big Four digital oligopolists, is replacing the Arkansan behemoth to become the world's prime retailer, as more and more commerce moves online, even groceries. Amazon has acquired Whole Foods supermarkets and is opening brick-and-mortar bookstores. One thing is certain, however: both Amazon and Wal-Mart are rabidly anti-union. Amazon's global workforce has grown by 20,000% in less than ten years (80% a year on average: from 17,000 in 2007, the year the Kindle was launched, to 341,400 in 2016, when the first Amazon Go grocery stores were opened). This is still a small number, compared to Wal-Mart's army of uniformed employees. However, Amazon is much more than a retailer. It sells its own hardware, commissions TV shows, and (most) crucially it dominates cloud computing with Amazon Drive. It also manages the largest platform for online labor in the world: Amazon Turk. The platform, in Smithian fashion, breaks down image-tagging and text-translation tasks in bite-sized parcels of work, which are then performed by the lowest bidder with the right qualifications and skills. Returning to the question of whether Amazon is supplanting Wal-Mart as America's largest retailer, the current transformation of Black Friday into Cyber Friday speaks volumes. Consumers are increasingly not willing to stand in line in the cold outside chains like Wal-Mart, or Target. The best post-Thanksgiving deals are already available online, from Amazon. Since Amazon set up a warehouse in Northern Milan in 2015, even pensioners have gotten used to receive packages with the smiling arrow on their doorstep. But in terms of productivity statistics alone, the Amazon effect is still unrecorded, while the Wal-Mart effect is well attested. In fact, the sheer impact of the big box supermarket chain on aggregate prices and employment shows that Wal-Mart (along with Carrefour, Tesco, and Lidl) has been a neoliberal template in terms of labor relations.

Industrialization vs Tertiarization

Manufacturing vs Distribution

Rustbelt vs Sunbelt

(Northern and Midwestern union shop vs Southern and Western open shop)

Male Blue-Collars vs Female Pink-Collars

Full-time vs Part-time employment

Union with High Benefits vs Non-Union wih Low Benefits

High Employment Security vs Low Employment Security

Low incidence of Migrant Labor vs High utilization of Immigrant labor

High, Living Wages vs Low, Poverty wages

Integration of working class through high consumption vs working poor and social disintegration

Long-Term Permanent Employee vs Short-Term Precarious Employee

Table 10: The Shift from Fordist to Walmartian Labor Relations

Although wages crept up during the latest years of the Obama presidency, this was not enough to quell the rage of impoverished white America. As a self-serving real estate developer holds office, one who despises women, African-Americans, Latinos, and labor unions in equal measure, the prospect of an insurmountable anti-labor stance by the new regime looms. It will take the mobilization of the whole of American society to counter the racism, misogyny, and elitism that are the trademarks of Trumpism. However, I am in fact confident that the current resistance of American society to national populism will take the Fight for 15 movement to its inevitable victory. Note however that, even with a doubling of the minimum wage, workers would still need as many as 30 hours per week of paid employment to stay above the poverty line. In fact, the magnitude of the redistribution from labor to capital that has occurred during neoliberalism is so large that, in order to reverse the trend properly, a much bigger hike in wages and transfers is needed to reduce affect poverty and inequality. Oxfam recently caused uproar by reporting that eight men, including Warren Buffett, Michael Bloomberg, Bill Gates, Mark Zuckerberg, and Jeff Bezos, currently have as much money as 50% of the population of the Earth. Forbes tells us that the wealth of known billionaires has greatly increased since the start of the Great Recession (call it the *Piketty effect*): already $2.4 trillion in 2009, by 2014 this pool of wealth had grown by 266%, to $6.4 trillion.

The effect was a spectacular increase in inequality compared to the postwar period, with the greatest gains accrued by the richest classes (and especially the super-wealthy). Nothing – as you can see from the table below – went to the majority of the population. The top 10% grabbed the lion's share of economic gains, leaving crumbs to the bottom 50%, even the middle 40%. Conversely, note how Fordism boosted the incomes of the working, and middle classes, while it prevented the wealthy and super-wealthy from gaining too much.

	Neoliberalism: 1980-2014	Fordism: 1946-1980
Total Population	61%	95%
Bottom 50%	1%	102%
Middle 40%	42%	105%
Top 10%	121%	79%
Top 1%	205%	47%
Top 0.001%	636%	57%

Table 11: Pre-Tax Income Growth. Who Gets the Goods: Neoliberalism vs. Fordism, 1946-2014. Source: Robert J. Gordon, *The Rise and Fall of US Productivity*; post-tax data are not significantly different, indicating a lack of government redistribution

The Irresistible Rise of the Precariat

After three decades of neoliberalism, the precariat has emerged as the fundamental labor provider, as well as the provider of services enabling social and cultural reproduction across society as a whole. They are still relegated to the margins of political and social citizenship; the contribution of precarious workers to the postindustrial, informational, service economy has steadily increased, but gone largely unnoticed. Amidst the booms and busts of the global economy, the precariat has relentlessly grown in size in the European Union, America, Japan, and elsewhere. Japanese youth fear for their future if they are without a job immediately after graduation: they will lose in the *shuktatsu*[76] race, and end up confined in the second-class, contingent workforce, while the luckier ones will be offered a tedious job and long hours working in a *keiretsu*,[77] one of the country's numerous multinationals. Even there, lifetime employment and guaranteed career advancement are memories of the early 90s. In South Korea, a quarter of recent graduates face unemployment, in spite of their parents having

76   *Shuktatsu* means 'job hunting' in Japanese.
77   *Keiretsus* are successors of war-time *Zaibatsus*, Japan's main industrial conglomerates, such as Mitsubishi, and Toyota. They are usually centered around a trading company, or an investment bank.

paid for costly *hagwon*[78] classes to gain them entrance to the country's top universities. We are unaccustomed to thinking of these groups – spanning industries and continents – as having any strong commonality. Yet the indignities suffered by the precariat are essentially the same at any latitude of global capitalism. They can be read on the faces of young and prepared temporary employees who are short-changed and made to feel disposable, precisely because they are overqualified and threaten the existing social hierarchy. The precarious face an uncertain future and a fearsome present, no matter the industry, no matter the political orientation of unions and employers in their respective countries. The time has come for a global union of the precariat.

The emergence of precarity is evidenced in a jump in the share of non-standard and short-term employment in the overall labor force, particularly new hires. In Europe, between two-thirds and three-fourths of the jobs created since the Great Recession are of a precarious nature. In France, 83% of new jobs created in 2013 were short-term contracts, two thirds of less than one month in duration; the same year broke all records as the number of temps reached 4.4 million, up from 2.5 million in 2000. In June 2013, the American Labor Department similarly reported the country had more temporary workers than ever before (2.7 million). With over 10 million people still jobless, America has almost 20% of its employees working part-time, with 7.5 million of them unwillingly working shorter hours than the standard 40-hour workweek. They are underemployed, in the sense that they would prefer to work more hours in order to earn more, since they are currently not making enough. However, the economy is too sluggish to enable them to find better jobs, either in terms of hours worked, or pay earned.[79]

Today, a little over 15% of all those employed in the Eurozone work on temporary contracts, according to Eurostat data and definitions. Since the total number of European employees in early 2013 was in excess of 115 million, we can say that – according to a rather narrow definition of precarity: a short-term position – today there are over 17 million precarious people in the Eurozone. In Spain, a quarter of employees are precarious. Mostly they are *permatemps*: they have been working short-term contracts for a number of years.

Short-time labor, as a percentage of total dependent employment, is a proxy for the rate of precarity, which is equivalent to the share of non-standard forms of employment on total employment. Short-time employees make up 15% of all employees in France and Germany. The same figures hold true for Finland and, outside the Eurozone, Sweden. In North America, the share of temporary employment had climbed to 14.5% of the total working population by the end of 2012. Examining the generational cross-section, in Europe short-term employees account for about a quarter of the people in dependent employment aged between 15 and 39. In Mediterranean Europe, the numbers are higher still. In both Spain and Portugal, roughly a

---

78   *Hagwons* are private schools, which most young Koreans have to attend in order to train for arduous state examinations that determine their employment status.

79   Jeff Kearns and Jeanna Smialek, 'Part-Time Workers a Full-Time Headache on Yellen Radar', *Bloomberg News*, 18 August 2014, http://www.bloomberg.com/news/2014-08-18/yellen-dashboard-warning-light-glows-as-millions-work-part-time.html

third of workers under the age of 40 exist with an expiration date written on their foreheads, while in France and Italy roughly a quarter of workers (23% and 21% respectively) are temps, without hope of permanent employment. In the Netherlands, the corresponding percentage stands at high 31%, but unlike most Eurozone countries, this is offset by high, rather than low, employment rates for people under 40. Specifically talking solely of people under 25 years of age, the OECD reported that in Europe more than 39% of employees were temps (up from 36% in 2000). Contrast this with older employees aged between 25 and 54; only 12% were temps in Europe, and 6% in North America, according to the same OECD figures.

As the Great Recession progressed, employment rates for people under 40, not so high to begin with, fell continuously. In the trough of the euro crisis, during the second quarter of 2011, only 61% of millennials were employed. This fell to 58% in 2013, and in Southern Europe it is now below 50%. In Spain, Italy, and Greece, the employed are actually a *minority* of the people under 40; only 44% of Greek millennials are employed at all. This stands as a colossal waste of human talent. People are most productive in their twenties and thirties, yet young Europeans are either forcibly unemployed, or employed on sub-standard contracts.

Within the 25-29 age bracket (which contains all recent college graduates), the incidence of part-time work is higher than average, both in Western Europe and America. In Canada, 13.6% of the labor force was working part-time in 2012, in America the corresponding figure stood at 10.6% (about the same as France). This proportion was markedly higher in Britain and Germany, 15.8% and 16%, respectively. The incidence of part-time is typically higher amongst women, young women in particular; in Germany, over two thirds of part-time employees are women.

Each successive economic recovery has led the proportion of the working population in short-term employment to grow exponentially. During the 1992-1993 recovery, formerly the golden age of American temp agencies, temporary employees made up 11% of new hires. By 2010, agency employment accounted for 26% of job creation by private firms. Temporary labor has become an entrenched feature of labor markets, and permatemps are the norm in the gig economy. Intermittent employment, once considered the temporary condition of the young and marginal sections of the labor force, has now become standard for all employees. The *temps* (temporary employees) now outnumber the *perms* (permanent employees). Recent data on the nervous employment recovery in America, and continuing stagnation in the European Union, provides confirmation that we are truly living in a permatemp economy, which has led to a precarious society where fear, anguish, and division thrive.

In the late 20th century, young people, women, immigrants, and those in the service industries were the first to be affected by flexible employment relations, and the ensuing state of precarity. Beginning in the 80s, temporary employment started crowding out permanent employment across the western world. Precarious employment grew relentlessly in the subsequent thirty years of neoliberal hegemony, opening up larger labor markets while simultaneously atomizing employment relations. By the early 21st century, this condition affects people of all ages, in all industries. Due to austerity measures adopted by neoliberal governments in response to the crisis, increasing numbers of people are now denied basic social rights such as health, housing, education, and the right to a fair wage.

Precarity as Driver of Inequality

From the fundamental work of Thomas Piketty,[80] we know that the share of total income going to capital has overshot in all advanced capitalist countries since 1990. This share ranged between 15% and 25% in 1970, but grew to between 25% and 30% in 2010, a huge shift in the span of just four decades. This was just one impact of neoliberal regulation on distribution (or lack thereof). The capital-output ratio has dramatically increased, returning to early 20th century levels, while the rate of return on capital has stayed more or less constant at the historical levels of between 4% and 5%. Differently to Marx's prediction, there has been no long-term tendency of profit rates falling. Similarly, however, to what Marx foresaw, capital has become more concentrated. The share of income going to labor has correspondingly decreased. In Germany, for instance, the labor share fell from 80% to 70% of aggregate income in the period between 1980 and 2010. Piketty demonstrates that the capital share is positively correlated with the savings rate, and negatively correlated with the growth rate. He outlines how the capital-output ratio has doubled during the era of neoliberalism. Since the savings rate stayed constant throughout this period, growth has suffered as a result.[81] This leads him to formulate what he calls the second fundamental law of capitalism:[82] if the profit rate exceeds the growth rate, as has been true since the start of the Great Recession, inequality will inexorably increase, and wealth will become ever more concentrated at the top. Thus, he demonstrates both empirically and theoretically why capitalism has grown more unequal since Reagan and Thatcher, as the share of Gross Domestic Product (GDP) going to capital owners has risen, and that going to wage earners has declined, making financiers and managers the main beneficiaries of the recent period of inequality.

In fact, Piketty's claims go further than merely proving the cause of wage inequality. He argues that, theoretically, there is nothing stopping the growth of capital from further outpacing output. If growth drops to zero permanently, as during the worst of the Great Recession, the capital-output ratio can rise above measurable level, and capital share can reach 100%: all work is automated, in this scenario. Piketty demonstrates that inequality has increased since the crisis: the already rich have gotten richer, while the precariat have merely become even more precarious.

Piketty argues that this is simply due to the internal logic of capital accumulation: absent countervailing factors, such as wars, inflation outbursts, labor unrest, and strongly progressive taxation, the power of accumulated wealth leads to increasing inequality. The historical

---

80   Thomas Piketty, *Capital in the 21st Century*, Cambridge: Harvard University Press, 2013.
81   This is because from the Harrod-Solow model we know that $g = s/v$ where s is the economy's saving rate, and v is the capital/output ratio. In the long run, the equation collapses, so that growth is equal to the sum of productivity growth and population growth.
82   The first is the tendency to rise of the capital share to rise as a function of the capital-output ratio: $a = r\,v$, where a is the capital share and r the real profit rate, which is empirically constant.

tendency of capitalism has been for the profit rate to stay above the growth rate, save for exceptional periods of recent history (such as the three decades following World War Two, the era of Fordist capitalism). According to Piketty, left to its own devices, capitalism is not a growth machine, but an accumulation machine that reproduces inequality.

In current times, this describes a situation of reproduction and intensification of precarity; a situation where jobs are scarce, and incomes consistently cut. In fact, precarity has been the fundamental factor in keeping wages low and driving down labor's share of total income. The wage fund (the number of people employed multiplied by the average number of hours worked, multiplied by the real hourly wage) has decreased both in absolute terms, and relative to total capital income. Employment levels have not recovered to those pre-2008, the average hours worked have gone down due to precarious employment, and both average and median wages have stagnated. How then do we escape the trap of inequality?

Only a progressive wealth tax, says Piketty, can prevent 'the past from eating the future'.[83] Fiscal redistribution should take the burden of accumulated wealth off the shoulders of precarious workers, a burden that currently acts as an engine of inequality. If democracy excludes these countermeasures, the lasting effect of the Great Recession could be the transformation of liberal democracies into financial oligarchies, enforcing an authoritarian brand of formal democracy. In fact, he claims that without these measures, the season of prosperity and reduction of inequality enjoyed by working people under Fordism cannot be repeated. This is the only aspect of Piketty's analysis that I do not find persuasive. In fact, his book leaves strangely unanswered the question of how to act politically, in order to tame capital's totalitarian instincts, as was successfully done for a generation after World War Two, thanks to the struggles and the will of the working people.

Thirty years of Keynesian regulation and social-democratic policies delivered prosperity and stability in America and Europe; thirty years of neoliberal deregulation and fiscal conservativism have delivered inequality and geopolitical chaos. Thus, what really matters is the presence or absence of a redistributive institutional arrangement. If the social regulation of capitalism was already successfully tried, can't it be repeated? A new form of regulation that restarts growth hasn't yet been found. It is not only a matter of engineering a sustained recovery to keep the economy going, it is also a matter of fundamental political legitimacy. Neoliberal elites in America and Britain were swept away because they failed to see that, in the aftermath of the crisis they caused, unregulated free trade and rigged financial markets were breeding nativism and nationalist resentment. As a result, for the first time since 1989, liberal democracy and open markets are no longer hegemonic. Protectionism and closed borders, and the regionalization of global trade, are seemingly the new tenets of the international political economy.

A new form of regulation must come into being in order to rebuild today's discredited institutions, and provide a strong and permanent demand stimulus. Regulation could be radically democratic, emancipating economically disadvantaged people, or authoritarian, justifying

---

83   Piketty, *Capital in the 21st Century*.

existing inequalities and scapegoating minorities for the sufferings of the majority. Whichever way, it will have to deliver growth, jobs, and an increase in the average standard of living. A progressive outcome of the crisis is not impossible, but it will have to be actively sought and fought for. Everything depends whether the collective action of the precariat can succeed in imposing redistribution of wealth, and confront the oligarchy with a stark choice: implement basic income, or we will revolt, and burn down your corporate headquarters and luxury condos. Reducing or blocking capital mobility – abolishing global financial parasitism – is a necessary condition for this to happen.

Instead of 'euthanizing' the rentier, as Keynes had hoped in *The General Theory*, Friedman-inspired financial deregulation has created a new class of super-wealthy people with immense clout over the workings of supposedly democratic governments. The Occupy movement was correct: the 1% is happily riding out the crisis, and turning liberal democracy into a patrimonial oligarchy. Short of movements for radical democracy that take power away from neoliberal and authoritarian regimes, strike waves that achieve redistribution from profits and rents towards wages, and social investment funded by wealth and corporate taxation, present capitalist trends are leading to levels of inequality incompatible with democracy.

Since its inception in Classical Athens, democracy has always been about restraining the privileges of the propertied classes, and protecting the well-being of the laboring classes, in order to advance the common prosperity of the polity. In modern times, democracy has come to depend on the existence of a sizable middle class that all can aspire to join through college education and salaried employment. This is precisely the class that has lost the most in terms of economic and social standing since the Great Recession, with many educated professionals now living in poverty.

The Value of Human Labor in Classical and Neoclassical Thinking

While the ravages of the crisis still exact their social toll, automation of service work, coupled with the expropriation of professional skills by machine learning, are exacerbating unemployment, making many ponder whether there will indeed be a place for humans as wage-earners in a fully-automated digitized economy. This would be a society, as Piketty observes, where capital gets all the share of output (all the money is invested in machines) and labor none (no money is spent on human workers). How would people survive in such a world? The emerging policy answer coming from the eco-populist left, and liberal billionaires such as Bill Gates and Mark Zuckerberg, is that of a universal basic income funded by the taxation of robots and artificial intelligence. The fact that driverless vehicles might endanger the jobs of truck drivers has caused labor leaders like Andrew Stern, the man who turned the Service Employees' International Union (SEIU) into a mighty organization, to reconsider the traditional hostility of trade unions toward basic income. He now agrees that universal basic income will soon be needed to give a share of the digital dividend to everybody, and guarantee all a decent livelihood. Work may no longer be the exit route out of indigence. Mass youth unemployment is keeping idle the most knowledgeable and skilled generation that has ever existed: the internet natives. Work could soon lose the central place it has enjoyed in society since the industrial era.

David Graeber observes that most existing jobs are in fact 'bullshit jobs': zero-productivity jobs that add nothing to, or even subtract from, the social product.[84] Rising numbers of employees are declaring their work to be useless and stultifying. The question to be resolved, however, requires a foolproof definition of 'productive labor'. Smith was especially concerned with the question of productive and unproductive labor, and argued that the wealth of nations depended on the growth of productive labor in factories, at the expense of unproductive labor at the service of the aristocracy. However, economists have been unable to firmly establish on a theoretical basis what actually constitutes 'productive' and 'unproductive' labor.[85] In Classical economics, the distinction between productive and unproductive labor is based on the labor theory of value, such that value is proportional to the hours of work required to produce a given product. However, translating labor values into prices is not possible unless heroic assumptions are made, as one of the founders of modern economics, David Ricardo, first realized. Ricardo defended the interests of the early profit-making bourgeoisie against the rent-seeking aristocracy. Similarly, his liberal predecessor Adam Smith[86] argued in favor of what he considered productive labor – the labor of workers and capitalists, peasants, and farmers – but railed against the unproductive labor commanded by royal courts and wealthy landowners. When Marx put forward his labor theory of value aimed at demonstrating the existence of exploitation of the proletariat in the capitalist labor process, the political left began considering only industrial labor as productive labor. This politically alienated the majority of peasants and farmers, as well as the urban middle classes, who have mostly sided against the socialist working class since the Industrial Revolution, notwithstanding the attempts made by Russian populists and Spanish anarchists at organizing the rural poor, and the efforts of social-ists and communists to recruit technical employees and middle-class artists and intellectuals.

Conservative opposition to the rapidly expanding socialism of the Second International, and the logical flaw intrinsic to the labor theory of value (the so-called transformation problem, which would be later solved by Tugan-Baranovsky and Piero Sraffa), caused economic thought take a sharp turn to the right of the political spectrum. As such, the materialist theory of value, which intended to objectively demonstrate that workers were underpaid, was shelved during the Second Industrial Revolution by the first neoclassical economists, Léon Walras and Vilfredo Pareto,[87] who instead sought to demonstrate that free markets were superior to other forms of economic organization, and that economic exploitation does not exist. In this theoretical setting, government intervention only made the situation worse. The labeling of this school of thought as 'neoclassical' is misleading, since it has little interest in the issues of growth and distribution; issues that preyed on the minds of classical

---

84   David Graeber, On the Phenomenon of Bullshit Jobs, *Strike*, 17 August 2013, now available as 'Why Capitalism Creates Pointless Jobs', http://evonomics.com/why-capitalism-creates-pointless-jobs-david-graeber/, *Evonomics*, 27 September 2016. See also 'Workers of the World Despair', *New Scientist*, 10 December 2016.

85   In layman's terms, the issue is a lot more straightforward: if you get paid for what you do, then it's work. Folk wisdom, I think, suffices here.

86   Adam Smith, *The Wealth of Nations* (1776). David Ricardo, *On the Principles of Political Economy and Taxation* (1817). Both of these texts have been recently reprinted by CreateSpace.

87   Léon Walras, *Éléments d'économie politique pure*, 1874. Vilfredo Pareto, *Manual of Political Economy*, 1906.

economic thinkers like Smith, Malthus, Ricardo, and Marx. Whereas Ricardo saw the reality of class struggle over income distribution, and Smith warned against the evils of monopoly and financialization, early neoclassicals (also known as 'marginalists', for their application of calculus to economic problems), were apologists of laissez-faire capitalism. They wanted to rescue property owners from the assault of socialism, and thus dispose of the theory labor of value that revealed the antagonism that existed between capitalists and workers. They only cared for the omnipotence of the market, wherein egotistic individuals sought to maximize personal advantage, at the lowest cost for themselves. As expressed by Pareto's welfare economics, the utility theory of value prevents any kind of economic redistribution due to the non-comparability of individual utilities (I cannot say what a dollar or an apple is actually worth for you, I can only say what is worth for me). These are the political reasons why methodological individualism and ordinal utility are at the heart of neoclassical economics, the clearest intellectual apology of neoliberalism. Neoclassical economics mathematically demonstrates that free market competition leads to an optimal, and efficient, economy. In particular, for neoclassicals there can be no exploitation in the labor market, because the wage is always set at the level of marginal productivity determined by technology and paid by profit-maximizing firms competing in free markets. If workers asked for more than the equilibrium level, for instance by striking for higher pay and / or shorter hours with the help of unions, they would cause other workers to become unemployed. Thus, if there exists unemployment, it's because wages are too high, and must fall. In the end, all unemployment is voluntary, the consequence of the free decisions of people asking for too much money for their work. The liberal mainstream has in general shied away from this conservative doctrine, a doctrine that seeks to justify existing wealth and income disparities as eternally given, refutes the intervention of governments in the economy as reducing unemployment, and opposes the role of unions in defending labor. In liberal politics, Rawlsian neo-con-tractualism[88] rather than Paretian neo-utilitarianism has usually prevailed, thus justifying government redistribution in favor of the economically deprived.

Keynes and Kalecki

Keynes' progressive liberalism consciously broke with laissez-faire tradition, and returned to the classical problem of determining the appropriate level of output, and its subsequent distribution among social classes. Whereas Marx wanted to replace capitalism with socialism, Keynes sought to salvage capitalism from itself, and make sure that liberal capitalism would defeat fascism, since this was a more attractive option than statist communism. Keynes, although not caring much for Marx's theory of value, saw that Marx was correct in seeing crisis as a normal feature of capitalism, rather than as the anomaly that neoclassicals were trying to expunge from academic economics. Marx saw the possibility of under-consumption leading to a realization crisis, where the inability of capitalist companies to sell their goods

---

88   John Rawls, *A Theory of Justice*, Cambridge: Belknap Press, 1999. Rawls sees liberal political society arising from a contract between citizens who do not know in advance where they will end up in the distribution scale: they might be rich, and they might be poor. In this situation, individuals have an incentive to want a system that offers as much welfare as possible to the poor, since they could end up being poor themselves.

for a profit would cause involuntary unemployment. The occurrence of insufficient market demand for capitalist firms was eminently possible, and indeed the norm. Keynes saw that unregulated capitalism had produced mass unemployment. Its speculative excesses had led to deflationary crises, when the economy became mired in a high-unemployment equilibrium. It was investment decisions that determined the business cycle, and if private companies were not doing their part, then the state had the right to step in to ensure full employment. The Great Depression was thus a crisis of private investment, and a crisis that needed to be solved by the socialization of investment. Keynes also described the particular role of money in depressions. He argued against the gold standard, for imposing wage reductions to deficit countries, and being intrinsically deflationary. Against monetarist orthodoxy, he showed that money was not a veil over real transactions, but that it had a measurable effect on the level of activity and employment through investors' varying preference for liquidity, which could be influenced by monetary policy via the interest rate. However, in the Great Depression the economy had fallen into a liquidity trap, such that even an expansionary monetary policy could not restart the economy. He instead favored increased government spending in public works and welfare programs, which kickstarted growth, and restored business confidence from which investment, and thus employment, crucially stemmed. Keynes thought that austerity and wage cuts were uselessly worsening the crisis, and that the mass unemployment was dangerous for democracy.

A more radical proponent of the theory of effective demand, who came independently and simultaneously to the conclusion that investment determines the cyclicality of output and employment, was the Polish Jew Michal Kalecki, who had been strongly influenced by Rosa Luxemburg in his youth. Kalecki's revealing aphorism – that workers spend what they get and capitalists get what they spend – succinctly revealed the logic of his argument. While wages limit the consumption of workers, the profits and consumption of capitalists are determined by how much they decide to invest. Given that they will invest based on expectations of demand, if this is composed mostly of workers' incomes, then cutting the latter will reduce the former, and hence capitalist investment. In a depression, cutting wages reduces effective demand, whilst raising wages increases effective demand. Keynes and Kalecki, the two founding fathers of macroeconomics, thus respectively found the two post-keynesian solutions to the problem of mass unemployment adopted by social democracies the world over: high government spending, in order to pay for welfare and public investment, and high wages, to finance high consumption. This last solution also meant that governments had to explicitly promote the unionization of labor.

After World War Two, full employment was indeed attained by capitalist economies through Keynesian policies, while high wages were kept rising by wild productivity growth. Blue-collar workers agitated for, and eventually won, social security for all. However, it was white-collar workers who mostly benefited from this victory without having to fight for it. They were rewarded for supporting centrist governments and upholding of values of moderation in both social emancipation and economic progress. For three decades, capitalism barely felt a moment of crisis, as production, employment, and wages all grew at unprecedented rates. Corporations reaped economies of scale (productivity grew as the scale of production increased) making larger volumes of consumer goods more readily available worldwide. The fall in the production costs was facilitated by the low prices of oil, and other raw materials. The postwar liberalization of trade after the protectionism of the interwar period boosted export-oriented economies like Germany and Japan, who had managed to catch up with America in terms of technological advancement. The return to free trade occurred under the auspices of Adam Smith, meaning that protection of industries in their infancy was possible, and that trade concerned the exchange of manufactured goods between industrial economies, rather than the exchange of industrial goods for primary goods as theorized by Ricardo. This mode of free trade, however, was in fact slowly condemning the Global South to chronic underdevelopment.

From Bretton Woods to the Euro

At the Bretton Woods international conference, Keynes lost the battle on gold, since the dollar was nominally tied to it, but won the argument in favor of fierce restrictions on capital mobility. These were necessary in order to maintain the fixed exchange rate system put in place, and ensure that the financial crises and competitive devaluations of the interwar period would not return to haunt the world economy. Governments ratified his advice, rationing foreign currency purchases, and restraining international investment. Capital mobility was indeed kept low well into the 60s, until international investments made by American multinationals, combined with the export surpluses of Germany and Japan, began to create an offshore, dollar-based market. This market enabled financiers to circumvent jurisdictions, and create the basis of the international financial market we know today. Keynes also wanted to abolish gold as international measure of value in favor of a multilateral currency, the bancor. However, during the conference, American delegates argued that they would rather much see the dollar replace gold as the international monetary standard. Thus, a new international monetary system was born, setting parities between the U.S. dollar and various European currencies, parities later extended to the Japan Yen. However, as Volkswagens and Toyotas began to flood the American car market, and the American administrations asked the Fed to monetize the debt accumulated during the ill-fated Vietnam War, serious pressure was placed on the dollar to depreciate its parity with gold. Rather than giving in to this pressure, however, then-President Richard Nixon decided to suspend the gold convertibility of the dollar in the summer of 1971, and allow its value to float in international currency markets.

Europe, destabilized by the sudden introduction of exchange rate flexibility, then set out to establish the monetary unification that led to the introduction of the euro in 1999, when the EU just had only 15 members (having recently been extended to include Austria, Finland, and Sweden). All member states, save Britain, Denmark, and (eventually) Sweden, decided to adopt the single currency, and relinquish their monetary sovereignty, which was now exercised by a powerful, independent central bank headquartered in Frankfurt: the European Central Bank (ECB). The ECB has an explicit monetarist mandate, set out in the Maastricht Treaty: to ensure that inflation never rises above 2%. For its part, the Commission have made sure that budget deficits of state governments not exceed 3% of GDP (by way of comparison, the U.S. deficit hit 12% in 2009, although this was orchestrated in order to save the American economy). As deflation plagues the Eurozone, unorthodox measures, such as the purchase of government assets, and negative interest rates to incentivize lending, have been adopted by President of the ECB Mario Draghi, in spite of the opposition of the Bundesbank and German Finance Minister Wolfgang Schäuble, the custodian of ordoliberalism and neomercantilism. Even with these measures in place, the euro, which was sold to the European people as a catalyst for economic prosperity, has made life far more precarious for millions of Europeans. It has led to a massive contraction in both GDP and social spending in Greece, cementing the understanding that debtor countries must pay back their loans, or else. The break-up of the euro has been averted, but at the cost of potentially having the majority of the citizens of the Eurozone despise it for what it has brought them. Living conditions across Europe are deteriorating, since the weaker economies of the South cannot devaluate, and the stronger economies of the North will not recycle their trade surpluses by reflating either their own economies, or transferring resources to debtor countries. By refusing to mutualize sovereign debt and European banks' toxic assets, Germany has achieved European supremacy, but has endangered the European project possibly beyond repair, by breeding resentment in Greece, Spain, Portugal, and Italy. We can say the euro is the political equivalent of the return to gold standard, enforcing a blanket wage deflation as a way of realigning the productivity differentials between the various Eurozone economies. The euro is the last remaining symbol of European unity. Furthermore, political sociologist Claus Offe has recently noted[89] that, no matter how poorly-conceived the euro is, Eurozone countries would be worse off, were they to leave the single currency. If the euro disappears, it means that the dissolution of the European Union at the hands of right-wing populist forces is complete.

This crisis is of course no random phenomenon, it was caused by the venality of financial and political elites. The political backlash, and solution, to it either involves right-wing authoritarianism, or a new, populist left. While America has chosen the right-populist path, Europe's future still hangs in balance (although Macron's election as president of France portends the unexpected resilience of European liberalism). The aftermath of the Great Recession can either fan the flames of xenophobia and islamophobia, further scapegoating immigrants, or it can give rise to a social-populist response that empowers the precariat to obtain universal entitlements like basic income and free higher education, new forms of urban democracy and social participation, as well as new forms of solidarity between service and cognitive workers.

A Theory of the Great Recession: Capitalist Crises and Ideological Bifurcations

At the heart of the Great Recession is a basic imbalance between informational accumulation and neoliberal (de)regulation. In other words, the new technological and media paradigm is no longer compatible with the principles of economic governance laid out by neoliberal doctrine. The Great Depression signaled the incompatibility between Fordist mass production and laissez-faire capitalism, that is, between the need for mass demand and unregulated labor markets. The Great Recession signals the incompatibility between

---

89   Claus Offe, *Europe Entrapped*, London: Wiley, 2015.

the mass diffusion of the means of information, and the concentration of wealth in few digital oligopolies, which make fortunes by exploiting precarious labor, while reaping profits from their monopoly.

This book is about how the Great Recession set the precariat in motion, triggering an egalitarian, populist-revolution that, although followed by a succession of right-wing reactions in the Middle East, Europe, and America, is not over yet; it could still go either way.

In the television series *The Man in the High Castle,* Germany and Japan win World War Two. Remember that the Great Depression sent Hitler and Tojo to power, consolidated Stalin's hold on the Communist party, and for three long years partitioned Spain in Europe's bloodiest civil war, which was ultimately the fight between the European fascism of Hitler, Mussolini, Franco, and leftists of all stripes. International brigades composed of anarchists, socialists, and communists came to support the Popular Front, and keep Barcelona and Madrid in republican hands. Although socialist France and conservative Britain ultimately let the Spanish Republic be overtaken by a fascist dictatorship, the Popular Front's strategy was behind the progressive turn of capitalism in America and France, as a wave of sitdown strikes led to Roosevelt and Blum's social reforms for the working class. In fact, the Dimitrov doctrine, which ended the Comintern's suicidal hostility to reformist socialists after Nazism seized Germany, opened up the possibility of a broad, leftist camp, one which made the alliance between capitalist America and communist Russia possible. This alliance was, of course, formed to prevent Europe being ruled by national-socialist Germany, and the Pacific sphere ruled by nationalist Japan.

The uchronic science-fiction of Philip K. Dick,[90] which was subsequently serialized for television, outlines how an alternative outcome to World War Two was entirely possible. It describes life in an alternative dimension during the early 60s, where America is under Nazi rule between the East Coast and the Rocky Mountains, and imperial Japan holds California and the rest of the West Coast. Whilst the Midway, and Stalingrad, prevented this scenario from actually occurring, it could have easily been the Axis powers prevailing over America and the Soviet Union in 1942. Eventually, the Allies defeated the Nazis, the world was freed from the worst genocidal regime in history, and Germany was partitioned by Allied Powers. In the Pacific, Japan's military regime was defeated by American nukes, before the subsequent invasion transformed the country into a temporary protectorate, in order to westernize it permanently. In 1947, negotiations between the victorious powers broke down, and the Cold War began, a titanic competition between two ideological, geopolitical, and geoeconomic camps: capitalism, liberal in the Global North and authoritarian in the Global South, and communism in Russia, China and a host of countries in the Global South fighting for national liberation from western imperialism. Both superpowers engaged in massive government spending, in order to boost economic growth, and increase material well being, making sure that within each bloc, rising prosperity would prevent a return to the economic and national rivalries that had caused depression and war. America and the Soviet Union rebuilt the world's

---

90   See Philip K. Dick, *The Man with the High Castle*, New York: Putnam, 1962.

institutions to stave off nationalism and depression, and, by grudgingly accepting their geopolitical coexistence, created something of a sphere of co-prosperity spanning both sides of the Iron Curtain.

The fall of the Berlin Wall and the end of the Cold War conversely led to the victory of a less equal version of capitalism: neoliberalism. The neoliberal age (1980-2008) was never as dynamic as the post-keynesian age (1950-1979) in economic terms: with the major exception of China, growth rates were lower across the board. While the British economy deindustrialized, and American industry offshored many tech and industry jobs, the beast of financial capitalism kept being fed, until the tumble of its enormous carcass overwhelmed the real economy. Years of financial deregulation eventually ushered in the Great Recession, and mass precarity. Neoliberal ideology will never recover from this blow, although something nastier might be rising to take its place.

At the root of both the Great Depression and the Great Recession was same structural demand crisis: the economy simply could not produce enough jobs with fair wages for people to buy the goods it produced. In the 30s and 40s, these goods were cars and white goods, and in the 00s and 10s, they are instead smart phones and digital services. Both crises of capitalism were preceded by a severe concentration of financial wealth in few hands. This was done by redistributing income away from labor, and towards capital, combined with the effective banning of unions from many workplaces, in reaction to earlier working-class victories, such as the introduction of the 8-hour workday in the 20s, and the shop floor democracy of the 70s.

The end of the Great Depression came as democracy defeated fascism, and the working class was given its fair share, thanks to social democracy (both in the form of unions and political parties), and socialism. The Great Recession will end when real democracy is re-established, and the precariat is able to redistribute the wealth and power accumulated by oligopolies, and oligarchies.

Just as postwar recovery was predicated on Keynesian regulation of the economy, strong unions, and constant wage growth providing enough demand to sustain Fordism, the way out of the Great Recession requires major fiscal redistribution, redressing the balance between capital and labor, and expansionary social and environmental spending.

The Great Recession is a capitalist crisis, but it's not the crisis of capitalism. It's the crisis of neoliberal capitalism, a specific historical configuration whose unraveling we are currently witnessing. A different institutional form of capitalism will emerge out of the crisis, and the political earthquakes we are experiencing are due to the global repositioning of those actors that give economies and societies their coherence. Capitalism in the near future may well be fascistic and xenophobic, even dystopian, but it could also be reformist, progressive, and transformational. The Great Recession has opened a historical bifurcation, a fork in societal development which, similarly to what the Great Depression led to in the 1930s and 1940s, is causing a global civil war between reaction and reform. The ultimate outcome of the battle between democracy and authoritarianism, will depend on the victors of the various ideological and political battles that have been raging around the globe since the revolutions of 2011.

The state is back, but its intervention has so far been solely in the interests of the owners of capital, rather than the creators of wealth. Also, unlike the world of the Great Depression, when much of the world was still rural, and carbon emissions were still low, in this crisis humankind faces both economic *and* ecological predicaments. We must create jobs and incomes for all, while simultaneously ensuring ecological balance for future generations. This twin challenge is what defines 21st century movements, for social and climate justice are indissoluble from an *egalitarian* perspective, the cosmopolitan philosophical stance adopted herein. A victory against emerging national-populist forces needs to be also to be a victory against fossil-fuel capitalism, in order to count as real progress. However, this is a three-way game where declining neoliberalism faces a stronger threat from the political right than a challenge from what used to be called the left. Thus, movements have to be very careful with what they wish for. For instance, the dissolution of the euro and the abolition of the Eurocracy would be a defeat for European liberalism, but a victory for nationalist forces in France, Germany, Hungary, and Poland, not a victory for social movements. The end of Europe wouldn't have any leftist fallouts, while its survival allows movements to campaign for a full implementation of the European Charter of Fundamental Rights, and alter the balance of European Union network power though political action, and institutional change. More to the point, while there have been social movements that have successfully contested national state power, we have yet to see a political movement of the European people that sets out to provide citizens across the Eurozone with guaranteed income, housing, health, and education. This is just for starters. Most of the radical left prefers to question the legitimacy to exist of the admittedly non-democratic European Union, something radical movements in America would never do: they accept that the United States of America should exist. '*Europa is meine Heimat*' ('*Europe is my home*'), I once said in a radio interview; we should consider Europe as our motherland, finally superseding the nation-states and national patriotism that led to so much blood being spilled, especially that of workers and people of the left.

Since the euro crisis, European integration has been in political and geographic retreat. Particularly damaging for the European liberal agenda was Brexit, which appears to be leading to an increasingly nationalist England. Combined with the rise of Trump (which entails an increasingly nationalist America), the rules of the game have changed from those applicable when neoliberal Europe was conceived of in the early 90s. Europe is now a paradoxical construction; the single market arose through implementation of Anglo-Saxon, neoliberal principles, but now Atlanticism is dead, and the Continent is facing a political legitimacy crisis while confronted with a growing external threat in the form of Putin's Russia. Eurocrats increasingly look like the priests of a religion whose prophets have finally denounced it as farce. Not only are European elites in ideological disarray; monetary unification has led to the exact opposite of the prosperity and unity they promised, and now the people of Europe are furious. Many have started to wonder what Europe is for, if it cannot resist rising unemployment, and help weaker member states. This, however, is an objectively reactionary sentiment that should be resisted. The radical left can only be transnationalist, and must keep red-brown temptations at arm's length. European social movements are fighting a two-sided battle, one to assert that no one is illegal and refugees must be protected from racism, the other against the neoliberalism with a human face that Macron wants to establish in France and across Europe, on the basis of a new Franco-German alliance with Merkel to adapt Europe to the new political and economic circumstances. High unemployment in France and rising poverty in Germany signal the limits and constraints of the centrist, liberal and christian-democratic project for post-crisis Europe, in the attempt to regain popularity and consent among the citizenry.

The progressive way out of the reactionary morass we are seeing across the globe, in my view, involves a geopolitical order based on a structural compromise between informational capitalism and radical democracy, between digital capital and the social precariat. The liberal wing of Silicon Valley is ready to compromise with precarious labor on basic income, for instance. Similar to the Fordist compromise between industrial capitalism and social democracy of the post-keynesian era, such compromise would warrant growth while reducing inequality and increasing inclusion. In political terms, such an institutional arrangement would similarly pull the carpet under the feet of the forces of nationalism, and bring prosperity and emancipation to the world. Since this entails major tax redistribution, expect stiff resistance from financial and corporate lobbies.

Democracy has always been the only way to tame the unequal and unstable tendencies of capitalism. Factory laws, the suffrage of men and women, industrial planning, public education, the welfare state, and gender equality were all imposed on capitalism by radical movements.[91] It will take persistent struggle, and possibly global civil war, for ecosocial populism to prevail over ecocidal national populism. Social reform and environmental progress are attainable, even though the current mood of the world is dark, and reactionary forces appear to be succeeding.

The Great Recession of the 10s (as did the Great Depression of the 30s) has opened a historical bifurcation in the normally stable process of capitalist accumulation, and the evolution of regulatory institutions. Only in capitalism's major depressions (1873-1879, 1929-1938, and 2008-2012) possibilities open up for radically new political ideologies and economic structures to establish themselves, such as industrialism, socialism, populism, anarchism, communism, social democracy. Today the new ideologies emerging are ecofeminism, in the form of Pink Tide, People's Climate March, LGBTQ movements, and cyber-populism, either in the anarchist jeer for the lulz that has made Anonymous an anti-authoritarian avatar worldwide, or under the form of political movements based on online democracy and deliberation. Times of historical chaos signal that new modes of regulation need to be found, in order to manage the existing technological paradigm (such as heavy industry in Victorian times, mass consumerism in Fordist times, and digital informationalism in Jobsian times). This management is necessary due to the productivity potential of a given paradigm being squandered by a crisis, whose root causes are to be found in a faulty mode of regulation (imperialist, conservative, and neoliberal, respectively). Thus, new mental frameworks and novel redistributive institutions are required, so that the major technological transformations that have already transformed society and the economy beyond recognition can properly distribute the wealth they have created for capital owners. Just as urban craftsmen and

---

91   Polanyi would say 'countermovement'. For the relevance of the Polanyian approach with respect to the
      current crisis, see Nancy Fraser, 'A Triple Movement? Parsing the Politics of Crisis', *New Left Review*,
      May-June, 2013.

industrial workers acted to determine what direction their societies would take after crippling depressions and fight back against capitalism, the informational precariat must forcibly expropriate digital wealth to fund a new universal welfare system, in order to cope with rising poverty, and the extinction of permanent employment.

For a long time, the availability of easy credit masked neoliberalism's singular inability to widely distribute purchasing power, but in the end the adepts of Hayek and Friedman proved incapable of creating demand at a sufficient level to match the 1996-2004 productivity boost, brought about by the completion of the information economy. The advent of neoliberalism at the end of the Cold War was crucial for unleashing the digital forces of productivity which have since transformed the world. In spite of the exponential rise of computing power and the liberalization of computer networks and telecommunications in the 80s and 90s, the Great Recession showed that the neoliberal ideology that conquered politicians and pundits with its weird mix of amoral individualism, market theology, and social conservatism, was in the end incapable of being true to its promise of technological abundance for all. Damningly, it was on this point that neoliberal ideology claimed to hold superiority over socialism. State socialism floundered because it was incapable of technological and consumer innovation, and market capitalism is now floundering because it is no longer capable of delivering jobs and prosperity.

During depressions, monetary policy normally doesn't work, since the economy falls into a liquidity trap when the nominal interest rate hits zero. Quantitative easing has been a way to circumvent the problem, but expansionary monetary policy just makes sure recession doesn't turn to depression; it cannot restart the economy. Trillions of dollars were created to save international banks from going bankrupt, and prop up stock markets. Yet this further exacerbated the structural imbalance in income distribution that is itself the root of the Great Recession. Only redistribution through fiscal expansion (more social spending and public investment), is going to do the trick. After immense suffering, the Great Depression led to innovative solutions such as demand management, union counter-power, and the welfare state. We must act to make sure that the exit from the Great Recession leads to economic redistribution, social emancipation, and ecological community, rather than racism, war, and climate disaster.

Capitalist accumulation and reproduction depend on the creativity, and docility of the precariat, without whom the wealth shot to offshore financial centers would simply not exist. Neoliberalism is losing its hold on power in Europe and America. It long sought to present itself as the natural state of things in economic affairs (and nearly succeeded), but was in fact a deeply historical phenomenon, motivated by political vindictiveness of the capitalist class against the considerable gains achieved over the 60s and 70s by the working class, and ethnic minorities. Inequality was restored under the justification that it fostered profit and investment, and intervention in capital-labor relations began to be strongly biased in favor of business owners, and against labor unions, which were increasingly considered a dangerous interference in the workings of capitalism. The neoliberal gospel made laissez-faire respectable again. The free market preaching of Hayek had fallen on deaf ears in the 40s and 50s; memories of the Great Depression, and World War Two, were just too painful to allow a return to the kind of free market logic that had destroyed the world economy. From 1950 until the first oil crisis in 1973, faith in government intervention to combat unemployment and poverty was predominant. In conjunction with the opening of America to European and Japanese imports, Keynesian demand management produced the biggest economic boom in the history of capitalism.

However, by the 70s, what became later known as the Fordist regime of accumulation had fallen into crisis. Declining productivity, working-class insubordination, and rising inflation were undermining the economic basis of the social compromise between organized capital, and organized labor. Samuel Huntington wrote that the long period of nearly full employment was making people unruly, ungrateful, and hostile to the profit motive; women, ethnic minorities, and students were behaving as if they were entitled to something, and capitalism had to give it to them.[92] The early 80s job crisis, engineered by monetarism, showed them otherwise. Forty years later, those same groups are mobilizing in an attempt to bring back equality and democracy to America. While Huntington, shortly before dying, railed against the Latinization of America, which was supposedly seeding a breed of Catholic egalitarianism, and undermining the country's white, Calvinist, individualist ethos.[93] Trump won on the basis of hostility to Latino immigrants and African-American civil rights; Huntington is not dead after all.[94]

Whereas baby boomers grew up under the comforts of mass consumerism (1950-1979), millennials reached maturity during the dizzying transformation of society brought by personal computing and networking technologies (1980-2016). I propose we call this *Jobsism,* after the late Steve Jobs, the entrepreneur that embodied the personal computer revolution much as Henry Ford symbolized the assembly-line revolution in productivity. In the following pages, I present 'the Grid & the Fork', the model which enabled me to predict the Great Recession (terminology my own) around 2004. I have since refined this model, particularly regarding future scenarios, because the ideological and geopolitical contours of the historical bifurcation are now clearer. The basic idea is to describe the 'capitalist laws of motion' via changes in two endogenous variables (accumulation and regulation), and two exogenous variables (ideology and geopolitics). It stands as my attempt to explain the critical dynamics of advanced, informational capitalism, via comparing historical accumulation regimes and modes of regulation, before drawing parallels (and differences) between the crises of capitalism, particularly with regards to their political outcomes.

This model, essentially, combines the French theory of regulation with Nikolai Dmitriyevich Kondratiev's theory of long waves. I am thus intellectually in debt to Robert Boyer, Michel Aglietta, and Alain Lipietz,[95] for their theory of Fordism, and Carlota Perez, for her neo-Schum-

92   Samuel P. Huntington, *The Crisis of Democracy: On the Governability of Democracies*, New York: Simon & Schuster, 1976.

93   Samuel P. Huntington, *Who Are We? The Challenges to America's National Identity*, New York: Simon & Schuster, 2004.

94   Of course, he's also well known for the clash of civilizations thesis embraced by both Bush Jr and Trump Jr against Muslims. Samuel P. Huntington, *The Clash of Civilizations and the Remaking of the World Order*, 1996.

95   Robert Boyer, *La Théorie de la Régulation: Une Analyse Critique*, Paris: La Découverte, 1986. Michel

peterian resurrection of long wave theory in the 80s (although I significantly depart from both). My approach also differs from that of Paul Mason, who combines long wave cycles with phases of working-class insurgency, rather than political regulation. He thus offers a different historical portrait of modern capitalism, which he breaks into only two periods, 1890-1945 and 1947-2008, conflating very different ideological and geopolitical discontinuities of capitalism's history. Mason also overlooks the crucial role of political power in determining income and wealth distribution through state institutions; why should capitalist accumulation be soon over? It doesn't look that way today, as an excess in global savings is funding a major new round of investment into artificial intelligence, robotics, smart services, and the green energy industries. In fact, Mason's historical model doesn't predict the advent of postcapitalism, it's just the author hoping that non-profit-based industries will grow in size, until some political threshold is reached.[96]

In the model below, the critical dynamics of the capitalist system is conversely explained by the interplay between capitalist accumulation and social regulation (including workers' agency but also state regulation), and the exogenous effects that ideology and geopolitics have on these two key variables. The basic mechanism is simple. When there is too much accumulation, and too little regulation, a demand crisis arises, leading to mass unemployment (investment and consumption are too low to keep the economy going). When there is too much regulation, a supply crisis ensues (costs rise too much due to hikes in wages and prices of raw materials), depressing profitability below the level capitalists are ready to accept. The 30s and the 10s are examples of the former type of crisis, and the 1910s and the 70s examples of the latter. Regulation crises are deflationary crises, while accumulation crises are inflationary crises. The Great Recession is thus a regulation crisis, brought about by the inadequacy of neoliberal regulation with respect to the technological paradigm of informationalism that, since the 80s, has changed the logic of capitalist accumulation. Note that the same technological paradigm can be associated with either prosperity (as in the 50s and 60s) or stagnation (as in the 30s and 40s), depending on the set of regulating national and international institutions. The technological and organizational features of Fordism were already in place after World War One, but only when wage earners were brought into the circuit of mass consumption after World War Two did industrial society prosper. Regulation crises are particularly momentous, because they create historical bifurcations, whose potential sociopolitical outcomes tend to be drastically polar. While in normal times decisions and investments are predictable, and keeping in the middle of the road is the best political course, in depressions anything can happen, and the times reward the bold, both on the radical right and on the reformist left: Trump, but also Tsipras, can unexpectedly rise to power.

The geopolitical balance of power tends to reflect (albeit with a slight lag effect), the international shifts in economic hierarchy, such as China's rise as a world power following its transformation into a global exporter of manufactured goods. Of course, an ill-chosen war, or a crumbling defeat, can rearrange the distribution of international power in unexpected

---

Aglietta, *Régulation et Crises du Capitalisme*, Paris: Odile Jacob, 1994. Alain Lipietz, *La Société en Sablier: Le Partage du Travail Contre la Déchirure Sociale*, Paris, La Découverte, 1994.

96   Paul Mason, *Postcapitalism*.

ways. A key example of such an unexpected shift in power is George Bush Jr.'s thwarted push for global hegemony in Iraq, which transformed the unipolar world that arrived with the end of the Cold War into the multipolar world of today, where America, Europe, and Japan are challenged by rising regional powers such as China, India, Brazil, Turkey, and Iran, and where a diminished Russia is reasserting its international stature as a military power. The world could evolve toward a bipolar system based on America and China, reminiscent of the Cold War's bipolarism, but not based on a fundamental ideological antagonism; if anything, Xi Jin Ping's China seems more committed to the global capitalist order than Trump's America. Although the summit of capitalist powers has been expanded from the G8 to the G20 (soon to be held in Hamburg, and the NoG20 are preparing their 'welcome'), if there are only two global superpowers (China and America), and they go to war, then global suffering will ensue. Certainly, rivalry between the two nations is rising over the ongoing South China Sea land dispute with Japan. North Korea will be more likely to launch missiles if enmity continues to rise between the two economic superpowers.

Yet what are the main ideological forces pushing people into political confrontation today? We have already discussed the rise of national populism in America, Russia, and Turkey (where Erdogan has recently consolidated his Sultanat by plebiscite). The three strongmen all share religion as an ideological base for their nationalist agenda, namely fundamentalist versions of Protestantism, Orthodox Christianity, and Sunni Islam. Let's now consider the alternatives to nationalist populism.

Leaving behind the ideological conundrums of the Middle East aside, and venturing into the wider world, green liberalism is certainly an emerging ideology (one that is discussing how to differently manage capitalism, and is attracting popular support). Green capitalism cannot be dismissed as simple *greenwashing*, because the apparatus of production, transportation, and consumption is undergoing a deep change thanks to the shift to green technology and waste reduction (usually eulogized under the rubric of the 'circular economy'). China and America are fast upgrading their energy infrastructure by massively investing in photovoltaics. In America, there are currently more people employed by the solar power industry than by the coal industry. While investment in renewable energy and energy efficiency is bound to rise (in spite of the last gasp of fossil-fuel capitalism occurring due to Trump), it is unlikely that this will result in the drastic cuts in emissions needed to mitigate the effects of climate change. A more drastic approach is needed, as Naomi Klein reminds readers in *This Changes Everything*.[97] Eco-populism is this approach. It is a mass political movement, born from the climate justice movement, and foreshadowed by the People's Climate Marches: global days of action networked by 350.org, the most active climate advocacy in the world. Global feminism is another mighty force, as demonstrated by international mobilizations that, from Argentina to America, have united an entire new generation of young women against rape, abuse, and gender discrimination, and for full equality in the economy, in society, and in politics. Together, feminism and eco-populism form the basis of a viable antagonist to right-wing populism: social populism. The constituents of these two movements command the allegiance of the majority of the

---

97   Naomi Klein, *This Changes Everything: Capitalism vs. the Climate*, New York: Simon & Schuster, 2014.

global population, comprised as they are of women, precarious youth, migrants, and the inhabitants of ecologically devastated regions. Every *partido morado* (*purple party*) which, modeling itself on the Podemos, stands for the precariat, must articulate a sophisticated gender-oriented discourse, and support the pink, queer tide that is undermining the political machismo of demagogues and dictators.

Rojava's feminist guerrilla war against ISIS has attracted anarchists and communists from Northern Europe and North America in a way reminiscent of the International Brigades in Spain during the civil war. The ideology that gave birth to Rojava – Syria's only free canton – rests on two pillars: Abdullah Öcalan's marxist-leninism, and Murray Bookchin's anarchist bioregionalism. Turkish President Recep Tayyip Erdogan an wishes to violently remove this expression of Kurdish autonomy, as it constitutes a serious danger to his absolute rule. It remains to be seen whether America will let him do just this. The Pentagon is (finally) arming the Kurdish fighters of the People's Protection Units (more commonly known as the YPG) with heavy weaponry. Kurdish support is vital if the two ISIS strongholds in Raqqa and Mosul are to be retaken and controlled. However, Trump clearly feels an affinity for the anti-democratic instincts of the Erdo an; the arming of the YPG in the fight against ISIS should not be read as a wholesale endorsement of Kurdish independence by America.

An ideological schism concerning Aleppo is consuming the left. Most sane people see in Assad a ruthless dictator who has turned Syria into a cemetery, after plunging the country into six years of bloody civil war. Within the radical left, there are those who oppose genocidal Assad, and thus support both the Turkey and Qatar-backed Syrian rebels. Others instead support Russia and Iran, ostensibly against the imperialism of America and Israel. Autonomists and anarchists have sided with the rebels of Aleppo and Idlib, while communists, particularly of the red-brown variety, have generally sided with Putin and Assad, in spite of the aerial bombings and gassings which have devastated the civilian populations of Aleppo, Damascus, and Homs.

The Tunisian and Egyptian revolutions of early 2011 tried to establish secular Arab democracies. Although Tunisia is still a democracy, the Egypt of Tahrir Square has fallen, and is now under Abdel Fattah el-Sisi's dictatorial rule. Backed by Saudi Arabia, el-Sisi ousted the democratically elected president Mohamed Morsi, who belonged to the Qatar-supported Muslim Brotherhood. Since the 2013 coup, the organization and its members have been outlawed, yet the Brotherhood's project of an Islamic democracy is popular across the Middle East, and is destined to prevail in one form or another. The outcome of the 2011 Arab Spring may be the Muslim Brotherhood's eventual rise to power after decades of foiled attempts, from Algeria to Palestine. On the other hand, Saudi Arabia's regional influence is fading, hence the House of Saud's aggressive reactions against Iran and even its neighbor Qatar, defending across the region its own brand of reactionary Wahhabism that is fueling ISIS and other jihadist groups, as well as providing them with economic support. The victory of Iran and Hezbollah in Syria (on the side of Assad and Putin) can only mean that the regional influence of Saudi Arabia's traditional rival will continue to rise, with the effect of creating a Shia crescent across the Gulf, and the Levant.

At the red end of the ideological spectrum, we have Bolivarianism. Named after South Amer-ica's 19th century liberator, Simón Bolívar, it is a leftist political ideology that combines top-down, communist *Castrismo* with the participatory philosophy of Indio-liberation movements. Articulated by Hugo Chavez after his successful counter-coup in 2002, *Bolivarismo* succeeded in holding off the spread of American neoliberalism into Latin American for almost a decade, granting left-populist governments time to consolidate power in Venezuela, Bolivia, and Ecua-dor. Thanks to Bolivarianism, the long-awaited climb out of poverty began. In Brazil, previously the most unequal country of the world, the rise to power of the leftist Workers' Party led to major anti-poverty reforms under the leadership of Luiz 'Lula' de Silva. While the economy has now sputtered to a halt, leading to President Dilma Roussef being overthrown in a coup, social movements remain active across Brazil, sparked by the mass protests of 2013 and 2014.

Systemic Variables	Description
Accumulation	Capital (endogenous)
Regulation	Capital-Labor-State Relations (endogenous)
Ideology	Political Mobilization (strong exogenous)
Geopolitics	Balance of World Power (weak exogenous)

Table 11: The Model of Capitalist Crisis: Variables

Brazil aside, the Bolivarian model itself has been in crisis since the deaths of Chavez and Fidel Castro. Venezuela is now rioting, vocally rejecting the Bolivarian regime that is unable to feed the population, Rafael Correa is no longer the president of Ecuador, and the Bolivian administration of Juan 'Evo' Morales faces allegations of systemic corruption. For their part, Brazil and Argentina have been stagnant since the Great Recession. Economic populism has diminished poverty, but neither solved macroeconomic imbalances nor removed obstacles that prevent sustainable productivity levels and global exports. The truth is that Latin America is still too heavily reliant on the exports of commodities, rather than the export of manufactured products. Economies as different as Germany, Italy, South Korea, and China, have shown that export-led growth is the only way to catch up from a position of relative backwardness in regard to technological innovation. The protection of certain industries, allowing them to attain competitive advantage before opening them to the global market, is necessary for successful economic development. As Korean economist Ha-Joon Chang shows,[98] you can ditch neoliberalism without killing the capitalist goose. Almost the entire population of China lived in poverty during the 80s. Yet by embracing capitalist enterprise, and the world market, on its own terms, the Chinese economy has since grown enormously, almost completely

---

98   Ha-Joon Chang, *Bad Samaritans: The Guilty Secrets of Rich Nations and the Threat to Global Prosperity*, London: Random House, 2008; *23 Things They Didn't Tell You About Capitalism*, London: Penguin, 2011.

eradicating poverty and illiteracy in the space of a generation. It is Deng, and not Mao, that the Chinese have to thank for this amazing feat of socio-economic engineering. The current Chinese government is both nationalist and globalist, and is likely to have much to offer Europe, which has now been left out in the cold by America. The central party controls the economy, but does not yet control society. A political agreement between Europe and China is inevitable, the economic preparations for which are over a decade in the making.

Accumulation vs. Regulation: Critical Dynamics of Capitalism from the Great Depression to the Great Recession

FORDISM	
Macro variables	1890s-20s: Belle Epoque, War, Revolution
ACCUMULATION (Capital, Technology, Nature) main endogenous	Second Industrial Revolution and start of industrialism: electromechanic tech, electric lighting, industrial chemicals and dyes; combustion engine; diffusion of mass dailies, radio and telephone, silent movies; coal key energy input, Haber process boosts agricultural yields. Intensive: mass production of investment and intermediate goods, élite consumerism, international financial cartels, monopolistic competition. Crisis of gold standard, postwar inflationary crises, monetary stabilizations, American loans and German reparation, trends in terms of trade in favor of industrial goods, rising protectionism, wartime economic blockades.
REGULATION (State-Capital-Labor Relations and Business/ Union Organization) main endogenous	Decline and crisis of classical liberal regulation based on government-bosses alliance, subsistence wages, monetary and budgetary orthodoxy, low social spending, polarized income and wealth distribution; direct action, mass strikes, Second and Third International (mayday and international workers' movement) 8-hour working day, single-product firms, authoritarian/paternalist organization, mass migrations, craft unionism, industrial unionism, birth of the white collar and first feminization of labor.
IDEOLOGY (Political Mobilization) strong exogenous	Socialism, liberalism, anarchosyndicalism, nationalism, modernism, leninism.
GEOPOLITICS (Balance of World Power) weak exogenous	Unbalanced multipolar: first concert then League of Nations, German attempt at hegemony blocked by Franco-British with U.S. help; British primacy in decline, rise of U.S. and Germany; first anti-colonial movements, first genocides; two Russian revolutions, Mexican revolution, white army vs red army civil war, red-white civil war in rest of Europe, early spread of reactionary regimes, creation of Comintern.

FORDISM	
Macro variables	**30s-40s: BIFURCATION I: Regulation crisis: Great Depression & World War**
ACCUMULATION (Capital, Technology, Nature) main endogenous	Industrialism: motorization, aviation, tanks, rise of oil as key energy input; radars and early computers, sound cinema, mass propaganda; falling agricultural prices and wartime subsistence agriculture. Intensive: high productivity growth and low wages lead to Great Depression then expansionary war economy. Black Tuesday: Wall Street crash, currency crises, deflation and competitive devaluation, drop in prices of agricultural and other raw materials, manufacturing prices stay stable, widespread protectionism, autarky, bank failures, end of international financial system; financial reconstruction at Bretton Woods / industrial reconstruction with Marshall Plan.
REGULATION (State-Capital-Labor Relations and Business/ Union Organization) main endogenous	Regulation Crisis: Great Depression - right vs left class struggle and world war, employers' confederations vs industrial unions, sitdown strikes, militarization of labor force, paid weekend and holidays for white and blue collars, monetary and fiscal policies first restrictive then expansionary; crisis epicenters: U.S. and Germany. Rise of multiproduct/ multidivision firm, repression of working-class movement in Axis powers, stakhanovism and forced labor in USSR, curbs in migration, WWII full employment in U.S., interethnic industrial unionism, feminization of heavy industrial work.
IDEOLOGY (Political Mobilization) strong exogenous	Fascism/nazism, communism/stalinism, popular front/ liberal democracy.
GEOPOLITICS (Balance of World Power) weak exogenous	Potential hegemony Germany/Japan: systemic world war vs Allies and USSR: soviet industrialization and defeat of Nazi Lebensraum; genocide of European Jews and ethnic/ political/ sexual minorities; Communist Russia dominating land power in Eurasia after Stalingrad; U.S. is hegemon on Atlantic (inherits British naval power) and on Pacific (defeat of Japan's Co-Prosperity Sphere); civil wars: antifascism vs fascism.

FORDISM	
Macro variables	50s-60s: Fordist Regulation: Welfare/Warfare State
ACCUMULATION (Capital, Technology, Nature) main endogenous	Industrialism: white goods, autopia, aerospace, plastics, cosmetics, the pill and antibiotics; mass publishing, broadcasting television; gasoline and natural gas, petrochemicals, nuclear energy, regulated and subsidized intensive agriculture: green revolution. Intensive: scale economies, mass production and mass consumerism of consumer durables, multinational groups, oligopolistic competition, rising industrial prices, decreasing prices of agricultural goods and raw materials. Bretton Woods: dollar standard (fixed exchange rates), moderate inflation, low capital mobility, creation of GATT, IMF, World Bank, progressive liberalization of trade and reduction in tariffs, growing U.S. trade deficit, dollar and pound devaluation with respect to mark and yen, growth in Nippo-German reserves: imported inflation; prices of primary goods slowly decline, prices of secondary goods slowly rise.
REGULATION (State-Capital-Labor Relations and Business/Union Organization) main endogenous	Fordism: capital-labor compromise guaranteed by government, and employers' and union organizations, Keynesian expansionary fiscal and monetary policies, cost-of-living wage adjustments, full male employment, high wages, high social spending, balanced income distribution, some nationalization of utilities, banking and heavy industry, consumerized leisure: generalization of weekend and increase in overtime work. Vertical, integrated corporation: expansion of multidivisional multinationals, supply-oriented hierarchical/bureaucratic organization, human resource management, neocorporativism; big business big labor partnership, male re-gendering of wage labor, controlled migrations, rise of educated middle class, public sector unionism.
IDEOLOGY (Political Mobilization) strong exogenous	Social democracy, christian democracy, managerialism, anti-imperialist marxism, generational anarchism, third-world nationalism.
GEOPOLITICS (Balance of World Power) weak exogenous	Stable bipolar: creation of UN, Cold War, military/ideological competition between U.S. and USSR, NATO vs Warsaw Pact, Common Market vs COMECON, free world vs popular democracies; decolonization, non-aligned countries, pro-American and pro-Soviet dictatorships; Nippo-European economic miracle: reduction of technology gap with U.S.

JOBSISM	
Macro variables	70s: Social Crisis of Accumulation
ACCUMULATION (Capital, Technology, Nature) main endogenous	Accumulation crisis of Fordism: transition from industrialism to informationalism starting from U.S. West Coast, two oil crises, environmental limits to intensive growth. Transition from intensive to flexible: profitability crisis due to oil hike, labor conflict, diseconomies of scale; end of dollar's convertibility and crisis of Bretton Woods regime: floating exchange rates, high inflation and end of Phillips' Curve, euro/petrodollars: creation of world financial market, sharp rise in prices of primary goods: terms of trade favorable to LDCs and Soviet Union, which borrow massively from international markets.
REGULATION (State-Capital-Labor Relations and Business/Union Organization) main endogenous	Conflictual: crisis of neocorporativism, working-class protest and rank-and-file insurgency, distributional conflicts, stagflation and the return of unemployment, monetization of fiscal deficits, refusal of work ethic (stoppages, wildcat strikes, absenteeism). Transnational conglomerate (keiretsu): hierarchical (management)/ horizontal (line production), robotization / flexible automation, shop-floor radical unionism, white collars' democratic emancipation, flows of unskilled labor from former colonies.
IDEOLOGY (Political Mobilization) strong exogenous	1968, 1977, and the global democratic revolution; feminism and East-West antinuclear movement; Islamic revolution.
GEOPOLITICS (Balance of World Power) weak exogenous	Unstable bipolar: Soviet stagnation, post-Vietnam American crisis, China-U.S. rapprochement, reactionary counterrevolutions, secret wars, anti-imperialist terrorism. Unstable bipolar: Soviet stagnation, post-Vietnam U.S. crisis, U.S.-China rapprochement, marxist-leninist revolution, reactionary counterrevolutions, secret wars, armed struggle.

JOBSISM	
Macro variables	**80s & 90s: Neoliberal Deregulation: global corporate state**
ACCUMULATION (Capital, Technology, Nature) main endogenous	Flexible accumulation: Third Industrial Revolution and diffusion of personal computing and mobile telephony, low productivity growth, economies of scope, customized mass consumption, transnational market concentration, competition among global production and communication networks, decreasing prices of technology goods and raw materials, global environmental crisis. Flexible exchange rates and financial deregulation (repeal of Glass-Steagall Act): mark-dollar-yen realignments (Plaza & Reverse Plaza); stock exchange booms and busts, monetarism cuts inflation and budget deficits, liberalization of capital movements and trade: U.S. becomes net capital importer, drop in prices of commodities; debt crises in Latin America, Africa and Balkans; creation of E.U., Mercosur, NAFTA, WTO, European monetary integration, euramerican trade tensions and amerasian financial wars.
REGULATION (State-Capital-Labor Relations and Business/ Union Organization) main endogenous	Neoliberal: state subordinated to capital, monetarist macroeconomic policy, financial deregulation, growing unemployment, redistribution from labor to capital. Transnational network firm: horizontal organization, lean but mean, toyotism: just-in-time and zero-stock manufacturing; tertiarization and feminization of employment, downsizing of labor force, mass immigration, deunionization, Mitbestimmung, company unionism: dual labor markets.
IDEOLOGY (Political Mobilization) strong exogenous	Neoliberalism, postmodernism, environmentalism, liberation theology, ethnonationalism.
GEOPOLITICS (Balance of World Power) weak exogenous	Unbalanced unipolar: U.S. hyperpower, decline deflagration of Soviet Empire, neoliberal cosmopolianism, European integration, Asian tigers, ascent of China and India; nationalist civil wars and ethnic genocides, first Pan-African war.

JOBSISM	
Macro variables	**00s-10s: BIFURCATION II – Regulation Crisis: Great Recession & Global War**

ACCUMULATION (Capital, Technology, Nature) main endogenous

Flexible accumulation: mature informationalism, rapid expansion of net economy and diffusion of smartphones, high productivity growth, regulation crisis and drop in effective demand, oligopolistic concentration and gig economy. Crisis of New Economy (2000) and Financial Crash (2008) lead to Great Recession European monetary unification, euro, dollar, yen and yuan in competition for financial domination, creeping deflation in the system's core, currency crises in emerging economies (South-East Asia, Russia, Argentina), China enters WTO; decreasing manufacturing prices and increase in price of energy and raw materials.

REGULATION (State-Capital-Labor Relations and Business/Union Organization) main endogenous

Regulation Crisis: Great Recession: E.U. cuts and U.S. spends; global movement vs transnational corporations and US-sponsored wars, popular resistance to privatization and austerity: expansionary monetary policy, restrictive fiscal policy, growth rate < profit rate. Flat business organizations constrained by shareholders and corporate reputation; outsourcing/offshoring networks, mass precarization of labor, polarization of job tasks and pay scales, gaping income inequality but reduction in gender gap.

IDEOLOGY (Political Mobilization) strong exogenous

Neoconservatism, bolivarianism, salafism, cyberanarchism, climate Justice.

GEOPOLITICS (Balance of World Power) weak exogenous

9/11 and 7-7: first global war; Al Qaeda and ISIS (and rise of Iran); defeat of US drive for global hegemony, coopetition with E.U. and competition with China, rise of Russian revanchism, end of the Monroe Doctrine in South America, Afghan, Iraqi and Syrian wars, extermination of civilians and global refugee crisis.

JOBSISM	
Macro variables	20s-30s: ANTI-DYSTOPIAN FUTURE? Social populism beyond national populism
ACCUMULATION (Capital, Technology, Nature) main endogenous	Modulable accumulation: high productivity growth, decarbonization of economy, regulated competition between business organizations and economic regions, rising trend in industrial and agricultural prices. Re-regulation of markets: semi-fixed exchange rates among regional currency areas, limitation of capital movements, global environmental and labor standards in international trade.
REGULATION (State-Capital-Labor Relations and Business/Union Organization) main endogenous	Jobsian Regulation: expansionary monetary and fiscal policies, redistribution of productivity toward labor, flexicurity, Universal Basic Income, employee status for app workers, Schumpeterian welfare oriented toward individuals and pools of talent, right to continuous education, participated democracy/technology, alternative/ complementary currencies, redistribution from capital to labor, growth rate > profit rate. Dismbembering of digital oligopolies, andabolition of tax havens; enforcement of opensource technology and stakeholder capitalism, cooperative platforms of information/ knowledge/ service sharing, empowerment of precariat, global feminism, transnational unionism, climate justice movement.
IDEOLOGY (Political Mobilization) strong exogenous	Social populism, green liberalism, queer feminism, radical municipalism defeat authoritarian national populism and religious integralism and halt the extropian bent in digital capitalism.
GEOPOLITICS (Balance of World Power) weak exogenous	Balanced multipolar: North American Democracy, European Republic, Neo-Tsarist Russia, Neo-Ottoman Turkey, Democratic Federation of Arab States, Shia Crescent, China as East Asia hegemon, Pan-African Community.

Table 12: Critical Dynamics of Capitalism from the Great Depression to the Great Recession.

We can see from history that post-depression conjunctures tend to favor populist and reformist solutions to capitalist crises. The aftermath of the 1879 depression brought about populism and municipal socialism, and solutions to the global crisis of 1929 assumed the forms of the Popular Front, and the social reform of the New Deal. On the other hand, inflationary crises of capitalism tend to lead to revolutionary outcomes, as evidenced by the numerous revolutions that occurred after intense periods of global inflation during 1917 and 1973. By the end of the World War One, the legitimacy of capitalism itself was questioned by the Russian revolution, while after 1968 and the Kippur crisis, American imperialism (and western capitalism itself) were challenged by both the global student movement and the Iranian revolution in the Middle East. The consequences of the latter would prove to be more permanent than the former, with political Islamism affecting global political developments to this day.

Depressions favor the crystallization of new classes. Just as the industrial proletariat emerged from the crises of the Second Industrial Revolution, the postindustrial precariat has emerged from the crises of the Third Industrial Revolution, brought about by the exponential diffusion of digital and network technologies. However, unlike the industrial proletariat, which was poor in terms of cultural capital but held a lot of political capital, the informational precariat is rich in terms of cultural capital, but lacking in political capital. The industrial proletariat overcame its class inferiority by building party and union institutions capable of educating it and advancing its cause. Likewise, the informational precariat has attempted to overcome its political exclusion by building computer-mediated social networks and online platforms. Over the course of the 20th century, the working class managed to secure social inclusion by taming the industrial capitalism of large enterprises. Over a series of punctuated social outbursts, most notably in 1919, 1936, 1945, and 1968, blue-collar proletarians managed to secure fundamental social rights: the 8-hour work day, the welfare state, social security, union freedom, and co-management privileges. The Keynesian regulation of Fordism allowed for redistribution toward higher wages, as productivity soared thanks to increasingly automated mass production. The neoliberal regulation of Jobsism has brought precarity and low wages, while productivity growth has exclusively benefited the digital and financial oligarchy. In the 20th century, the organized working class curbed the power of the industrial bourgeoisie, and struck a deal with big corporations for relative social peace, all in exchange for a larger slice of the pie. In the 21st century, the still largely unorganized precariat has to undermine the profiteers of the sharing economy, and break the big banks' stranglehold on government policy. The objective is to achieve eco-social redistribution and economic expansion, and invert the tendency (recorded by Piketty) toward the total domination of capital (when the profit rate of an economy exceeds the growth rate). The precariat has to fight for an empowering, customer-oriented welfare state, rather than the current, control-obsessed workfare system. It can succeed in this fight by using the introduction of basic income as leverage for the growth of social and ecological enterprises producing immaterial and non-market goods, as well as demanding forms of Schumpeterian public investment in young talent and socially innovative firms.

CHAPTER 4. THE POLITICS OF THE PRECARIAT: REVOLUTION AND SOCIAL POPULISM

During the revolutionary wave of 2011, I was briefly in New York as Occupy Wall Street activists temporarily re-occupied Zuccotti Park. In 2013, I spent a fortnight in the still-revolutionary Cairo, with its charred government buildings and politicized soccer hooligans, in charge of public (dis)order in one of the biggest cities of the world. In Tahrir, as the sun set, I saw columns of bi-gendered black blocs (an unexpected sight in a Muslim country), ready to confront the police placed at the gates of a ministerial palaces. The clashes continued until dawn. The following day, my host - sociologist Paolo Gerbaudo – and I woke up to flames coming from the island in the middle of the Nile: soccer hooligans were torching the police officers' club and Egyptian football league offices, after news had broken of the verdict concerning the deaths of Al Ahly supporters in Port Said. The luxury island of Zamalek, hitherto spared by the 2011 revolution, was up in flames.

The precariat has already managed to wage creative and impassioned battles. Precarious creatives gave rise to the EuroMayDay network in the 2000s, which acted as a masthead for temps, intermittents, queers, and migrants across Europe, while the precarious underclass exploded in the mega-riots that took place in Paris (2005) and London (2010). In Paris 2006 and 2016, the mobilization of a whole generation against precarity challenged executive power with insurgent determination. Place de la République seethed with indignation at the flagrant corruption of elites and now-discredited political parties. Since the Great Recession of 2008, and the revolutions of 2011, the precariat has been the vanguard of the people in the Arab Spring, the Spanish May, and in the Occupy and Blockupy movements. These movements have all fueled the anti-establishment sentiments that burn strong today across the European Union, America, and the Middle East.

Great Recession and National Populism

The precarious have been shortchanged for a long time, and a sustainable solution to the Great Recession requires greatly expanding their purchasing power via higher wages and basic income. By doing so, aggregate demand can be boosted, and a progressive solution to the crisis can be found; this solution – most importantly – reduces inequality. These social conquests will have to be seriously fought for, against both the lingering forces of neoliberalism, and the growing influence of nationalist forces in Europe, bolstered by the victory of Trump. America is turning toward national populism and white supremacism thanks to Donald Trump's capitalizing on the discontent of the deindustrialized working class of the Rust Belt during the election. The forces of neo-conservatism are being revived and put to the service of a fascist agenda, one which includes the mass persecution and deportation of immigrants, and the reassertion of a white patriarchy.

The explosion of urban rebellions from Washington to Portland, the mass resistance to the Muslim ban, and especially the Women's March show us that resistance to national-populist aggression will be strong. Black Lives Matter emerged in the late Obama presidency to fight against police brutality; now the battle is against racist rule. European movements must provide solidarity to the mounting mobilizations of African-American militants, Latino migrant groups, LGBTQ groups, and ex-Occupy activists. The unprecedented election of a far-right president in America puts the seal on years of growing authoritarianism around the world, from Putin's neo-tsarist Russia to Erdogan's neo-Ottoman Turkey. Putin played a crucial role in Trump's victory. A KGB-agent-turned-president having his man in the White House is something not even Le Carré could have imagined. Yet all of this is frighteningly real. Trump was hailed as a savior by Nigel Farage in Britain, Marine Le Pen in France, Frauke Petry in Germany, Heinz-Christian Strache in Austria, Geert Wilders in the Netherlands, and Matteo Salvini in Italy. All of these figures are either funded or supported by Putin, and share his ultimate objective of dissolving the European Union. Most of the xenophobic European movements assembled in Koblenz in early 2017 are directly bankrolled by the Kremlin. Since 2008, Putin's Russia has engaged in active revanchism from Georgia to Ukraine, and now threatens both Finland and the Baltic Republics. Poland, which has historically feared Russia, has fallen into reactionary hands, sharing the fate of Hungary (however, unlike the former, the latter does not feel threatened by Putin).

The world created at Yalta by Roosevelt, Stalin, and Churchill is gone forever; a rising nationalist international (to use Yanis Varoufakis' expression) now threatens to rule the world from Istanbul to Vladivostok, in concert with a jingoistic America. Whereas the Great Depression led to the New Deal, the aftermath of the Great Recession sees America moving to the extreme right after the initial shift to a Keynesian center-left under Obama. In Europe, the liberal-, social- and christian-democratic concert that has governed since 1957 is being undermined by europhobic forces in France, Germany, Italy, the initial bedrock, together with Belgium, the Netherlands and Luxembourg, on which Europe was built. After the likes of Boris Johnson and Steve Bannon, liberal democracy has left Atlantic waters: the historical destinies of Anglo-Saxons and Europeans no longer seem tied. The empowered national populism of America and Britain has forced Europe to get its act together, culminating in Macron's victory and a new pact with Merkel to relaunch Euro-governance. Whilst Western and Eastern Europe are diverging politically, the Eurozone could reverse this trend by actively striving to deepen overall integration.

In this turbulent scenario, the precariat must become the voice of the people, and articulate a global project that pragmatically addresses the basic needs left unanswered by the terminal crisis of neoliberalism. This project is *ecosocial populism*. The precariat needs to develop an equivalent of 20th century socialist parties and labor unions, in order to defend its interests (which are themselves in the general interest). Social populist parties and syndicates are needed to counter the reactionary headwinds blowing in.

The imposition of precarity was the crime perpetrated by neoliberalism in order to profit from labor flexibility and globalization. Now that neoliberalism is meeting its demise at the hands of xenophobic and inegalitarian forces, the precariat, its size greatly increased by the Great Recession, must build an anti-fascist, anti-racist, and populist front. This front must challenge, on both physical and ideological terms, nationalist and xenophobic movements either in, or clamoring for, power across Europe, America, and Asia. The precariat attempted to start a global revolution in 2011. Now it must defeat reactionary forces, and establish an alternative to neoliberal society.

The Precariat as Vanguard of 21st Century Revolution

Tahrir, Sol, and Occupy Wall Street were the three topical moments of the 2011 people's revolution. Each of these movements were incubated, and led, by the vanguard of the precariat: young university graduates without a job, and young professionals saddled with a precarious one. In the third year of the Great Recession, the precariat seized squares in major cities around the world in a cycle of mass struggles unprecedented in their width and scope. Indeed, the historical significance of these upheavals may be greater than that of the global mobilization of students in 1968; it makes sense to consider the revolutions of 2011 as the 21st century equivalent of 1848, the Spring of Nations. The Arab Spring began in Sidi Bouzid, Tunisia, in 2010, and soon spread to Egypt, Libya, Syria, and Bahrein in 2011. This sequence of revolutions then sparked revolutions elsewhere, with protests soon engulfing Spain, Catalonia, Greece, America, Slovenia, Bosnia, Turkey, and Brazil in our century's Spring of the People. Three dictators (Ben Ali, Muhammad Mubarak, Muammar el-Qaddafi) were toppled in 2011 alone, and Bashar al-Assad's position was endangered to such an extent that he had to declare war on his own people, who had dared to question his regime. He bombed and gassed them. This reaction sparked the bloodiest civil war since 1945, with Syrian troops being bolstered by Russian air support. Libya in turn has become a failed state, partially post-Bush Iraq, where ISIS has similarly found fertile ground, and partially post-Soviet Afghanistan, with rival warlords vying for control of state resources.

Writing from the perspective of early 2017, it's important to resist the claim that the revolutions of 2011 brought unmitigated pain to the world. The so-called Movement of the Squares, led by educated but unemployed youth, meant to create agoras from which a parliament of the people could rise and challenge the power of political and financial elites, by reclaiming democratic sovereignty and campaigning for social measures that would redress the exploding inequalities caused by the 2008 financial crisis. The Great Recession, by causing mass youth unemployment (a phenomenon still plaguing contemporary capitalist countries worldwide), created the conditions for revolutionary movements to expand and cross-pollinate across borders. Occupying city squares around the world were vast sections of the citizenry, enraged at the bailouts being handed to bankers and politicians who had been scheming with global financial institutions and transnational corporations. The Revolution of 2011 demanded political democracy in the Middle East, and a return to popular democracy and welfare rights in what used to be the West, until Trumpism rose to power in America. In Europe and the Americas, the people loudly questioned austerity and inequality, by denouncing the culprit of the crisis: neoliberal capitalism and its inherently inegalitarian project of empowering the few at the expense of the many. 2011 meant to empower the many at the expense of the 1%. Its fighting troops were a societal aggregate plucked from across the spectrum of civil society, and bound together by a common cause. The young, who had been made jobless and (supposedly) useless by the crisis, demonstrated alongside the unionized working class and members of the aggrieved petty bourgeoisie. The revolutionary contribution of the precariat was vital to the mobilization of these previously disparate groups; the propagation and organization of the logistics of protest were spread overwhelmingly via social media platforms. Facebook groups, like the April 6 Youth Movement in Egypt, and Twitter accounts like *Democracia Real YA!* in Spain, were pivotal in spreading the message of the revolution. Authoritarian regimes invariably tried time and again to censor – or even entirely shut down – the internet, but in doing so they simply signaled their terminal weakness.

Anarcho-Populism as the Ideology of 2011

2011 marks the irruption of the precariat into political history. As Paolo Gerbaudo argues,[99] the ideology of 2011 was a mix of cyber-anarchism, no globalism, and true populism, of the sort seen previously across Russian and America in the late 19th century, which sought to educate the people (the *Narodniks*), and stop the depredations of trusts and robber barons (the People's Party). The Anonymous mask became the veritable symbol of the Revolution, and was sold in street markets from Cairo to Oakland (this also made money for Warner Bros., as sales of trademarked masks of Catholic dissident Guy Fawkes boomed). In fact, the revolution was also about pop culture, as the author of *V for Vendetta,*[100] Alan Moore, crossed swords with the author of *Dark Knight,*[101] Frank Miller, over the patriotism of the Occupy Wall Street Movement. This tension presaged the two fronts of the cultural and political war which was soon to come: the war of social and national populisms.

Many of the cadres of the 2011 revolution were also part of the anti-globalization move-ment of the 90s and 00s, and brought with them their knack for media subvertising, and consensus culture rooted in general assemblies and affinity groups. However, whereas the anti-globalization movement fought global neoliberalism as a largely abstract enemy which temporarily materialized at World Trade Organization, G8, International Monetary Fund, and World Bank summits, the movement of the squares fought national oligarchy first and foremost – worrying less about ideological purity, and caring more for inclusivity – by involving ordinary people in public discussions, reflecting on their needs and aspirations, and thus aggregating a set of disparate demands into a mighty whole, which converged on one issue: the lost legitimacy of the existing political and business classes. Neoliberal elites created the financial crisis and then profited from it thanks to bailouts and quanti-tative easing, throwing millions into poverty and precarity in the process. The revolution loudly proclaimed what many had already come to think: that incumbent governments had broken the democratic pact by failing to secure the livelihood of the majority of the population, and the protection of liberties that are fundamental to a fair society: welfare, labor, gender, and cyber rights.

99   Paolo Gerbaudo, *The Mask and the Flag: Populism, Citizenism and Global Protest*, London: Hurtst
      Publishers, 2014.
100   Alan Moore, *V for Vendetta*, New York: DC Comics, 2008.
101   Frank Miller, *The Dark Night Returns*, New York: DC Comics, 2005.

	Anti-Globalization Movement	Movement of the Squares
Ideology	Black anarchism, red marxism, pink feminism, green ecology	Social populism and cyber libertarianism
Values	Anarchy, autonomy, diversity	Inclusiveness and unity
Actors	Global activists	National citizens
Enemy	Neoliberalism aka the Washington Consensus	Political caste and financial oligarchy
Media	Indymedia, discussion mailing lists, hacker groups	Anonymous, Twitter, Facebook, Reddit
Organization	Squatted social centers, affinity groups, social forums	General and neighborhood assemblies
Aim	Organizing the unorganized and the excluded: precarious, migrants, peasants	Mobilize the enraged citizenry, defend society from austerity
Campaigns	Third World debt, climate crisis, persecution of migrants, labor precarity	Financial and political scandals, impoverishment of middle class, government repression
Protest Tactics	Mass blockades, White Overall resistance, black bloc rioting	Mass encampments in central squares, mass demos and encirclements of government buildings
Projection	Transnational	National
State and Civil Society	Global civil society vs neoliberalism: anti-statist	The people vs the elite: reclaiming democratic sovereignty
Relation with Left	Collaboration	Competition
Geopolitics	South vs North	Democracy vs authoritarianism
Economics	Fair trade and social responsibility	Basic income and social expenditure
Historical Utopia	End of capitalism	End of inequality

Table 13: Social Movements: the 00s vs the 10s.

It makes sense to compare the anti-globalization movement in Genoa (2001) with the Indignados movement in Madrid (2011). To do so, see the table above from *The Mask and the Flag*, in order to illustrate how the political landscape has shifted, and how the precariat should continue the counteroffensive against national populism. I have done so by adding elements that further highlight the differences between the anti-globalization movement and the Movement of the Squares (as the revolution of 2011 is also known), given its method of occupying the central squares of cities in order to stir the population against the elites.

Revolution and Reaction

Every revolution engenders a counterrevolution. After the French Revolution came the Vienna Congress, and the repressive armies of the Holy Alliance of Austria, Russia, and Prussia - the three reactionary powers who had been defeated by Napoleon Bonaparte at Austerlitz and Jena, but had ended up winning the war in alliance with Great Britain at Waterloo. After the Bolshevik revolution, the counterrevolution triggered the Russian civil war, which was eventually won by Leon Trotsky's Red Army on behalf of Lenin's Communist Party, against the White Army which was supported by Western powers. In Europe, reactionary *Freikorps* and fascist Blackshirts ensured the restoration of the bourgeoisie by dismantling council communism in both Italy and Germany between 1919 and 1922, while in America, President Woodrow Wilson destroyed the 'red threat' by persecuting wobblies and socialists, painting them as traitors to the nation.

The every-revolution-is-followed-by-reaction thesis has been confirmed by the aftermath of the 2011 revolution, which deeply alarmed capitalists and dictators around the world. During the Arab Spring, and the demonstrations in Gezi Park, Hong Kong, Oakland, and Brazil, the people clamored for equality and democracy. What they got instead was repression and greater inequality; movements must now confront a reactionary backlash sponsored by Putin and Trump, while the (hopefully subsiding) terrorist actions of ISIS are fanning the flames of anti-immigrant parties in Europe, emboldened by the unexpected turn to nationalism in the heartlands of neoliberal capitalism. The double threat that Putin and Trump pose to the existence of Europe becomes more apparent every day. Trump wants more countries to leave the Union and imitate Britain's increasingly europhobic Brexit, and chastises open-border policies favored by Germany and the European Commission. This is the reason Merkel has greeted Macron's victory with a sigh of relief and is ready to compromise on German economic domination. While the potential catastrophe of disintegration has been averted, the Eurozone is still in deep trouble.

Neoliberalism and National Populism Compared

The rich might still rule the world, but neoliberalism is economically, politically, and ideologically dead. The Great Recession of 2008 killed the illusion that neoliberal democracy was the end of the history, and that free markets led to prosperity. The Revolution of 2011 questioned and subverted the legitimacy of neoliberal governance, but failed to dislodge global neoliberalism from power. With the hindsight of 2017, we now know that neoliberalism has been substituted in its Anglo-Saxon core by neo-isolationist and reactionary forces that I place in the umbrella category of national populism, while the European liberal center has held. Still shocked by the unexpected electoral victory scored by Bannon and Trump, many leftists have rushed to conclude that Trumpism is government by and for corporate executives that brings neoliberal tendencies to their logical conclusion, the highest stage of neoliberalism (to paraphrase Lenin's interpretation of imperialism). I think this interpretation runs against basic political facts, and that national populism is a distinctive political current that is opening up a new phase in the history of capitalism, as its toxic mix of nationalism, xenophobia, and military escalation signals the death of Friedmanite neoliberalism (1980-2008). Indeed, it undermines the entire concept of the western world that was initially built by the Anglo-Saxon liberal powers that emerged victorious from World War Two, and consolidated in the long Cold War against Communist Eurasia. We are navigating uncharted waters. As a provisional compass in stormy seas, below follows a comparison of the basic characteristics of neoliberalism and national populism, so we can better understand the nature of the threats posed to democracy.

	Neoliberalism	Nazipopulism
Economy	International free trade restrictive fiscal policy, expansionary monetary policy	Nationalist protectionism, restrictive monetary policy, expansionary fiscal policy
Geopolitics	Partnership with China, rivalry with Russia, European Union as NATO ally	Partnership with Russia, rivalry with China, European disintegration, rebalancing of NATO
Technology	Green capitalism	Fossil-fuel capitalism
Ideology	Conservative/ moderate liberalism, christian democracy, social democracy	Reactionary nationalism, racism, neoconservatism.
Population	Mass migration and multiculturalism	Closed borders and white supremacy
Culture	Individualism, liberal feminism, cosmopolitanism, scientific reason and technology as efficiency	Populism, misogyny, provincialism, manipulation of irrationalism and technology as domination

Table 14: Neoliberalism vs. National Populism.

Social Populism vs. National Populism

The politics of the precariat have emerged as a radical response to neoliberal policies that brought unemployment, insecurity, and exclusion to swathes of society. As a neoliberal empire consolidated after 1989, a global counterhegemonic movement coalesced around anarchist and autonomist principles, and engaged in grassroots practices. The struggles of the precarious and the unemployed retained this framework by fighting global corporations, and resisting global summits. Since the revolution, the politics of the precariat have been left-populist, or *social-populist*, and aim to restore political and economic equality. The precariat has shed some of its anarchist and communist purity in order to experiment with forms of radical democracy based on popular mobilization and electoral consent. Conversely, the politics of the oligarchy that constitutes the reaction to the revolution is right-populist, or *national-populist*. I argue that both constitute major departures from either the inherited left or the neoliberal right. Social populism is different from traditional leftist politics because it rejects class, and embraces the people as a democratic counterbalance to oligopoly and oligarchy. It is not explicitly anti-capitalist, although anti-capitalists are part of the social-populist front. Like classical populism, it favors direct producers and small firms over major corporations and financial concerns. It advocates an increase in social spending to escape the recession, and thus is a sworn enemy of neoliberal austerity. Similarly to national-populists, social-populists oppose free trade, as in the case of the protest movements against TTIP/CETA, but on grounds of fairness, not of protectionism. Whereas national-populists are hostile to immigration, and seek a return to isolationism and closed borders, social-populists are in favor of open borders, solidarity with refugees, and a rebalancing of both regional and global trade. Spanish *Podemistas* denounce international capital movements as ways for the corrupt bankers and politicians to further enrich themselves and are likely to reintroduce capital controls if elected.

National populism is authoritarian capitalism. Just as Putin filled government and Gazprom with his Chekist cronies, Trump is filling his cabinet with his own oligarchs: a racist Justice, an oilman at State, a climate-denier at EPA. The attempted appointment of a fast-food billionaire Andrew Pudzer as Secretary of Labor was thankfully defeated by the Fight for 15 movement, as it emerged that he was both exploitative *and* guilty of domestic abuse. National populism is pushing the oligarchic and oligopolistic tendencies of neoliberalism to their extremes and, unlike neoliberalism, it is deeply nationalist and irrational. Neoliberalism had an irrational faith in markets, but espoused scientific rationality in the name of efficiency. National populism is so enmeshed in the world of 'post-truth' that it no longer believes in science when it is not politically advantageous (exemplified by Trump's exit from the Paris climate treaty). Bush, however jingoistic and inegalitarian, remained an Atlanticist who refrained from racism and gynophobia. Trump, on the other hand, is a gleefully immoral and corrupt person. More importantly, he is a post-neoliberal who openly rallies for the disintegration of the European Union and NATO, to the dismay of Germany and France. Romano Prodi, long-time Italian prime minister and head of European Commission during enlargement to the East in 2004, recently proclaimed that his Europe (meaning the European Community born in the 50s) 'is dead', and that he, a progressive catholic, could only pray to fend off what comes next. This leaves social-populists in the Eurozone with a big question: what are they going to do with Europe? The time has come for movements across the European Union to take up strategy that seeks to seize Brussels and Frankfurt against the remnants of neoliberalism, and defend Europe from internal and external aggressions. It will not be easy; the populist right is singing the tune of democratic sovereignty to better effect, because people instinctively attach it to the notion of national sovereignty, and this is the central theme of their entire position.

	Social Populism	National Populism
Ideology	Egalitarianism, feminism, anti-racism	Nationalism, white supremacy, male chauvinism
Actors	Precarious youth, indignant citizens	Oligarchs, xenophobic working class and petty bourgeoisie
Enemy	Financial elite, political caste, police state	Cosmopolitans, women, minorities, muslims, immigrants
Geopolitics	Southern Europe, Middle East, Latin America	U.S., Russia, Britain, Turkey
Demands	Radical democracy, living wage, basic income, climate justice	Cronyism, nepotism, fossil-fuel capitalism
Economics	Fair trade, local development, alternative currencies, expansionary fiscal	Protectionism, restrictive monetary policy
Distribution	Egalitarian	Inegalitarian
Technology	Open source, sustainable energy	Proprietary, fossil-fuel energy
Media	Neighborhood councils, protest social media	Charismatic gatherings, fake news viralization
Tactics	Women's Tide, mass civil resistance, labor rights campaigns	Moral crusades, immigration walls, Muslim bans, criminalization of protest
Slogans	No Es Una Crisis, Es Una Estafa (Indignados), Fight for $15 (Fast-Food Workers), Rêve Général (Nuit Debout), Refugees Are Welcome (No Borders), Ni Una Menos (Feminist Strike)	Make America (Russia, Turkey) Great Again

Table 15: Social Populism vs. National Populism.

In fact, 'sovereignty' has become a fascist buzzword today, even though the origins of the concept lie in the work of Jean-Jacques Rousseau, and the French Revolution. A European citizenship would be much more inclusive than national citizenship, especially in this period of widespread anti-immigrant sentiment. 'I thank Italy, I thank Europe', the Gambian president of the Black Panthers Football Club said while accepting an anti-racist prize in Milan. This soccer team is composed of young African refugees, and is supported by the local autonomous movement (they are also frighteningly good). It struck me that he thanked *Europe*. Much like the Syrian refugees waving the European flag as they walked along Balkan highways to reach Germany in 2015, Milan's Black Panthers grasp that Europe is the land of human rights, a political entity that is greater than the sum of its parts. Left-wing Europeans should ponder this, and not leave the European cause to the likes of Macron and other European neoliberals. Do not expect liberals to stop fascism, though. They are vulnerable because they are not people of action, as they are only trained to administrate the world, not to defend it. They are too attached to existing institutions to make the leap necessary to save Europe from nationalism.

The revolutions of 2011 have been defeated everywhere, except in Spain. In molotov-torched Athens, the crisis brought the Trotskyists of Syriza to power, but the Tsipras government was unable to resist the draconian demands made by Germany and the Eurogroup to extend international loans. The Tsipras' government relented in spite of the result of the so-called Oxi referendum in 2015, the only tangible consequence of which was the resignation of Finance Minister Yanis Varoufakis, the only policymaker in Europe with enough intellectual weight to denounce the falsehoods of austerity-centric macroeconomic policy (namely that government spending must be cut in times of crisis, and that the payment of international debts comes before the welfare of the people).

Neoliberalism lost its intellectual credibility when it crashed in 2008, and its political legitimacy due to the ineptitude with which its technocratic lackeys handled the crisis in the subsequent decade. The Great Recession was very much self-inflicted, and neoliberals' pavlovian response - advocating for smaller government and a reduction of the welfare state - has proved suicidal. Neoliberalism is now being supplanted by nazi-populism. Its thirty-year rule won't be missed by the majority of society. However, since 1989, neoliberalism has been decidedly cosmopolitan, preaching open markets and open societies. Neoliberalism means free trade and the free movement of capital, which means open borders to let people move around the world in search of jobs and opportunities. National populism is none of that. It is protectionist, racist, and misogynist. It pursues the wages of war rather than the business of peace. It seeks to reinstate the power of whites in societies made multiethnic by neoliberal globalization.

Europe: From Dream to Nightmare

For a moment, imagine you are suddenly back in the year 2000 again. Europe was optimistic. The economy was strong, and Al Gore seemed poised to succeed Bill Clinton as president of the United States. Whilst noglobal protesters had emerged as spoilers of the party of monetarism and neoliberalism, and the cinders of the Balkans were still smoldering, the West appeared triumphant, and neoliberal hegemony inevitable. The European Union seemed one of its most civilized achievements, having abolished war and created prosperity, all the while setting out to absorb post-cold-war Central Europe into its body of supranational institutions. The euro was just one year old when German politician Joschka Fischer, in a famous lecture at Humboldt University, sketched out a plan for a federal, multicultural, and liberal European Union that united the East with the West. Subsequently, members of both the European Parliament and European Convention drafted a constitution that would give a political skeleton to the single market and the single currency.

However, this fledgling constitution was rejected by French and Dutch voters in 2005. The tide propelling neoliberal eurofederalism had irreversibly turned. European elites tried to patch over the problem with the Lisbon Treaty in 2009, but the europhobic cat was out of the bag. This sentiment only grew as the Great Recession made its bite felt between 2010 and 2011 during the euro crisis, when the sovereign debt of indebted Eurozone countries such as Greece and Portugal was downgraded by international speculation, prompting the European Central Bank to intervene, in order to save the euro and restore financial stability.

Seventeen years later, eurofederalism, once the progressive ideology commanding the allegiance of European elites, is definitely *passé*: Britain is leaving, Greece is bleeding, and the European Union, enlarged to the East in 2004, is weakened by the joint threat of Putin and Trump. Germany is putting its national economic interest above that of the Union, while Southern Europe fails to counterbalance Northern Europe's pressures for fiscal probity and budget cuts in EU institutions. The much-touted European miracle of a transnational polity turned out to be a mirage. The currency is shared, but the debt burden is not. Money is in the hand of a temporarily enlightened technocracy that buys debt that is issued by separate national governments, each of which has a different degree of credibility in the eyes of international investors. Because of differing credit rankings, German Bunds pay negative interest and Spanish Bonos pay positive interest rates. Belonging to the monetary union has actually amplified financial shocks, and debtor countries are now sitting ducks for international financial speculation. The neoliberal project that propelled the idea of a united Europe forward with the Maastricht and Schengen Treaties now lies in shambles. The euro did not lead to growth, but to austerity and unemployment. The free circulation of goods and labor has yielded to closed borders, and hate for refugees. National-populist forces are warping politics in France, Italy, the Netherlands, and even in Germany; all core countries that began the process of European integration 60 years ago. In short, political Europe lies in ruins, as nationalism and xenophobia are dangerously on the rise in both its Western core and Eastern appendix. Reverting to the warring age of nation-states seems an eminent possibility as America turns its gaze inward, and long-buried rivalries reemerge from the dark past of European nationalism.

Yet the populist answer to this scenario – exiting the euro – is a mistake, not only because it would signal the end of Europe, but because leaving would be a lot costlier than remaining, as sociologist Claus Offe has argued.[102] Protectionism and a return to a national economy are right-wing options that would cut real wages by drastically increasing the price of imports. The only reformist option for softening the external constraint, which dictates restrictive fiscal policy in all European countries with adverse consequences on the population, is to change the terms of the Maastricht Treaty, and create a parliament of the Eurozone, one which would hold the Bank, Commission and Council accountable to European citizens and residents. France is leaning toward this position. The revolutionary option would instead be to seize power in

---

102 Offe, *Europe Entrapped.*

the European Union and orient all politics and institutions towards popular, egalitarian, and environmental ends. A revolutionary call of this kind would read as such: *we, the precarious and immigrant generation of Europe, must seize power in Brussels and Frankfurt to establish a neutral, social, and radical Europe.* However, there is no existing European movement or party that can command the kind of mass appeal necessary for such a radical social-populist transformation. Mainstream European unions, composing the European Trade Union Confederation (ETUC) have been content with sitting in purposeless discussion over social Europe with EU employers' lobbies for years, having little effect on actual EU employment and social policy. Green parties have a European policy, but this mostly comprises green lobbying and embracing liberal capitalism. Red parties sit together in Strasbourg and Brussels, but have only sporadically expressed a unified position on Europe, especially regarding what the European Union should be. National politics remains paramount for all leftists, while communists in the various countries of the Continent have historically opposed European integration.

Right now, Europe seems to be coming apart at the seams, with an unloved political structure, an outdated economic policy, and an outmoded foreign policy. Trump is betting on the dissolution of the Union, hedge funds are betting on the dissolution of the euro, and Germany is repatriating gold from France and America. The Great Recession hit Europeans harder than Americans, due to the neoliberal and monetarist inertia built into existing European institutions. In fact, the European Union had never weathered a major recession before. Will it survive the economic crisis its institutions never thought possible? After Macron's election, I think it will, since the Franco-German entente upon on which modern Europe was built is solid (although it should at least be tempered by a special relationship between Italy and Spain). What is clear is that the European Union's enlargement to the East has failed to integrate those countries into the political idea of Europe. However, this aside, the Baltic Republics are firmly inside the Eurozone, and as such should be defended from any potential future aggression from Russia (or elsewhere). What is emerging, in the liberal European center represented by Macron and Renzi, is the need to create political institutions for the governance of the euro, the need for which was made painfully apparent when the unaccountable Eurogroup,[103] the Eurozone's group of finance ministers, laid out draconian (and ultimately unsustainable) conditions for rescuing the Greek economy in 2015 (taking their orders from Schäuble, the German finance minister).

Fearing Brexit and its consequences, I wrote a piece for Euronomade titled *The revolution of the European Continental Republic,*[104] proposing a movement for the establishment of a European republic in the euro area. As Britain leaves and the European Union is in retreat, my idea is to strategically consolidate the remnants of Europe into a single state with open borders and federated cities, regions, and nations. The eurocracy is too

---

103 Its head, the Dutch Labour politician Jeroen Dijsselbloem, recently attacked southern European countries, comparing PIGS to males wasting all their money on alcohol and prostitutes, then asking for financial forgiveness for their behavior.

104 Alex Foti, *La Rivoluzione della Repubblica Continentale Europea*, Euronomade, 20 February 2016, http://www.euronomade.info/?p=6759.

scared by recent events to even consider this. In Juncker's five scenarios for Europe,[105] a step toward political unification was not even contemplated. Angela Merkel said she was interested in 'doing less more efficiently', while France is clearly for the position 'those who want more do more' on debt and defense. At the moment, no country wants to do 'much more together'. I think the only politically viable solution is the Eurozone does so much more that it becomes a federal republic. In a future parliament of the euro area, German economic power would be finally counterbalanced by the deputies of France, Spain, and Italy. An alliance between any two of these three countries would put Germany in the minority.

Euthanasia of the Left

If the precariat is to resist the nazi-populist onslaught in Europe and America, it must develop a persuasive populist alternative in the institutional realm. The precariat simply cannot win the battles it is currently fights across the world if it does not develop its own distinctive ideology, organization, and strategy. The precariat could be the core of a transnational political movement, defending society from national-populist reaction, and engendering its emancipation from neoliberal subjugation. In order to do so, the reliance of the precarious class on communist ideology in the fight for equality would be dangerous. Today, equality is a populist concern, not a socialist demand.

The red left has little to offer the cause of the precariat, save old memories of 20th century working-class insurrections in what today are industrial wastelands which overwhelmingly vote right-wing candidates, and the now-dead guerrilla revolutions led by Giap and Che Guevara. The left instinctively defends full-time employees and pensioners, whose interests are always put ahead of the vital needs of precarious people. However, the interest of the precariat is in fact the general interest, because the young (and their children) are the future of society. Defending high pensions at the detriment of welfare has made younger generations both impoverished and existentially insecure, reducing birth rates and the formation of new households. The left has decided to turn its back to the future, by adopting what is essentially a defensive, and ultimately conservative, posture that will end in certain defeat. Capitalism is in crisis, yet communism will never recover, because it stands at odds with contemporary social reality. Its geopolitical worldview is hopelessly dated, and its understanding of online society and culture is very limited. The left has only rhetorical gestures with which to respond to the plight of the precariat, and its thirst for social and climate justice. Time and again, unions have spurned basic income for the young, and stayed away from organizing temporary and posted labor.

Although it is true that Occupy Wall Street brought about a socialist revival in America, both in terms of ideological debate[106] and political mobilization, there is still no socialism

---

105 They are: 'Carrying on', 'Nothing but the Single Market', 'Those Who Want More Do More', Doing Less More Efficiently, 'Doing Much More Together', and can be found on the Commission's official website: http://europa.eu/rapid/press-release_IP-17-385_en.htm.

106 Publications such as *n+1* and *Jacobin* being the most important examples, as well as the newborn *Catalyst*.

in America, a century after Sombart first analyzed American exceptionalism, and there is no longer democracy in America, two centuries after Tocqueville investigated its fledgling democratic society. Bernie Sanders and Michael Moore notwithstanding, Trump's white supremacy program finally carried the day against Clinton's tone-deaf interpretation of Obama's cosmopolitan liberalism. It's possible that the movement around Sanders will create a successful brand of radical populism that can be embraced by Blacks, Latinos, Native Americans, and militant sections of the white precariat in their fight against the encroaching nazi-populist regime.

But 'Feeling the Bern'[107] aside, wherever red flags are waved, the crowd consists mainly of gray-haired pensioners. Socialist and social-democratic parties are declining and out of government in all European countries, save Sweden and Portugal. It's a telling sign that the traditional left has no future. Today, the ranks of the left are mostly made up of people who were radical in the 70s, and are now approaching old age. When the wind of public opinion changed, and began to oppose the sanctity of free market deregulation and liberal technocracy, the left was unable to successfully resist austerity, and propose an economic alternative to neoliberalism. This crucially weakened its relevance and weight. What neoliberalism ultimately failed to achieve – the complete destruction of the left in Europe and Latin America – the Great Recession is accomplishing. Christian-Democrats and Liberals still rule Europe, largely due to fear of what might come after them: full-blown fascism across the Continent. Spanish left-populist party Podemos, and its ally in Catalonia, En Comú, have been the only political movements wielding constituent power after the revolution of 2011, in order to advance a political agenda for and by the precariat. The social center run by Podemos in Madrid is named *Casa Morada*, (*Purple House*), since this is the color of the party's flags. Purple is also the color of anarcha-feminism. Indignadas and Indignados of the world, the new horizon of the people is *morado*! The hopes and struggles of precarious people could be enshrined in a purple flag with a shocking pink feminist fist. Precisely because it's an empty signifier, a new revolutionary flag could be a powerful symbol to express the unity of the enraged precariat, who is leading the people toward political and social change.

I argued in *Anarchy in the EU* that chromatology is essential to understand contemporary political movements. In that text, I discussed how the queer pink, black anarchist, green climate movements were superseding the red left. The book was published in the final phase of the anti-globalization movement and as the first convulsions of the Great Recession were being felt. Anarchy is not dead, but communism is, I argued. This sounds even truer now, as the Chekists (named after Lenin's secret police) that compose Putin's inner circle are scheming for world power, meddling in Europe and the Middle East with nefarious intent, and murderous consequences. On the centennial of the Russian revolution, my mind goes to the Soviets of workers and soldiers, who were betrayed by the Bolsheviks, just like the Kronstadt sailors and the Ukrainian anarchist army of Makhno, as well as the generously populist Social-Revolutionists, who won the only elections held after Lenin's October revolution.

---

107 'Feeling the Bern' was the campaign slogan of Bernie Sanders in the 2016 presidential elections.

I'm not questioning Marx's enduring importance as theorist of capitalism and capitalist crisis. With the Great Recession, Marx's work is more relevant now than it has been since the end of the Cold War. In the immediate aftermath of the financial crisis, *Das Kapital* became a surprise bestseller in Germany. When a capitalist crisis occurs, it is natural to turn to Marx, and Marxist thinkers. For example, the global revival of Gramsci and his theory of political hegemony stressing the role of popular culture is again relevant in the fight against right-wing populism. As Perry Anderson writes in his inimitable style, the Sardinian communist imprisoned by Mussolini has inspired some of the best Marxist writing since 1945, in particular the works of Stuart Hall, Giovanni Arrighi, Ernesto Laclau, and Ranajit Guha. Fordism is, of course, a Gramscian concept, on par with hegemony, and the notion of historical bloc. Laclau and Chantal Mouffe borrowed from Gramsci to define the essential discursive elements of a left-populist strategy.[108]

We have already noted how Negri's discussion of *autonomia* (*autonomy*) has strongly influenced anti-globalization movements, and the discourse on precarity. On another front, the critical sophistication of the Frankfurt tradition of Theodor Adorno, Max Horkheimer, and Herbert Marcuse, lives on in Judith Butler's philosophy regarding the queering and gendering of subjects and Streeck's political and economic sociology. Marxist feminism, as represented by the seminal works of Luisa Muraro, Bell Hooks, Nancy Fraser, and Selma James (among others) has become a stronger intellectual and social force than it ever was, even at the height of the women's liberation movement of the 1970s.

As long as capitalism exists, Marx and the Marxian body of thought will stay relevant in the 21st century. My polemic is not against Marxism, but against what's left of communism,[109] which looks like a dead-end strategy by which to emancipate society, and seize state power. Marxist formations look down on the precariat and secretly hope for an impossible return to the 70s, the heyday of red influence. They would like to rewind history to a time before their defeat at the hands of neoliberalism, and the subsequent dismantling of the world built by the Russian Revolution. However, Che Guevara will not rise from the dead, and *Sandinista* is now just a Clash album. The red left is moribund, and the Great Recession hasn't resurrected it. In fact, the longer the communist corpse is left unburied (to borrow a metaphor from Bifo), the harder the process of defeating inequality and oligarchy will be. It is revealing that the most important Marxist work written since the Great Recession, *Capital in the 21st Century,* has been vehemently attacked by Marxists everywhere for not being sufficiently faithful to the letter

---

108 In seminal works such as *Hegemony and Socialist Strategy, Agonistics*, and *The Illusion of Consensus*.

109 In practice, it is hard to distinguish between intellectual and political Marxism, because every Marxist wants to start their own party. Marx himself was a great theorist and a bad politician. The same can be said of Toni Negri, who still professes himself to be a communist, albeit on the side of the precariat, as he recently argued in an interview on Italian TV. This aside, today's last line of defense for communism is, in my view, the Zizek-Badiou Hegelian neo-orthodoxy. Communists without a cause, the two are ready to ridicule everything except their own failings (significant in the case of Badiou, the last survivor of French Maoism). Although I am no philosopher, and this is a book of social theory, I find that the conflictual democracy of Jacques Rancière best expressed the philosophy of the 2011 revolutions, certainly better than the hugely popular *Indignez-vous!* by old resistance hero Hessel.

of the prophet.[110] Having equality and democracy as twin polar stars, the leftist Post-Keynesian nevertheless exposes neoliberalism as the most unequal economic regime in living memory, and encourages people to fight against the financial oligarchy. Most communists, however, consider it ideologically impure.

Piketty was the main intellectual force behind the doomed presidential campaign of Benoit Hamon, who arguably had a forward-looking program: basic income, ecology, taxation of robots, and a parliament for the Eurozone. By waving the French flag, Mélenchon managed to annihilate him and the French Socialist Party built by Mitterrand in 1971. In Germany, former European Parliament President Martin Schulz is campaigning on a platform centered around universal free tuition (among other welfare measures) in a desperate bid to end Merkel's long hold on the German chancellorship. As things stand, he will be defeated, also because he's let Angie play the European card he should have been playing. Considering current political trends, it is hard to shake the feeling that social democracy is going the way of communism, fading into historical irrelevance. In Greece, the Panhellenic Socialist Movement (PASOK) has evaporated, the Spanish Socialist Worker's Party (PSOE) has been deserted by young voters, in France, the Socialist Party (PS) is dissolving in internecine strife, in the Netherlands the Labor Party (PvdA) was almost erased at the ballot, the Belgian socialists are out of government, and Scandinavian social democracy is threatened by populism and xenophobia much like the rest of Europe (a border post has been erected on the bridge linking Copenhagen to Malmö to stem the tide of refugees into Sweden). Collaboration with neoliberalism in the 90s and 00s, most evident in Tony Blair's Third Way, is the curse that is keeping the left out of power now that the crisis could restore its appeal. Today, most people, frightened by precarity and unemployment, would subscribe without a thought to the old social-democratic compact of universal welfare from cradle to grave. The fact is that both socialists in Latin Europe and social-democrats in Northern Europe sold out to neoliberalism, and have lost any credibility they once had, undermining their attempts at campaigning on issues such as equality and the welfare state.

The inherited culture of socialism has often proved conservative with regard to recent social, technological, and intellectual developments. By remaining focused on the working class and public employees, it has refused to acknowledge the precariat as the new class produced by neoliberal globalization, and thus overlooked precarity as a structural social condition specific to neoliberalism, the harbinger of a new radical subjectivity evident in the revolutionary wave of 2011. Just as the industrial proletariat led the struggle for emancipation in the 20th century, the postindustrial precariat will lead the fight for 21st century radical democracy for all and by all across the globe, by defeating fossil-fuel capitalism, thus staving off catastrophic climate change and the end of civilization. In order to fix the metabolic rift with the biosphere (to use theorist McKenzie Wark's expression), we have to adopt the 'labor perspective':[111] the perspective of precarious labor. The left is descending into political irrelevance. It will not be resurrected by its historic socialist parties, or commu-

---

110   This unfortunately includes David Harvey, author of the best commentary available on the three
      volumes of Marx's *Capital*.
111   McKenzie Wark, *Molecular Red: Theory for the Anthropocene*, London: Verso, 2015.

nist movements. The precariat needs to look elsewhere for its ideological arsenal, namely, populism, feminism, and environmentalism. Red is dead, but pink is very much alive.

As such, my basic message is that we should retain Marx, but let go of communism. There are two main sources of communist nostalgia. One is Trotskyism, the minority tendency in international communism that resurfaced after 1991. It was a major influence on C.L.R. James and Marxist cultural studies, but the political parties it has inspired in France, Britain, and elsewhere tend to be sectarian beyond repair. The 4th International usually stands on the right side of geopolitical issues, because, due to the historical opposition to Stalinism, Trotskyists instinctively reject authoritarian regimes. The other source of this nostalgia is none other than Red China, led by a communist party which embraced neoliberal capitalism and thus survived, unlike the Soviet doppelganger. Giovanni Arrighi (formerly an Italian Maoist) wrote that a Smithian China committed to global free trade could usher the world toward a post-imperialist phase, no longer characterized by the center-periphery dichotomy which had shaped all previous cycles of capitalist accumulation.[112] As the Braudel-Wallerstein tradition of historiography tells us, the world economy has been governed by a succession of dominating financial centers: Amsterdam until the 18th century, London until the 20th century, and New York until the 21st centrury. The election of Trump makes Arrighi's prediction highly relevant. In my view, the only form of intellectually coherent communism is to support China's rise to global hegemony, similar to what European communist parties did by supporting Communist Russia during the Cold War. Since I side with Hong Kong and Taiwan's young democracy activists, I don't recommend anybody should go that far. However, now that Europe is caught between Putin and Trump, a deal with China seems a good idea. It's the last remaining world power committed to peace and free trade, because the former is the condition of the latter and China's only pursuable path to mass prosperity. Furthermore, in a world plagued by increasing irrationality, the Chinese leadership remains rational and committed to a long-term plan, as evidenced in Xi Jinping's charm offensive at the World Economic Forum, and now his rapprochement with Trump, after China rattled its nuclear sabers over maintenance of the One-China policy.

The Precariat at Davos

What used to be the annual ritual of self-congratulation held by corporate elites and their political allies (a ritual that the anti-globalization movement used to vehemently target), has now become a soul-searching symposium attempting to understand why neoliberal globalism has been voted out of office in Britain and America. Guy Standing chaired a session on the precariat and its political makeup,[113] his thesis being that the shift to the populist right is due to the precariat becoming xenophobic and nationalistic. While I do not buy into this premise, let us examine it more closely. Fundamentally, he argues that there are two precariats: one nostalgic and atavistic, and the other progressive. In a nutshell, one

---

112 Giovanni Arrighi, *Adam Smith in Beijing: Lineages of the 21st Century*, Verso Books, 2009.
113 Guy Standing, 'Meet the precariat, the new global class fuelling the rise of populism', *World Economic Forum*, November 9, 2016, https://www.weforum.org/agenda/2016/11/precariat-global-class-rise-of-populism/.

voted for Brexit, the other for Podemos. Many mistakes aside (*lumped* precariat, instead of *lumpenprecariat;* the weird category of *proficians* for neoliberal careerists and entre-preneurs; immigrants labeled as *nostalgics*, considered intermediate between right-wing atavists and left-wing progressives) evidence disproves his claim that precarious millennials ever dreamt of voting for either Farage or Trump. The precariat is not the gelatinous mass of middle-aged people losing their jobs, as he argues, but is the multicultural multitude of young people stuck in temporary employment and unemployment, as this book seeks to point out. This kind of precariat has overwhelming anti-fascist and anti-racist sentiments, as mass protests have shown time and again since 2011.

My experience is that migrant labor and precarious labor have joined forces against racism, abusive work practices, detention centers, gender inequality, homophobia, and many other kinds of social discrimination. Second-generation immigrant youth are already prominent actors in social conflict and labor organizing; if you are young (and thus precarious), you tend to care more about class than ethnic or religious identity. In fact, for Generation Z, multiethnic-ity is a way of living. The precariat is spontaneously social-populist, always seeking the welfare of the greatest number of people possible. You have to look elsewhere for nostalgia, in the white working class and the white lower middle-class of shopkeepers, artisans, pensioners, and other social strata still attached to the nation-state. All things told, this is what the class pyramid in contemporary capitalism actually looks like:

Financial Elite

Office Salariat

Petty Bourgeoisie

Industrial Proletariat

Service Precariat

Urban Underclass

Table 16: The Class Pyramid of Advanced Capitalism, 2010s

Below the commandeering 1% of financiers and tycoons, there is a privileged stratum of salaried employees and professionals. They are the insiders of the informational job market, and upholders of the neoliberal regime now damaged beyond repair. Government employees and officials also belong to this category. The salariat mostly votes center-left and center-right, and tends to be immune to the worst forms of racism. Below them come the traditional petty bourgeoisie and working class, which have mostly shifted towards the right in the last two decades, after a century of voting for socialists and communists. Considering the role of Wisconsin, Michigan and the Rust Belt states in securing the electoral vote for Trump, we must look to the white working class and underclass if we want to locate people fueling right-wing populism today. The precariat either does not vote, or votes for left-populist candidates. Millennials have fewer social guarantees than the salariat, and display stronger individualism, but have moved to the left since the Great Recession. They have also been harbingers of innovation in political communication; from the victory of Zapatero in 2004 (the SMS chain the spread the news of the right-wing government's deception, after media outlets were shut down), to the victory of Obama in 2008 (strategic use of social media in winning primaries and presidential elections), and, most importantly, in the revolutions of 2011, where the alliance of the cognitive precariat with the insurgent population through social media was central in achieving large-scale participation in protests.[114] It's the precarious Millennials that are also behind the rise of Sanders in America and Corbyn in Britain.

In my own country, the precariat largely votes for the Five Star Movement, the populist force led by mercurial comedian Beppe Grillo, which defies easy classification. The movement practices a warped form of online democracy, embraces environmental issues (especially of the unscientific kind), and has an overall egalitarian stance. It also has a left-leaning mayor in Turin, who, unlike her colleague in Rome, is competent and sufficiently respected. However, the movement – founded by Grillo and now deceased internet entrepreneur Gianroberto Casaleggio – has also flirted with the kind of Europhobia and racism practiced by Lega and the fascist right. They could well win the upcoming general elections against Renzi's Democratic Party, which has been in disarray since their stinging defeat over the referendum on whether to reform the constitution and abolish the Senate, a personal reversal for the Florentine leader. One of the most popular points in their program is the introduction of a basic citizenship income, in order to combat poverty. This priority clearly makes them social-populist, while their hostility to the euro and immigration places them in the national-populist camp. Also, whilst their online deliberation platform – Rousseau – is similar to that used by Podemos, votes can be reversed if the omnipotent leader says so, as recently happened in Genoa, where internal elections for candidate to mayor were voided, and the winning candidate replaced by one favored by Grillo, who miserably lost the election (Berlusconi's right-wing coalition won). In order to classify the Five Star Movement, I often use an analogy from chemistry. They are like sodium chloride (table salt) neutral on the political litmus scale, but the result of a combination of a left acid and a right base. Territorially, of the two large city administrations they currently control, Turin leans to the left (the NoTav movement voted massively for Chiara Appendino), while Rome leans to the right (the incompetent mayor, Virginia Raggi, and his collaborators come from right-wing formations). A significant minority of the precariat, influenced by social movements in large cities, instead votes for Italy's fragmented left, or is anarcho-autonomist (and thus refrains from voting at all).

The Italian precarious workers' movement rose and fell with the fortunes of the anti-globalization movement and of the European project, but is now adapting to the new political framework created by the Great Recession, the revolution it spawned, and the global reaction against it that is currently taking place. The politics of the precariat must be to occupy the state to defeat precarity. The conquest of basic income is fundamental, but, politically, is only the first step. The precariat must seize the city, as the proletariat once sought to seize

114   I owe this synthesis to Emanuele Cozzo of *Fundación de los Comunes*.

factories. This is the reason the revolution of 2011 occupied metropolitan squares, not industrial workplaces, and led to the conquest of municipal, rather than state power.

The ultimate defeat of national populism and the superseding of neoliberalism depends on the mobilization of the precarious youth, who will lead the people in a broad front against financial oligarchy, and form new transnational municipal and labor alliances. Traditional parties are lost, but the people are not, and labor unions are reawakening thanks to the pressure of grassroots movements. However, expansionary policies for a leftward solution to the Great Recession will have to be bitterly fought for against vested money and oil interests, and ecological constraints are likely to put limits on an egalitarian growth strategy.

It is the precarious youth that have lost the most because of the Great Recession. Their disillusionment and rage has, however, made history, from Tahrir to Occupy Wall Street, and Madrid to Istanbul. The Indignados Movement that paralyzed Spain in the spring of 2011 was started in Plaza del Sol, Madrid's central square, by a group of precarious young workers and students who erected their tents and refused to move until their demands were heard by the rest of society (they put little faith in the then socialist government). People from all walks of society responded in huge numbers (although young precarious individuals made up the single largest section of those involved), and set up permanent protest camps (*acampadas*) in all the major cities of Spain, including Barcelona's Plaça Catalunya, on 15 May. It was a social upheaval that involved between 6 and 8 million people, and was supported by the majority of Spaniards, according to opinion polls. Occupy Wall Street followed suit on 17 September 2011, and the protest camp in Liberty Square became a magnet for all those outraged at how the financial class had been bailed out at the expense of the people. Student workers, disgruntled temps, interns, and the unemployed were at the forefront of the protests, and were the main social force behind the popular assemblies that vented the anger and articulated the demands of the 99%. A form of anarcho-populism is evident in both movements, as sociologist Paolo Gerbaudo[115] wrote in *The Guardian*. They both talked on behalf of a wronged people against economic and political elites, as in traditional populist discourse, but they shared with traditional anarchism a passion for direct (online) democracy, and renewed anarchist praxis in their quest for free social networks and transparent democracy (evident in associated movements like Anonymous).

It is the precarious who are the revolutionary activists of the 21st century, from Tahrir to Plaza del Sol, Zuccotti Park to Gezi Park, and far beyond. The precariat is not the working class of communist lore, it is the digital generation politicized and radicalized by the crisis, even though, much like the industrial proletariat of yore, it occupies a central position in the production of value under capitalism, particularly in the lucrative information and creative industries. The precarious are at the core of contemporary accumulation, but remain on the periphery of political and social citizenship. Even in Europe, they are excluded from the social contract and the inherited welfare state, which is largely conditional on full-time employment, and thus cannot address the generalization of precarious work.

---

115 Paolo Gerbaudo 'Why it's time to occupy the state', *Guardian*, December 10, 2013, https://www. theguardian.com/commentisfree/2013/dec/10/occupy-protesters-electoral-politics.

In 2011, the precariat combined technical expertise, creative forms of struggle and popular mobilization, giving birth to the largest protest movements the world has seen since 1968. Cross-fertilized by the Seattle-Genoa antiglobalization protests of the early 00s, a generation of activists has become a generation of revolutionaries. Government employees went on strike and protested, while young people built barricades and rioted, until the invariably heavy hand of the state squashed budding social alliances that threatened incumbent governments (which, of course, included members of the elite who had a stake in the existing financial system). The Indignados Movement (locally known as the 15-M Movement) survived the repression, and morphed into a catalyst, turning public employees against austerity economics (Mareas Ciudadanas), from the defense of public health and education to the huge movement against evictions (PAH), to damning revelations of financial corruption (Partido X) plaguing the austerity government led by the conservative, centralizing, and militantly catholic Popular Party (PP) in power. In America, the Occupy Movement was squashed by concentrated police repression orchestrated at both the local and federal level, and further declined after the partial success of the 2012 May Day General Strike (the flashpoint of which was Oakland, a trade port, rather than the financial marketplace of New York). These defeats aside, the precariat is still on the move, from Korea to Brazil.

Precarity is both exploitation and liberation. It deprives young workers of their labor and welfare rights, but leaves them uncommitted to the work ethic and strict discipline of their forebears. Precarious people express themselves outside work, establishing communities of scope and support. Yet with the crisis the exploitative element of flexible jobs is increasingly apparent: the precariat must flex its muscle and fight for its own rights, for its interests are at odds with those of traditional blue- and white-collars. Fundamentally, the left sees the precarious as lacking in a fundamental quality that would make them fully-fledged workers and citizens: steady employment. Precarity is thus perceived as a lack thereof, rather than as a new condition that calls for new types of organization and conflict.

No matter, for the precarious have bypassed unions and parties and gone straight to the heart of the state, by being at the vanguard of the barricades and *acampadas* that have rocked the world since 2011. In fact, it is hard to explain the success of Podemos in European and local elections without continuous reference to the problems created by *precariedad laboral (labor precarity)* and the financial abuses committed by the political caste. Spain is a country where half of the country's young are unemployed, and one in four workers are precarious. Indeed, almost all of the political cadres of Podemos, as well as the activists behind the urban coalitions rising to municipal power in Barcelona and Madrid, belong to the precarious generation. The precariat is behind the rise of Bernie Sanders in America and the expressions of civic power in Iceland, Slovenia, Bosnia, and Romania (to name but European examples). Syriza's growth and victory at the polls in Greece was crucially due to the mobilization of the precarious generation. A transnational network of progressive municipalities on immigration and the environment is being led by Ada Colau and other left-leaning city administrations. A coherent social-populist international has yet to coalesce, though, not least in Europe, where it is vitally needed in order to shake off neoliberal austerity and defeat national-populist reaction.

A new class comes into being only when it has forged a new culture and a new ideology, new forms of self-organization, and a sense of political activation. The precarious need to build their own organizations. Timidly, some have begun to emerge: for instance the Freelancers Union in North America and the Freeters Union in Japan, as well as the network of Italian anti-precarity activists that has launched the very successful national strike dubbed #scioperosociale in November 2014, and especially the Coordination des Intermittents et Précaires, the leftist network that managed to organize France's stage hands against cuts to unemployment subsidies, in a labor dispute that has been ongoing since 2003.

I think that what the precarious absolutely need is a transnational advocacy, one that spreads news of the worst injustices that they suffer via sophisticated, non-violent direct actions and media interventions, while at the same time pressuring governments and supranational institutions. *Precariat Syndicate* is currently my favorite name for such a labor advocacy. It would combine media subvertising and workplace picketing with knowledge of the legal and political issues surrounding precarity, in order to affect social legislation and revert the deterioration of labor standards. Precarious individuals from all over the globe could join and fund it. It would be the Act Up! of the precarious. Such an advocacy would spearhead the cause of the precariat and defend the rights of protesters, migrants, strikers in solidarity with antira and antifa movements.

People are taking to the streets and the networks to make their demands heard by governments: a halt to austerity, an expansion rather than a contraction of welfare benefits, less leeway for corporations to evade taxes and impose precarious employment relationships, open borders and hospitality to refugees, the extension of citizenship to long-term immigrants, the resolute defense of the existing welfare state, social security, healthcare, public education and public housing, and an ecological commons. The syndicalist platform of the precariat can be summarized as a simple triad: gender rights, cyber rights, and labor rights.

In a regulation crisis such as the current one, ideological power matters enormously, since it provides the ideal blueprints to rebuild the failed economic and social institutions of the previous phase. I tend to share activist-cum-theorist David Graeber's point that the Seattle-Genoa movement was mainly about anarchism and black blocs,[116] although autonomous Marxism played an influential intellectual role. Also, the main geopolitical effect of the anti-globalization movement was the wave of red Bolivarianism across South America - the Porto Alegre effect critically underscored by Michael Hardt.[117] Anti-capitalism has been the ideology of protest movements since the anti-globalization movement. This is a catchall term that hides very different positions, from communist to anarchist groups, and from autonomist to queer movements.

---

116 David Graeber, 'The New Anarchists', *New Left Review*, 1999. https://newleftreview.org/II/13/david-graeber-the-new-anarchists.
117 Michael Hardt, 'Porto Alegre: The New Bandung?', *New Left Review*, 2002. https://newleftreview.org/II/14/michael-hardt-porto-alegre-today-s-bandung

In the table below, I take the revival of anarchism as a starting point from which to offer a sociological taxonomy of contemporary anti-capitalist movements that combine anarchist ethics and tactics with the three other major sources of resistance to capital: Marxian autonomy, green environmentalism, and pink genderism:

	Anarcho-Green	Anarcho-Syndicalist	Anarcho-Autonomist	Anarcho-Feminist
Aim	Defend the Earth	Subvert the economy	Smash the state	End the Patriarchy
Issue	Climate justice	Social inequality	political domination	Male violence
Ideology	Radical ecology	Revolutionary unionism	Autonomous Marxism	Queer theory
Direct Action	Ecotage	Wildcat strike	Urban riot(s)	Pink protest tide
Actors	Ecohacktivists, vegans, animalists, indigenous peoples	Precarious/migrant workers, landless, unemployed	Unemployed youth, immaterial labor, multiethnic underclass	Women, LGBTIQ persons
Movements	ZAD, Climate Camps, Earth First!	EuroMayDay, Spanish CGT, IWW	Nuit Debout, No Border, Antifa, Invisible Committee	Ni Una Menos, #Feministrike

Table 17: Anti-Capitalism: Anarchy, Autonomy, Ecology, and Feminism

It's vital for anarchists and autonomists of all stripes to look out to the wider world, and open up to the queer and creative influences coming from contemporary society and popular culture. Concerns with ideological purity and historical fidelity are usually hindrances to the effectiveness of political strategy, especially now that national-populist reaction threatens everything anti-capitalists hold dear: labor is under attack, nature is under threat, and patriarchy is regaining ground.

Anti-capitalist movements have adopted queer pink, anarcho black, and radical green ideological forms. Pink, black, and green insurgence seems the name of the game. Pink, because since the rainbow flag threw the gauntlet of protest against homophobia, queer has become revolutionary for all sectors of society: it's no longer simply a matter of identity politics and civil rights, it speaks of a radical social transformation, such as the contemporary women's movement fighting for the end of patriarchy and sexism. Pink because it refers to deviant *pinko* political tendencies in non-pacified urban subcultures, experimenting with the radical mixing of codes, genders, and ethnicities. Pink like a clown insurrection. It's also ecotopian green, because its calls for reclaiming the streets, guerrilla gardening, critical mass-vélorution, climate action are setting a new template for ecological protest. It's a DIY, eco-hacking way of dealing with environmental issues, exploring how to empower the people in adopting alternative forms of socialization and social organization. It is also black like an urban insurgence, much like those which have mobilized the Europe's autonomous youth to defend to the last social squatting as a way of life, a way of life which has become integral to the notion of European urban culture over the last three decades. Self-managed zones and radical collectives are federating all across the world, making sure that the political legacy of anarchism and autonomism survives in contemporary cities of the globe.

We have to act in defense of the biosphere, and remove carbon lobbies from power that prevent action against climate change, while maintaining the digital civilization which common labor, information, and knowledge has created. Revolutionary direct action needs to be employed for ends that are ultimately reformist: a new welfare system favoring precarious individuals and families, an urban environment friendly to disadvantaged sections of the population, a reregulated labor market to prevent wage fraud, posted labor, and other anti-union practices, levies on individual wealth and corporate profits, carbon taxation and an energy and transportation system based on renewables. NGOs and civil society cannot mount an effective resistance and transformation of society without the help of radicals, because they are best activists and most imaginative organizers. Even if the precariat hates capitalism and what it does to people and the planet, its anti-capitalism and opposition to neoliberalism is likely to trigger fundamental reform, rather than the abolition of capitalism. It will finally tax the rich, rather than hang them.

A new (pink, black, green) political ideology is needed to give substance to the anti-capitalist movement, which (in a nutshell) is the interbreeding of the autonomous, anarchist, anti-fascist, queer, and vegan tendencies that have been brewing in metropolitan subcultures. I think anti-capitalism stands a better chance if it acts in conjunction with a social-populist project, in order to prevail over nationalist authoritarians and military-carbon corporatists.

It is important to not just showing rage at capitalist inequality, but to reverse it. It is important not simply to denounce the self-destruction of civilization, but to prevent it. The fight is not to return to pre-industrial nature (whatever that was like), but foster non-capitalist relations between society and nature.

CHAPTER 5. THE EMANCIPATION OF THE PRECARIAT: URBAN POWER, BASIC INCOME, CLIMATE JUSTICE

Since the 90s, radical movements across Europe have targeted resurgent racism and fascism. Mass unemployment is giving new life to fascists and Nazis across the globe. Just like in the 30s, the depression is fanning the flames of nationalism. So for the radical left the *antifa/antira* organization of precarious, immigrants, unemployed is now a matter of survival. Radicals are building bridges of social solidarity between the precarious and refugees, while the children of immigrants are already active in student and labor movements. Organizations are being born where *mixité* and *métissage* are the norm, where the precarious join in common struggles and campaigns against borders and precarity, no matter whether they are black or white, Christian, Muslim, or Jewish, red or anarchist. A cross-border movement is defending the disenfranchised in Europe, helping refugees arrive safely, and defending them from expulsion and deportation. *No One Is Illegal!* Second-generation immigrant youth are at the forefront of the social conflicts confronting securitarianism and cryptofascism; islamophobia is the contemporary equivalent of anti-Semitism during the interwar years, the fault line between left- and right-wing politics. In deteriorating conditions, only communally minded efforts can bridge the gulf between immigrant and native workers, service and creative labor, and rebellious immigrant youth and dissident White youth. In short, only political solidarity can root out the social causes of mounting xenophobia.

Young members of the global precariat need to organize around the kind of demands that were popularized by a 2014 article in *Rolling Stone*:[118] guaranteed work, basic income for all, taxation of the wealthy, public ownership of common goods, and socialized credit. This should be the minimal political program of the precariat.

The precariat is the sum of people working precarious jobs in both dependent and independent employment, and those suffering unemployment, either intermittently or permanently. We can distinguish a service precariat (working at Wal-Mart, Amazon, Uber, McDonald's, etc.) and a cognitive precariat (such as those engaging in the struggles of the Graduate Employees and Students Organization since the mid-90s), but what is most important to recognize is the emergence of the precariat as a class in the making, a class that is becoming a class for itself through the exploits of the 2011 revolutions, the global social mobilizations against austerity and inequality, and currently against right-wing populism.

The precarious are the children of wage- and salary-earners shut out of meaningful social and professional advancement. The precarious are the contemporary equivalent of plebeians and proletarians. They are the class that nobody wanted to name because it was

---

118 'Five Economic Reforms Millennials Should Fight For', *Rolling Stone*, 3 January 2014, http://www.rollingstone.com/politics/news/five-economic-reforms-millennials-should-be-fighting-for-20140103.

a condition lived in shame. Now that temps are the norm, and the perms the exception, the time has come to acknowledge the precariat as the maker of contemporary digital and financial wealth. The precariat has nothing, but shall be all.

As conclusion to this essay, I propose four main planks to emancipate the precariat from its subjugation: seize municipal power; obtain universal basic income; organize the syndicate of the precariat; lead the de-carbonization of the economy.

The Spanish Experiment with Democratic Populism and Ecosocial Municipalism

Spain has been a hotbed of political experimentation with social populism. In aftermath of the occupations of central squares in Madrid, Barcelona, and other major of Spanish cities in 2011, the Indignados Movement caused a sharp break with politics as usual, uncovering the network of corruption linking bankers with politicians of the Christian-Democrat (PP) establishment, and gaining mass consensus among the populace. On 12 May 2012, the countrywide mobilization of millions of people was repeated in a more organized and dis-ciplined manner. A section of the movement then decided to create its own party for the European election of 2014: Podemos. Millions of voters rallied behind its purple flag - mostly the young, surviving on unemployment benefits and short-term jobs - while the brain drain adversely affected the country's already stagnant economy, as educated youth poured out of Southern Europe in search of a better future in Northern Europe and America. Podemos also surpassed, and embarrassed, the existing party of the left, Izquierda Unida (IU), which had been a staple of Spanish politics for twenty-five years. Podemos' young, telegenic, pony-tailed leader, Pablo Iglesias, borrowed from Gramsci, Negri, and Chávez, in order to create a new political vocabulary which was used in online deliberations regarding the party's platform. A former anti-globalization activist in Madrid, Pablo Iglesias, who had been rejected by Izquierda Unida (IU) as a top candidate for the European Parliament, decided to form his own party. Yet still his heart belongs to the left; he has recenly brought the IU into an (not very effective) electoral alliance with Podemos, and sits in the GUE/NGL (red) group of European Union legislators in Strasbourg and Brussels. The party's ideologue, Iñigo Errejón, is a more intellectual and less charismatic figure, and a more straightforward heir of Laclau's theorizing on left-populism. A student of Laclau's partner, political theorist Chantal Mouffe, he coherently articulates a fully egalitarian, populist project, which is based on the political and economic demands articulated by the majority of the Spanish population. Eschewing anti-capitalism and a narrow focus on poverty, in the recent congress Errejón pleaded for a more effective cultural strategy, as well as a focus on parliamentary struggle, in order to effectively wield collective power within the Spanish state. In Spain's political stalemate of 2015-2016, with two general elections in less than a year, Podemos – now combined with IU – lost votes and failed to surpass the PSOE, the Spanish socialists, to the chagrin of Iglesias. In my view, this failure was confirmation that only a decisive break with the leftist tradition, as argued by Errejón, can permanently anchor social populism in Spain and, hopefully, the rest of Europe. However, Podemos' recent congress, held after their nemesis Rajoy renewed his hold on government, resulted in the triumph of Pablo Iglesias' leftism, and the defeat of his deputy's populism.

The greatest legacy of the Indignados' revolution has arguably been the conquest of municipal power in Madrid and Barcelona. In Madrid, Podemos heads a rather conventional leftist front, but in Barcelona, a related but distinct political formation, En Comú, made Ada Colau, leader of the Platform for People Affected by Mortgages (PAH) – a mass movement against home foreclosures caused by mortgage defaults – mayor of the city. Colau gave a credible face to an urban movement that distilled a novel synthesis of the political demands that I dub ecosocial populism. In her heart-warming electoral appeal to the people of Barcelona, she said:

> We are the precarious, we are the women, we are the queers, we are the barrio dwellers, we are the feminists, we are the immigrants, we are the environmentalists, the workers, the intellectuals.

Her electorate contains the people that make Barcelona a vibrant city and an example of tolerance for the rest of Europe.[119] Thanks to a clear municipal program, which focused on the struggle against inequality, the development of public services, a curb on mass tourism to put a stop on rent increases, sustainable energy and waste management – entirely the result of online and in-person consultations – En Comú ended up the victor of a thrilling, three-way race against the PP-PSOE duopoly, and ruling Catalan secessionists.

When a program sponsored by central Podemos failed to elicit the same enthusiastic response in the subsequent regional elections of Catalonia, the circle of social-media-savvy activists that built the Ada Colau campaign prevailed on Madrid to present a distinct list in Catalonia for the upcoming national elections, En Comú Podemm. It was a resounding success, and constituted a serious leap forward (in terms of seats and votes gained) for Podemos as a whole. In Barcelona, a regional party is now being created, in order to run against the bourgeois Catalan independence movement who control the Generalitat, the radical Catalans of Esquerra Catalana, and especially Popular Unity Candidacy (CUP), a marxist-leninist formation fanatically focused on Catalan independence, symbolized by the increasingly proudly waved Estelada flag. The hope is to repeat the exploits of the municipal elections. Still, the calling of referendum on Catalonia's secession from Spain hangs like Damocles' sword over the future of eco-feminist and social-populist *colauismo*. In my view, her success depends on the urban and Catalan questions to be framed in terms of class, rather than identity. If the polarity opposing the mercantile bourgeoisie of Gracia and Barrio Gotico to the urban precariat of youngsters and immigrants in Raval and Poble Sec is replaced by the Yes/No chasm on Catalunyna as a sovereign state separate from Spain, the damage to the egalitarian cause could be similar to the one caused by the Remain/Leave debate in the British referendum to secede from Europe. The first reason for this is that over a million people in Catalonia are non-Catalans, having migrated there either from other areas of Spain, or other countries entirely. Secondly, it would be hard for En Comú to position itself in the eventuality of such a referendum, when Podemos in Madrid favors autonomy, but not independence from Spain. Thus, their alliance would be endangered if En Comú opted to support independence as the lesser evil. Furthermore, from a populist perspective, it would be hard to both argue otherwise, and remain politically relevant.

---

119 Now being severely tested by the carnage in the Rambla perpetrated on August 17, 2017.

Today Barcelona is a city that has 200,000-strong demonstrations demanding greater refugee intake from the central government, which bans Uber and limits commercial tourism, where neighborhoods like Poble Sec and Barceloneta thrive with associations, social centers and environmental initiatives, and good old sociability. The city has definitely become more livable for locals and visitors after the decrease of sort of the hit-and-run tourism endemic before the crisis, and Ada is a popular mayor, who has made social participation in city politics and local economic sustainability efforts the hallmarks of her municipal program. The queer and green brand of municipalism being experimented with in Barcelona is something that can be exported, and is already being endorsed by other world cities. Mayor of New York Bill De Blasio is a fan of Ada Colau's. His election as mayor (replacing media financier Michael Bloomberg) was probably the biggest single political change achieved by Occupy Wall Street (although other city administrations have also taken a decidedly leftward turn in recent years).

The realities of institutional power, and municipal government, pose formidable challenges for social movements that decide to make the leap from contestation and protest to counterpower and counterhegemony – from destituent power to constituent power, in Negrian terms. No matter how daunting, the emergence of a reactionary rival, steeped in xenophobia, homophobia, and hard-fisted police repression, namely the nationalist international currently in power in Washington and Moscow (not to mention Budapest and Warsaw, Cairo and Ankara, and Tokyo and Dehli), forces radical-democracy movements to up the ante, and occupy the state (or at least some of its parts) in order to resist the assault on democratic freedoms and multicultural communitarianism, currently masterminded by the Trump-Putin-Erdogan triangle of evil.

Universal Basic Income: The Wage of the Precariat

The precariat clearly needs to craft alternative institutions to overcome the deflationary tendencies of neoliberalism, and the repressive tendencies of nazi-populism. Institutions are social and political technologies that co-evolve with information and material technologies. The Great Recession has exposed the fact that existing property relations are hindering the further development of an informational and automated economy; maldistribution depresses the economy by killing the buyers. Compressing the precariat's aggregate income has reduced the wealth of nations. Thus, the precariat needs to design and impose institutions that redistribute wealth and productivity in the general interest.

So far, trillions of dollars have been given to perpetrators of the financial crisis, and peanuts to its victims - the precarious and the unemployed. The more the rich accumulate wealth, the more demand sags, and unemployment rises. The structural root of the crisis lies in the crushing inability of thirty years of neoliberalism to redistribute the gains in productivity to the precarious population at large, thus undermining demand, and causing stagnation.

Given capitalism's long-term tendency to higher inequality, absent wars and social upheavals, the precariat needs to keep pushing for subversion and insurrection. However, it also needs to secure redistribution with a new social allocation of wealth, independent from increasingly scarce work, namely Universal Basic Income (UBI). This would be funded through general taxation, representing the technological dividend of each individual's contribution to social knowledge.

The basic concept behind UBI stems from American and French revolutionary Tom Paine, who proposed a universal dividend from the land in his work *Agrarian Justice* to achieve an equitable commonwealth. It was proposed to Nixon by policy expert Daniel Moynihan, as social remedy to ongoing race riots at the end of the 60s. Since the 80s, it has been discussed as either a complement, or a substitute, to the existing welfare system. It is also known as 'citizenship income' or as 'income of existence', and is, in essence, an unconditional social transfer. Negative income tax is not basic income, because the recipient must work to get the rebate (thus there is conditionality involved). The philosophical implications and justifications of UBI were first investigated by libertarian philosopher and political economist Philippe van Parijs who, in *Why Surfers Should Be Fed*[120] provided an unassailable liberal justification for unconditional basic income. It was justified on grounds of individual freedom and basic human rights, as imposing work on people was a violation of their individual freedom. There are people who would work fewer hours (or not work altogether), and people who desire to work but are left out of the job market. A universal allocation based on average purchasing power (such as $/€1,000 a month from the age of 18 until death) would thus free people to pursue their projects and dreams, and thus enhance total welfare.

I will not delve into the details of the topic here. Those interested should read the research done on the social desirability and economic feasibility of a universal transfer written by the Basic Income Earth Network (BIEN) and Scott Santens.[121] All I wish to note here are the salient features of a potential basic income for the precariat, which is a *Utopia for Realists*, as Rutger Bregman aptly titles his hopeful and well-researched book.[122]

First of all, the introduction of an unconditional basic income would abolish workfare and cease the persecution, and eventually the stigmatization, of people on welfare. These are already enormous political results. Strictly in regard to welfare, it would give precarious workers a bridge by which to move between jobs without having to go through complex bureaucratic procedures simply in order to collect unemployment benefits. It would especially abolish income uncertainty attached to temporary jobs – a major political victory for the precariat.

The most liberating aspect of basic income is in how it would free people's time, thus unleashing the potential to do the things they really want to do, from caring for children to engage in social activism, or idling around playing *Grand Theft Auto VI* before starting digital co-ops

---

120 Philippe van Parijs, 'Why Surfers Should Be Fed: The Liberal Case for an Unconditional Basic Income. *Philosophy & Public Affairs*, vol. 20, no. 2, 1991, pp. 101–131, www.jstor.org/stable/2265291.

121 See Scott Santens, 'Why we should all have a basic income', February 2017, http://basicincome.org/news/2017/02/scott-santens-basic-income/.

122 Rutger Bregman, *A Utopia for Realists. And How We Can Get There*, London: Bloomsbury, 2014.

in Lagos. For squats, social centers, and hacklabs, basic income would be a boon, because it would allow people to become full-time activists. It would also put commercial co-working spaces out of business.

Crucially, basic income makes people really free to choose whether they wish to work, or not, and for how long. In other words, it makes flexibility advantageous for temps. Basic income would also give precarious the option of refusing bullshit jobs, since they can rely on alternative source of income – namely UBI. By removing conditionality, the unequal exchange on which capitalism has always been based – work, or starve – would be abolished. And this is the greatest political weakness of basic income: can capitalism survive without fear?

This is what capitalist management and party commissars always held over people. Either under private capitalism or state communism, it was the specter of hunger that sent peasants into factories. In the England of the of the early 19th century, in order to make the population of the countryside more willing, the Poor Law was reformed, thus the rural masses had no choice but enter the satanic mills of the First Industrial Revolution. It was Stalin's collectivization of agriculture that, by bringing about famine, forced peasants to migrate to industrial towns during the first Five-Year plan (1928-33).

Whilst capitalism has always asserted that there's no such thing as a free lunch, basic income buys you lunch without you having to work. It's a subversion of capitalist discipline. Being paid to do nothing goes against the culturally ingrained work ethic, and doesn't encourage people to work tedious jobs for little reward.

There will be strong political resistance on the part of employers, especially low-wage employers, to the introduction of basic income. However, the progressive sectors of capital have already come to accept it as the inevitable price to pay, in order to avoid a reactionary backlash against globalization. The time has come to make them finally pay for the crisis. The economic cost of UBI is definitely bearable by the government budgets of advanced economies. A basic income scheme in the U.S., comprising of $12,000 dollars per year, per citizen above the age of 18, would have a net cost for government of around $900 million. This is equivalent to less than 3% of federal tax receipts. UBI is not impossibly costly; the hurdles are fundamentally political.

Regarding the political left, the problem with basic income is that it goes against the socialist labor principle of *to each according to their work*, or in other words, *to each according to their productivity*. If you do not work you are not entitled to an income, only to an unemployment subsidy. While social redistribution efforts have never had a better chance, the left is seriously out of step, still attached to socialism (and communism), and praising the value of work, an element understandably shared by labor unions. Culturally, most leftists have yet to come around to the idea that the area of non-work is a tangible, and growing, social reality – one that makes basic income unavoidable. It is only the political pressure of the precariat that will make UBI a reality.

The Precariat Syndicate

In Malmö at the 2008 European Social Forum, Michael Hardt hailed the General Freeters' Union in Japan as the first revolutionary syndicate in the world committed to the migrant and precarious' cause, and commended EuroMayDay in Europe for trying to do the same. Movements of the precariat have been usually working in tandem with radical and / or syndicalist unions, while keeping true to their anarcho-autonomist ideology and adopting a repertoire of 'fluffy' and 'spiky' practices, from the irreverent Pink Clown Army to confrontational black bloc tactics.

Traditionally, trade unions have been largely unwilling or unable to organize precarious workers in countries with two-tier labor markets. In Japan, casual workers and immigrants are excluded from official labor organizations and stigmatized by conservative public opinion. This is why young precarious workers have come together in Tokyo and Osaka, and formed a union, which organizes temps of all genders and ethnicities. This union constitutes my template for the Precariat Syndicate.

After unemployment started to be a European problem in the 80s, movements soon emerged to stage the fight against against the purveyors of precarity and unemployment. It was in France that the first actions undertaken by organized unemployed youth took place. Many took to the streets and destroyed property, earning the enduring nickname of *casseurs* (*breakers*), in prolonged campaigns, the most enduring example of which is the Action Chomage! (AC!) campaign that, born in the early 90s, lasted well into the 00s.[123] In 2001, strikes in Paris involved the occupations of various McDonald's and Pizza Hut outlets, were supported by the Stop Précarité campaign led by radical sections of French Unionism (CGT, CNT and Solidaires) and the European Marches against Precarity, which themselves were part of the anti-globalization movement. Abdel Mabrouki emerged as spokesperson of the fast food strike movement in Paris, and reflected upon his experience in the tellingly titled *Génération Précaire*.[124] He, along with the other strike delegates, were invited as guests of honor to Milan's first May Day Parade, a few months ahead of the massive protests and riots of the Genoa G8 countersummit (actions which were ferociously repressed by Berlusconi's government). The French movement of *Intermittents*, which paralyzed French culture festivals in the mid-00s, was also deeply enmeshed in the development of protests and reflections on the issues of precarity, intermittent work, and the new kind of welfare that had to address the plight of the precariat, symbolized in Italy by the popular San Precario icon.

These early attempts at organizing the precariat placed emphasis on the need for autonomous, self-managed, and transnational organizations which could potentially see their demands responded to. These demands usually centered around putting an end to the labor discrimination of young people, the persecution of migrants, and the need for a strong minimum wage and a decent universal basic income - fundamental steps that must be taken in order to defeat precarity.

---

123 See Cyprien Tasset, *Intermittents et précaires. Significations et origine d'une relation.* Cyprien is the emerging academic researcher on French precarity.
124 Abdel Mabrouki, *Génération Précaire*, Paris: Le Cherche Midi, 2004.

In 2006, students and unions repelled the first-employment contract (CPE) as Place de la Sorbonne was rechristened as Place de la Précarité. The French presidency (then held by Chirac) had to concede defeat after millions took to the streets. In 2016, Place de la République was occupied for months by Nuit Debout, protesting against Loi Travail making labor cheaper and more precarious, which was hammered through Parliament by the Socialist president and prime-minister, whose careers in politics were terminated as a result.

Precarious labor advocacy groups have emerged in many parts of Europe over the last decade, while Sciopero Sociale (Social Strike), part of the Blockupy movement that lay siege to the ECB's Eurotower between 2012 and 2015 and organized by radical precarious workers' collectives, managed to paralyze Rome, Milan and other major cities in the fall of 2014. The ChainWorkers in Milan, Yo Mango in Barcelona, Prekariaatti in Helsinki, Precarious Superheroes in Berlin, Precarias a la Deriva and Oficina Precaria in Madrid, Bob le Précaire in Liège and Brussels, Officine Zero in Rome, Precarious Angry Brigade in London, la Rede investigadores contra a precariedade cientifica in Lisbon, and Prekaer Café and Precarity Office in Vienna, are among the many noteworthy past and present precarious collectives that have made global anti-precarity action a viable option today.

Colau gained national popularity as leader of the PAH movements against home forecloses, managing to confront Spanish banks for evicting thousands of indebted families. Housing rights have been important for the mobilization of Spain's precarious youth since the V for Vivienda campaign against rent increases in the mid-00s. In Berlin and Rome, too, movements have focused on the urban question, the protection of low-income neighborhoods from gentrification, while squatting public housing in order to house precarious and immigrant families.

However, a general union federation of the precariat has yet to emerge in Europe. We need to build a pan-European syndicate of the precarious, the unemployed, the excluded, and the exploited. The alternative is the slide toward the form of patriotic sectionalism and xenophobia that was noticeable in Brexit and the Dutch elections. Mass unemployment makes the sirens of proletarian nativism and racism very seductive. Transnationalist solidarity must be organized; it will not occur by default. We have to organize the precarious and unemployed youth, the generation that yearns for freedom from police persecution and equality of treatment and opportunity.

In America, since the Justice for Janitors campaign in the late 90s, service and retail unions like SEIU have been working with grassroots movements, work that has culminated in the Fight for $15 campaign that is currently seeking to redress the recent explosion in wage inequality. The movement for a national living wage has already achieved localized success in Seattle and New York, and was behind the (modest) growth in wages seen during the Obama administration. However, the rise of decidedly anti-labor sentiments across the country, evidenced in Trump's appointment, creates daunting challenges for the movement. Trump's hotels have been recently unionized in Arizona – perhaps evidence that the national-populist turn in American politics could be faced down by organized labor.

Social unionism, which sees local unions working with civil society in order to support labor struggles, seems to fit the left-populist bill. Social unionism is clearly egalitarian, and thus populist, in nature, and supports the emergence of labor organizations (and movements of the precariat) that fight to share wealth and opportunity. Whereas it is absolutely crucial, in this historical phase, to work together with diverse orientations that share widely-conceived common objectives (such as gender equality, civil rights, labor dignity, and lifetime social security), it is also important that the precariat fights to impose its own economic agenda. This agenda rests on two pillars: a doubling of the minimum wage, and universal basic income.

A precariat syndicate of the world, which would federate urban precarious workers within and across continents, is something I hope to see in my lifetime. Whilst this is a wobbly ideal, existing anarcho-syndicalism has too narrow an appeal to command the allegiance of a very culturally diverse precarious population. It is rightly libertarian, but is usually sectarian. It mostly organizes public workers in areas where memories of past radicalism persist, but is unable to deal with the transformations of contemporary society, save for a few exceptions, such as the General Confederation of Labor (CGT) in Spain, a national anarcho-syndicalist organization, centered around Catalonia. The French union of the same name is instead a solid red union, in spite of its syndicalist origins, and has been strictly communist in its ideology since the end of World War Two. It has long been the most combative labor organization in France (and possibly Europe), and gave support to Nuit Debout. However, the French CGT rests on the assumption that radical youth must support the union-led labor movement, the opposite of my suggestion herein (this assumption is unfortunately shared by red unions across of Europe). Every popular uprising in France has seen the CGT attempt to steer social protest toward concrete economic demands, rather than push for systemic change. It is also worth noting that, while the students were burning down the Paris stock exchange in late May 1968, CGT leader Henri Krasucki was signing the Grenelles agreements, in secret, with Jacques Chirac. The future president had been sent by De Gaulle to negotiate a labor truce at any cost, and conceded all wage demands in order to separate workers from students, and finally break the revolutionary dynamics that the students of Nanterre and the Sorbonne had set in motion.

In more recent times, it was dismaying to see the more reformist, but still red, CGIL (the largest Italian union) failing to back the feminist strike that hundreds of collectives of young women had painstakingly prepared. The secretary - a woman to boot - explained to dumbfounded queer activists that unions do not call general strikes for 'abstract causes'. The fact is that the CGIL themselves have never called a national strike against precarity. The union is utterly disconnected from the issues that concern Italian youth, and has been so since its leadership supported the police entering the University of Rome to evict the student occupation in 1977. Even in its opposition to the Jobs Act, Italy's watered-down version of Loi Travail, all the union cared about was defending the status of permanent employees, rather than improve the conditions of precarious workers.

Gender equality is the fundamental social thread running through the variously orchestrated struggles of women around the world. Women are united as a front in an attempt to end male violence, pay discrimination, patriarchal oppression, and misogynist regression. As

Micah Jones rightly predicted, the global women's movement is emerging as the successor of the international movement of the squares. A pink tide is changing politics around the world, and this should be reflected in the organizations and institutions of the precariat. The global women's strike that took place on 8 March 2017, was a major step towards the creation of a global precariat movement; it is no secret that women are disproportionately represented in precarious occupations. As Italian intellectual Cristina Morini has written, the #feministrike was 'the first global strike of the precarious era.'[125] We need a pink union, and we need a purple party of the precariat (or the other way around). The race is on to find the style of communication, and ideological models that works best in practice. My recommendation is to adopt a populist discourse based on simple slogans and pop irony, and really enable egalitarian forms of participation in defining planks and decisions affecting the precarious themselves.

Looking elsewhere, Catholic unionism has had a keener interest than communist unionism in the precariat, due to the Vatican's current position regarding neoliberal inequality. In fact, Pope Bergoglio recently sang a ringing condemnation of precarious labor practices, proclaiming (to an audience of scolded labor consultants) that 'families are suffering because of the lack of labor and its precarity'. Much like red unions, catholic unions recruit along multi-ethnic and multi-confessional lines (for instance, Jeunes organisés et combatifs (JOC) in Belgium). Christian unions are certainly not fixated on anti-genderism like the current Pontiff. White unionism is really catholic in the English sense, attracting all sorts of people, including atheists and Muslims, because the meek and precarious shall inherit the Earth.

A New Social Compromise to Stave Off Global Fascism

What are the fundamental social and political needs of the precariat that need to be addressed? The emancipation from precarity, the defeat of national populism and neoliberal oligarchy in order to achieve radical democracy, gender equality, and the end of ethnic discrimination. The precariat agitates for a fair-share, solar-powered information economy, an uncensored network society with open source practices and open borders, a new welfare system based on universal basic income, local and global mutualism, a green new deal creating millions of green jobs, and the upgrading of the gig economy to a real sharing economy - one that properly shares profits between workers and consumers.

The end of open borders in Europe (essentially signaling the end of the Schengen agreement), and the closing of America brought about by the Muslim ban, portend a more general reorganization of borders and trading blocs, with Britain seceding from the European Single Market, and the European Union embracing free trade with Canada, while a nationalist America drops the TTP with East Asia, shelves the TTIP with Europe, and wishes to renegotiate the terms of NAFTA. Clearly the precariat needs to be a major political actor in these geopolitical and geoeconomic quakes. A Continental republic of free cities and regions is the constitutional utopia that the precariat should aspire to create. Women, minorities, and precarious youth

---

125 Cristina Morini, 'Uno sciopero biopolitico', *Effimera*, 7 March 2017, http://effimera.org/uno-sciopero-biopolitico-cristina-morini/.

have the combined numbers to muster enough energy to ram through a redistribution of European powers, and dispense with Maastricht's deflationary strictures. A veritable democracy can finally rise in Europe, in lieu of the present fissiparous confederation of nation-states, if the people seize constituent power to defeat resurgent neoliberalism, and plant the seeds of a fully-fledged European democratic republic.

If the political implications of the socio-economic theory of the Great Recession illustrated earlier in this text are correct - namely that the historical bifurcation we face admits only either reformist or reactionary outcomes, and that only a novel compromise between democracy and capitalism can prevent the second coming of fascism - then the trial-and-error search is on for what the Jobsian equivalent to the Fordist industrial compromise might be. Much like Fordism, it would have to be expansionary, equalizing, inclusive, and democratizing. The answer needs to be found within contemporary class structures, and in the historical array of political forces that vie for state power. After the crisis of neoliberalism, a multiethnic precariat confronts political authoritarianism and digital oligopoly. The American national-populist solution to the crisis relies - much like Nazism did in the 30s - on fiscal expansion, in order to finance military rearmament and domestic infrastructure. It is similarly nativist, protectionist, anti-women, anti-minorities, homophobic, and anti-labor. However, even American capital is not united in supporting Trump's nazi-populist project. Domestic resistance - both in radical and liberal forms - remains fierce, especially from the feminist, labor, and African-American movements. Silicon Valley has been split asunder on the issue of whether to support Trump's actions. Xi Jin Ping made it clear during the Davos summit that globalization can proceed without America, and implicitly proposed that the new guarantor of the global capitalist order would soon be China. Furthermore, the World Economic Forum appealed for the creation of a universal basic income, as a way to defuse the populist threat to liberal capitalism.

On the new geopolitical and geoeconomic board, incredible dangers lie ahead, not least the final triumph of the Carbon Liberation Front (as McKenzie Wark ironically refers to the forces of fossil-fuel capitalism), which now commands America's strategic interests, and promises only climate destruction and the annihilation of civilization. Digital capitalism, however, is not reliant on the energy matrix that propelled the industrial revolution in manufacturing. Google, and other sultans of digital rent, have removed themselves from the fossil race by making most of their activities – including energy-hungry server farms – reliant on renewable energy. Elon Musk is a Trumpian anti-union boss, but has self-evidently placed his bets on the emergence of a post-fossil-fuel infrastructure. Even e-commerce mogul (and fiercely anti-labor) Bezos will eventually rely on electric vehicles for the delivery of Amazon products to both warehouses and individual consumers. His Washington Post is staunchly anti-Trump (unlike Murdoch's Wall Street Journal), while Uber has had to swiftly reverse its initial support of the Muslim ban. The American entertainment industry will never give up on displaying hostility to Trump and Bannon's illiberal agenda. Europe and Canada also remain firmly on the liberal side, although the former is besieged by nationalism, and the latter has strong carbon lobbies influencing its polity.

All this is to say that capital remains divided on Trump, both at home and abroad, and is amenable to social concessions that were unthinkable under conservative neoliberalism. Certainly, neoliberal elites are still in power in political and economic spheres – so much so that the battle for counterhegemony still needs to be won – but their influence is decreasing. Precarious labor and liberal sections of capital can strike a compromise on equality and openness, based on an expansion of liquidity and spending. The Jobsian compromise cannot be but conflictual, much like the Fordist one used to be, by intensely focusing on distribution issues in an expanding economy. The political viability of such a compromise is predicated on a major redistribution of wealth through progressive taxation of individuals and corporations, in order to fund basic income and free universal education, reducing the unbelievable concentration of global income that is currently in the hands of the 0.01%. The alternative to a reduction of inequality is national populism, and the destruction of democracy.

Social democracy gave flesh to the Fordist compromise by building collective bargaining institutions and universal welfare programs. Social populism should adopt a Jobsian strategy for securing universal basic income against the backdrop of mass precarity caused by financialization and automation, for the universal diffusion and implementation of open knowledge through free lifelong public education and training, for a sharing economy that actually pays precarious workers for the value they create, for the provision of health care irrespective of employment status, for major public investment in rental housing, and finally for the provision of child care. Digital democracy in the political sphere and social unionism in the economic sphere can mutually reinforce each other, in order to milk the cow of informational capitalism while keeping at bay the big bad wolves of ExxonMobil and Goldman Sachs.

The objection to the thesis that precarious labor should fight, but also find compromise with, digital capital in order to save the world from national populism, and the destruction of the anthroposphere is well known: capitalism cannot be reformed. History, however, has shown that capitalism can in fact be reformed. Indeed, its malleability has enabled it to survive major crises and geopolitical shifts, and upheavals in all areas, from technological capabilities to gender politics. Democracy and universal suffrage, racial and gender equality before the law, the welfare state, and social security, were all imposed on capitalism by a powerful combination of popular pressure and labor conflict. The same will be true for universal income and redistribution of the digital dividend to the precarious social strata.

A stronger objection is that capitalism is inherently ecologically unsustainable, because it pursues endless accumulation, and therefore requires ever-larger quantities of energy to operate on a global scale. My contention is that only a particular historical-technological configuration of capitalism – carbon capitalism – is opposed to the interest of human life on Earth and thus not amenable to reform. Capitalism needs energy to function, yes, but this energy is not necessarily fossil energy from oil, gas, and coal. Solar energy has unlimited potential, and is quickly becoming able to seriously compete with fossil sources across the world (no matter how US executive power is presently fixated on appeasing the oil and coal lobbies). Therefore, a form of informational capitalism that thrives, while cutting carbon emissions to the level required to prevent catastrophic climate change, can exist, although its growth path is admittedly very narrow, given that loss of biodiversity, drinkable aquifers, and soil nitrification also need to be held in check, if the production and reproduction of civilization is to continue.

Paul Mason sees postcapitalism as emerging out of the organic growth of Yochai Benkler's peer-produced, open-source information economy.[126] This seems an uncharacteristically non-Marxist ending, as oligopolists are unlikely to renounce their privileges without putting a fight. In the end, there is a class struggle to be won by the precariat, if the digital commons are to be secured as the basis of exchange and livelihoods. The very fact that postcapitalism has been chosen to replace anti-capitalism bespeaks of a vagueness of aspiration, and weakness of intent. Either we want to abolish capitalism and take part in anti-capitalist riots (a strong temptation, I admit), or we want to reform it drastically via a populist strategy involving mass civil disobedience and political mobilization. What we cannot do is simply claim postcapitalism is already here while we still exist under capitalism; this would simply be an expression of our own powerlessness.

We have to recognize that the victory of national populism in the core country of the capitalist system, the one with most weapons and largest financial influence, poses a threat that is of a different order and magnitude than the one represented by the neoliberalism which we fought from 1999 (NO WTO) to 2011 (Occupy Wall Street). A populist strategy for the left would be to create a broad social front that can appeal to the liberal middle classes, while simultaneously satisfying the long-repressed needs of the popular classes. Yet today's left lacks either the nerve, or the force, to make such a move. Thus, it will have to be the precariat itself that builds its own institutions with which to further its interests. Institutions are created to enable the repeated satisfaction of material needs reflecting certain political priorities. The precariat needs basic income to live free from fear, and unleash its creative power. It is crowdsourcing a new political and economic constitution after the degeneration of liberal democracy into oligarchy. The precariat must rise, so that the world can exit the Great Recession on a path leading to economic redistribution, social emancipation, and ecologically sustainable communities.

Neoliberal capitalism is the cause of the job crisis, and the ecological crisis. I believe that a replacement in the form of a socially regulated market economy is more likely to deliver what we need and want (the uprooting of the fossil economy, wealth redistribution, transnational solidarity, etc.), than either the violent overthrow of the capitalist state, or the highly probable 'common ruin of the contending classes'[127] – otherwise understood as environmental catastrophe.

Discourses on the Ecological Question

The emergence of global warming as the single overarching problem confronting humankind – and the prevalent role of energy extraction and consumption, capitalist manufacturing, and mass consumerism in all of this – has vindicated the warnings made by the green movement since the institution of Earth Day in 1970.

126 Yochai Benkler, *The Wealth of Networks: How Social Production Transforms Markets and Freedom*, New Haven: Yale University Press, 2016.

127 Karl Marx and Friedrich Engels, *The Communist Manifesto: A Modern Edition*, London: Verso, 1998.

Since then, greens have become part of the establishment, but also affected the way capitalism does business; companies ignore palm oil at their peril, because consumers will punish them for it. This was unheard of before green consumerism started growing in the 80s and 90s. In the late 00s, it seemed that everybody was going green, from Gore to Schwarzenegger, and Google to Toyota. A liberal response to the climate crisis seemed possible, but was repeatedly thwarted until the Paris Climate Conference of 2016. However, then rose Trump, who made petro-capitalism and the willful ignorance of climate science the backbones of his reactionary project.

	Reformist	Radical
Prosaic	Technocratic Pragmatism	Malthusian Survivalism
Imaginative	Environmental Sustainability	Green Radicalism

Table 18. Types of Environmental Discourse. Source: Dryzek (2005)

Green radicalism is the ideological discourse that mobilizes climate anarchists, engendering civil disobedience, unrest, and ecotage in the name of environmental justice. It is in itself a fairly wide spectrum, ranging from the NGO professionalism of Greenpeace to the militancy of the Earth Liberation Front (ELF) and Animal Liberation Front (ALF); from Monbiot to Zerzan. In the middle of this spectrum are the growing climate action movements who provided the main thrust for the protests at the Climate Summits in Paris and Copenhagen. All of these movements share, to varying degrees, the belief that existing forms of politics and business are the root causes of the climate crisis. Changing individual behaviors, like Malthusians and United Nations sustainability drives advocate, is not enough. There needs to be a political drive to change the social infrastructure itself. Whilst those belonging to the sustainability approach want to make capitalism greener by changing its sectoral composition, technocrats merely want to make existing energy and manufacturing systems more efficient.

The emergence of green capitalism signals the diffusion of the concept of corporate sustainability, the key policy concept first put forward in the 1992 Earth Summit in Rio, which has become the platform of choice for European green parties and other environmental reformists. Green capitalism clearly markets sustainable development as a way out of the twin crises. However, sustainability is more concerned by the relative, rather than the absolute, impact of economic activity. It aims to provide incentives for companies to go green, but it is reluctant to measure whether basic ecological targets are indeed met *ex post*. The result of this attitude is that all carmakers are cheating on emission targets. Until now, all the talk about sustainability has just served to postpone the radical action needed to wean the economy off of fossil fuels.

Environmental malthusianism was inaugurated by *The Limits to Growth* report, which, appearing in the aftermath of the 1973 oil crisis, seemed to capture the essence of those times, only to be later shelved when the oil prices went back to levels equivalent to those before the second oil crisis in 1979. Today it is the ideology of the outspoken James Lovelock, and the implicit discourse of many IPCC[128] reports, which correlate disaster in coastal regions with increases in global temperatures. The rhetoric is gloomy and survivalist, a 'we have to do this, or most humans will be dead before the end of the century' approach to bringing about sustainability – 'only polar regions and large, rainy islands will host the remnants of humanity', they proclaim. Many in this camp think that the backlog of emissions has already overstepped the critical threshold after which runaway climate change becomes certain – we just have to brace ourselves for when it happens. The creativity and imagination of the British climate camps, the Water Protectors at Standing Rock, or ecomovements like 350. org and Rising Tide, are missing from the minds of Malthusians. They care about objective constraints and cold estimates. Green radicals, however, believe in subjectivity, and collective possibilities for radical transformation. Still, if the survivalists are right, organizing for a post-apocalyptic society might be the only option left to the opponents of state hierarchy and corporate exploitation.

Adverting Dystopia?

Obama's switch toward environmental keynesianism has changed the nature of the economic game, and Trump cannot reverse the process. Green capitalism is a reality, as Silicon Valley switches from chips to panels, and billions of dollars are invested in renewable energy and green jobs. Global solar power capacity soared by 50% last year due to rapid growth in America and China, and local produce, growing one's own food, community gardens, and even permaculture are all the rage. The rich and famous are converting to green lifestyles. Hybrid and electric cars are no longer confined to the attention of green enthusiasts. Although the rise of Tesla rests on shaky financial foundations, internal combustion engines will soon disappear from the roads, as the Netherlands and a number of Northern European countries have instigated plans to phase them out of circulation in less than a decade.

A global network of organizations and collectives are animating the climate justice movement, and distilling a new DIY material culture centered around ecological education, sustainable living (minimization of eco-footprint through self-produced renewable energy, vegan food, water recycling, etc.), and non-violent mass direct action, successfully targeting the largest emitters of greenhouse gases, from Kingston to KeystoneXL.

In a 2009 article, *The Ecologist* questioned whether climate campers were anarchists, or the best hope for the environmental movement.[129] I would argue that they are both. Pink queer and black anarchist influences are crucial to making the climate justice movement the most important heir of the anti-globalization movement, one in which libertarianism is kept alive against police repression, technocratic regimentation, and top-down decision-making. Only direct action ultimately affects power. In our current predicament, *power to the people* also

---

128 Intergovernmental Panel on Climate Change (IPCC).
129 'Climate Camp: Saviour of the Environmental Movement?', *The Ecologist*, 6 August 2009. http://www. theecologist.org/News/news_analysis/296747/climate_camp_saviour_of_the_environmental_movement. html.

means *power generated by the people*. The core struggle between climate justice radicals and petro-capitalists will determine whether, and how, drastic cuts in carbon emissions are made, and how the ecological redesigning of cities and their logistics (such as energy, transportation, and food production systems) is implemented, if at all. There is no other social conflict more important for the future of the world today. Green capitalists and climate anarchists arguably both seek the empathy and support of public opinion regarding a climate crisis whose existence both fronts acknowledge. The objective is to make the rest of society understand that global overheating is humankind's top political priority. Ultimately, 'less climate change, more social change' (to quote a climate camp slogan), is what drives radical and reformist politics alike.

Today, oil interests still determine the direction of energy policy. If the ongoing climate conflict yields economic transformation, then the world might progress toward a carbon-neutral future, just as labor conflict made the world emerging from the ashes of fascism progress toward social reform, and welfare provisions. If instead green capitalism is too weak to confront fossil lobbies, and the climate justice movement fails to gain critical mass, then environmental collapse and eco-fascism are likely to carry the day, in a planetary-scale replica of what happened to the poor of New Orleans in the aftermath of Katrina. I surmise that the present ecological crisis can lead to one, or a combination of, the following macro-political scenarios:

Eco-fascism

Steampunk Anarchy

Ecosocial Populism

Green Liberalism

Green Maoism

Table 19: The Climate Question: Future Macro-Political Scenarios

If the biosphere becomes uninhabitable for much of the human species, a global war for resources is likely to ensue, leading to areas where military despots have absolute rule over the lives of the inhabitants – *eco-fascism*. In this nightmare scenario – a return, essentially, to feudalism – brutal overlords would rule over a present of misery, and a future of regression. Trump's Nazi-populism could lead us to such a dystopian future. In such a setting, pockets of *steampunk anarchy* could survive, similar to when free cities in the Middle Ages managed to hold their own against the feudal lords, bishops, and monarchs. These will be self-managed communities, surviving - and perhaps thriving - through the recycling and hacking of old machinery, enabled by the transfer of pirate knowledge across generations. They will be under constant threat from eco-fascists and climate refugees, forced rewilders in a Hobbesian world where civilization (drinking water from taps, public health and schooling, internet, etc.) has collapsed. Those who fail to organize will either prey and / or perish, with eco-hacking providing an important edge for survival. Are primitivists cheering for the imminent collapse of electricity-based civilization? Sometimes it is best to not get what you wish for.

However, a utopian scenario also exists. Dystopia turned on its head, and remade into utopia. An ecosocial future for the seven (soon to be nine) billion human beings that people Gaia. A Green Deal that is in the interest of society, not corporations. A social pact that imposes the binding regulation of emissions to power plants, factories, and vehicles, which is enforced thanks to carbon pricing and the social control and pressure of active multitudes who are watchful of large emitters, and mindful of entrenched interests. Overdeveloped countries finance the technology needed in undeveloped countries to curb emissions. Viral experiments in urban and rural communities lead to distributed energy production, economic mutualism, and social ecologism. Green jobs are created to compensate those lost to automation in industry and mining. Regionalization of trade, and relocalization of food consumption also takes place.

A multipolar world leading to transnational human rights governance, where green and populist parties take on the role of the socialism of yesteryear. A society where barricades are burnt and conflicts occur – for access to water or knowledge, for instance – but ones that are managed and solved, through reform and compromise. A society where the economy starts to dematerialize, downshifting from material goods to immaterial leisure, as climate change unfolds slowly, but surely. The climate crisis thus becomes an occasion for *catagenesis* (to use Homer-Dixon's expression), when the crisis becomes a green opportunity to change the structures of society. Environmental groups stand to become mass organizations in such a world. Climate action and opposition to green capitalism is likely to lead to *ecosocial populism*, not revolution. It was James O'Connor who first articulated the possibility of ecosocialism. However, I differ in one fundamental aspect from O'Connor, as I don't wholeheartedly accept Marx's labor theory of value, and thus do not assume that the ecological crisis will negatively affect profits, just as it was wrong to assume a trend toward impoverishment of the working-class, or that the accumulation of fixed capital would lead to falling rates of profit (the historical record says otherwise). Indeed, the possibility of green capitalism rests on the potential of a productivity boost, afforded by green technology that will allow both wages and profits to grow – the exact opposite of what O'Connor argues:

> Put simply, the second contradiction states that when individual capitals attempt to defend or restore profits by cutting or externalizing costs, the unintended effect is to reduce the 'productivity' of the conditions of production and hence to raise average costs.[130]

Global opinion remains in favor of *green liberalism*: technocrats, governments and international agencies overseeing the ecological modernization of the economy, by responding to, and reconciling the interests of, corporations and organized science. Lord Stern and Oscar-Nobel Gore have been the most credible salesmen of corporate capitalism's 'green face'. It is carbon

---

130 James O'Connor, *Natural Causes: Essays in Ecological Marxism*, New York: Guilford Press, 1997.

trading and industrial innovation, not carbon taxes and sustainable living, as in ecosocialism. Sacrifices for the many, not the few. Yet any return to decent macroeconomic conditions requires redistribution from profits and rents, to wages and salaries as *condicio sine qua non*, if (im)material consumption is to resume, and green capitalism is to be kickstarted.

A final setting, largely hypothetical but within the realm of possibility, might be defined as Green Jacobinism, or *ecomaoism*. Imagine an Earth Liberation Army motivated by a radical green ideology, made up of disciplined cadres, which manages to defeat petro-capitalism in open battle, and subsequently conquer the world. It would set up an intransigent government dedicated to the strict regulation of economy and society, in order to halt climate change. This would be the revolutionary army that enables a party of radical ecologists to seize power, and then limit material production and consumption levels to stay within atmospheric limits. This revolutionary government would have one mission, and one mission only: reduce CO_2 concentration in the atmosphere to 350ppm, the level at which mean global temperatures will not increase further than pre-industrial era averages. No person would be entitled to more than 3 tons of carbon dioxide emissions. Private possession of fossil fuels and internal combustion engines would be outlawed. Mountains of SUVs would be sent to the junkyards and their owners imprisoned, to show people the harsh rule of the new global government. Civilian air transport networks would be dismantled. Coal mines would be closed, gas production nationalized, and oil used only for pharmaceuticals and petrochemicals. Nuclear energy would be exploited until the Hubbert's Peak of uranium is reached. Any form of unauthorized combustion would be actively discouraged, including smoking. Ecology and science education would be mandatory from an early age, which would further enforce nutrition, mobility, and power consumption regimes. Mandatory free labor in public parks, forests, and victory gardens would be required from every adult citizen. Paramilitary corps would be assigned to reforestation projects, and scout-like formations of green bio-engineers would oversee these projects with dictatorial powers limited only by the fear of causing an insurrection.

What to make of this scenario? In effect, it's hard to see, without resorting to authoritarian measures, how to persuade producers and consumers to change their habits with the rapidity necessary to avert disaster (reducing emissions by 20-30% within a decade, and by 80% within forty years). It seems that only a benevolent planner, or a planetary salvation committee endowed with full powers, could achieve such a feat, and win over people who don't like to be bossed around, even if it is supposedly in the name of a good (green) cause.

The End of Precarity

To briefly sum up before concluding. We are in the midst of both an economic, and ecological crisis, where class and climate struggles have become central to geopolitics. The social actors of the class struggle are new, since capitalism is no longer industrial, but informational. This struggle is between the budding precariat and the fossil-fuel elites. The precariat is the new historical social subject, and social populism and radical ecology shall be its ideological tenets.

In a networked information economy, it is the precarious, not the capitalists, that control the strategic means of production – the computing power of connected smartphones and PCs – and enable the production and distribution of information, culture, and knowledge, through networks which are making the age of mass media obsolete. Immaterial labor puts a new, non-market, and non-proprietary sector at the center of wealth creation. However, capitalist domination strongly resists the encroachment of peer-to-peer (p2p) cooperation on its hitherto unchallenged prerogatives – the ownership of ideas, the management of production, and the marketing of innovation – and political power, and is attempting to defend its proprietary interests against the growing commonalism of the precarious class.

The solution to the precarious question is not going to be found in the return to the speculative, over-indebted, overdeveloped, ecocidal, and unequal consumer economy of the recent past, but in the fight for a new economic and welfare system that is built around the environment, and the social needs of the precarious sectors of society. Redistribution can be achieved thanks to massive strike movements, the taxation of capital and carbon to pay for universal health and education, basic income for all adults, a 4-day working week, free access to online knowledge, economic incentives for commons-based peer production, subsidized green housing and green job initiatives (for all those wishing to work), the introduction of a socialized banking system to fund renewable energy and sustainable living projects, the promotion of urban and labor rights in the form of solidarity strikes, self-organization and self-unionization, and most of all an end the scandalous discrimination and persecution of immigrants and asylum-seekers.

The politics of the common and the struggle around commons – and especially of the most precious common of all, the atmosphere – starts with the collective defense and expansion of the urban commons of the precariat: social centers, radical associations, alternative theaters, people's kitchens, and community gardens. Social cooperation needs to find its own organizational resources and political strategies, in order to prevail over capitalist enclosures of immaterial assets, and the privatizations of social space.

The redistribution of wealth and power toward the precariat, the growth of immaterial knowledge, the cultural enrichment of society, and a massive expansion of the value of leisure, are all fundamental social preconditions for the horizontal re-design of the economy. This will make the economy socially empowering and ecologically resilient, by freeing up individuals' time to pursue ecohacktive and permacultural activities; giving time and money back to precarious people will enable them to devise ways to repair society and the environment, and decide collectively about their own future, cutting the need for quick consumption and instant satisfaction. A strongly relational and solidaristic economy would fulfill many of the needs today obviated by individualized market transactions. The multigendered and multiethnic precariat can be the social driver for local low-carbon economies of cooperation, exchange, mutual aid, food, and energy production, and the cognitive precariat has so far been the core constituency of the climate justice movement.

Is the Ecological Regulation of Capital Possible?

Green capitalism cannot be simply considered as a marketing ploy. It embodies the faction of the global bourgeoisie that understands the reality of climate change and of its own declining political legitimacy in the face of the banking crisis and the consequent end of neoliberal, monetarist hegemony. Capital now seeks a top-down, as opposed to bottom-up, form of regulation, in order to reconcile market forces with ecological imperatives and social needs. Fossil-fuel capitalism, on the other hand, is purely reactionary. It has long denied the existence of man-made planetary heating, and it is now lobbying to seize upon the spaces opened by geopolitical and ecological disasters. It has spawned the growth of an oil-military complex that is the biggest threat to the peace and welfare of humankind.

Fordist keynesianism was incredibly wasteful in terms of energy. Oil was made so cheap, and consumer goods so abundant, that the biosphere was ruined as a result. In fact, the present ecological crisis is mostly the crisis of the industrial economy, not informationalism. Over the last three decades, informationalism has replaced industrialism as the dominant technological matrix of accumulation. Indeed, the failure of economies to transition from industrialism to informationalism (from the electrical engine to the electronic chip) is viewed by contemporary sociology as the structural reason behind the implosion of the Soviet Union. Now, the inherited neoliberal form of informational capitalism is morphing into green capitalism. The evidence for this is mounting: from Silicon Valley becoming a hotbed for solar energy, to green sectors, and huge battery plants. Industrialism is dependent on oil, coal, and other hydrocarbons in a way that informationalism is not. Steel needs coal, the internet does not. The problem with green capitalism is that the scale effect is likely to more than offset any improvements in energy intensity, thus emissions continue to rise. Left to its own instincts, green capitalism would be ecologically unsustainable; it needs to be socially regulated.

Yet, economic growth only has meaning if measured in monetary terms, not in physical terms. Thus, in principle, a social regulation of capital can be envisaged where there is growth in monetary terms (thus overcoming the economic crisis), but not in entropic terms (thus forestalling climate catastrophe). This would be a stage of the economy where immaterial growth becomes the norm, along with the maximization of collective knowledge and social well-being, rather than corporate profit or private wealth. An economy where people mostly exchange immaterial services, rather than material goods. In other words, a world where there is money to be made in the economy, because information-based, and green jobs are available in large numbers, and the paying of universal basic income checks by a central bank keeps the economy liquid.

Today, the call for *décroissance* has fallen on deaf ears, because it preaches parsimony to a population already impoverished by the global recession. The precarious must organize, across genders and ethnic groups, to create their own movement that fights for a larger slice of the pie. But if the pie is shrinking, as Latouche advocates – because people save more and consume less – many more will be made jobless, and the people will end up in an even more precarious condition than under neoliberalism.

It is true that capitalism is addicted to accumulation and growth. The recovery from the crisis can only occur if there are more euros, dollars, and yuans are put in the hands of those with less money and thus likely to spend it when given the opportunity: the poor and the precarious. Social regulation must ensure that this extra money is not spent on Amazon.com but in ways that are thermodynamically sound, and funding things such as sustainable mobility, local agricultural produce, reforestation, and renewable energy deployment. Social spending must be used to strengthen the networks of solidarity within and across generations and nations. Only generalized conflict can emancipate the precariat, and lead to sharp increases in environmental investment.

The distinction between bounded material growth and unbounded immaterial growth is useful when imagining a social scenario that progressively de-commodifies capitalism. Politically, this would also be a society where the aims of anarcho-syndicalists – who aim to construct a postcapitalist, egalitarian commonwealth – and eco-populists – who aim to create a society of peers, on a biodiverse planet, oriented around a thermodynamic understanding of redistribution – converge in a major transformation of capitalism. It is a social scenario where the autonomous, pirate, and queer practices of the immaterial precariat are able to defeat the reactionary offensive of petro-capitalism, and drive the ecological transition of the economy, where grassroots experimentation is encouraged, and regulation is horizontal and bottom-up, rather than vertical and top-down. To address both the economic and ecological crises, the precariat needs to push for a service-based, relational, commons-oriented peer-production economy, the aim of which is the growth of knowledge, leisure, and culture, as opposed to the growth of material wealth. This would be a society based on ecological remediation, immaterial accumulation, and the maximization of well-being among its participants, rather than on material opulence for a tiny minority of people.

The debate is open about whether green capitalism can be made ecologically sustainable. Ecomarxists, who believe in the labor theory of value, think that the ecological crisis entails a squeeze in the rate of surplus value, and thus reinforces the tendency for the rate of profit to fall. In algebraic terms, this means that S/V, the ratio between surplus and variable capital (wages and fuel), goes down. The rate of profit is equal to surplus value over total capital invested – $C+V$ – which is turn the sum of fixed capital (machinery and equipment), and variable capital (wages and raw materials). As V rises, the rate of profit decreases (divide the numerator and denominator by V to verify it is so). The same occurs as K rises, which is the case originally considered by Marx.

Empirically, if productivity declines because of the ecological crisis, due to increases in the cost of energy or to the internalization (inclusion in the business cost of products and services) of the environmental damages caused by the economic process, then ecomarxists are correct, and green capitalism is unsustainable due to falling profits. If, conversely, the ecological crisis triggers a green technological revolution, the rate of profit can stay equal as wages rise, so that green capitalism can create its own demand. In simpler words, if green capitalism is just green washing, ultimately the ecological crisis will end up endangering capitalist accumulation, thus leading to the common ruin of today's contending social classes: the global elite and the transnational precariat. If, on the other hand, green capitalism is the harbinger of a fourth industrial revolution – genomics and greenomics – productivity will rise, creating a favorable context for increases in wages and labor conditions, as well as ease political resistance to income redistribution via progressive taxation (when taxes hit the rich proportionally more than the poor; under neoliberalism taxation has instead been regressive). Another way of looking at this is to consider the fact that the price of a good is equal to the wage rate, divided by productivity (production per hour worked) and multiplied by one plus the rate of profit: the margin that rewards the entrepreneur, and pays interest to the banker. At constant prices, if productivity increases because of a rise in energy efficiency, either the wage rate rises or the rate of profit must increase (or a combination of the two).

Let's consider a class-neutral theory of value – a mark-up price equation: $P = w/\pi\ (1 + r)$, where p is the price level, w is the hourly wage, π is hourly productivity, and r is the rate of profit. Introducing energy costs, the equation gets transformed into $P = (w/\pi)\ (1 + r)/(1 - \theta pE)$, where θ is the energy requirement per unit of output, and pE is the relative price of energy (the price of energy divided by the general price level P) and $1 > \theta pE$. If θ decreases because of a rise in energy efficiency, this has the same effect as an increase of productivity π: in order for prices to stay constant, either w or r must rise.

Contrary to what Marx predicted, improvements in wages and living standards have been made possible under capitalism thanks to the combination of technological innovation and social redistribution. Have these improvements come at the cost of bankrupting the biosphere? Yes, if social resistance to capitalism is not strong enough to decarbonize the economy. If movements lose the fight for climate justice, Earth might become like Venus. From the experience of the poor and precarious of New Orleans and Houston, we know the horrors that lie in store when climate disaster strikes a class-polarized urban society. The climate question conceals a social question, because the precarious stand to lose the most in the biocrisis. On the other hand, the precarious need to be empowered to be effective antagonists to global financial elites; only if they secure income and leisure, can they have the freedom to erect a postcapitalist society.

Precarious-to-precarious community solutions to urban habitats, energy, food production, and social housing, will have to become increasingly common as answers to unemployment and environmental crises. Whole cities can be redesigned by expanding self-organized groups of precarious ecohacktivists living from their collective labor, and the sharing of what is produced and exchanged in their social networks.

If climate movements lose the battle, and fail to decarbonize governments and corporations, then by the middle of this century coastal cities will drown. What is at stake is neither the survival of capitalism nor industrialism, but of digital civilization, and the promise of universal access to information, knowledge, and culture, that the switch to informationalism has made possible.

The climate crisis makes everybody precarious. The precariat must rise to the challenge to defend the environmental rights of all, as it fights in the cities of the world against racism, and for the emancipation of all from enforced precarity.

REFERENCES

Michel Aglietta, *Régulation et Crises du Capitalisme*, Paris: Odile Jacob, 1994.

Giuseppe Allegri and Giuseppe Bronzini, *Libertà e lavoro dopo il Jobs Act*, Rome: Derive e Approdi, 2015.

Giuseppe Allegri and Roberto Ciccarelli, *Il Quinto Stato*, Milan: Ponte alle Grazie, 2013.

Giuseppe Allegri, Roberto Ciccarelli, 'What Is the Fifth Estate?', *Open Democracy*, 27 February 2014, https://www.opendemocracy.net/can-europe-make-it/giuseppe-allegri-roberto-ciccarelli/what-is-fifth-estate.

Giovanni Arrighi, *Adam Smith in Beijing: Lineages of the 21st Century*, Verso Books, 2009.

Emiliana Armano, Arianna Bove, Annalisa Murgia (eds.), *Mapping Precariousness, Labour Insecurity and Uncertain Livelihoods*, London: Routledge, 2017.

Yochai Benkler, *The Wealth of Networks: How Social Production Transforms Markets and Freedom*, New Haven: Yale University Press, 2016.

Murray Bookchin, *The Ecology of Freedom: The Emergence and Dissolution of Hierarchy*, AK Press, 2005.

Mirko Bozzato, Alex Foti, 'La Geografia dell'Antidistopia: mappare l'ecologismo contemporaneo', *Lo Squaderno*, n.7, 2007.

Robert Boyer, *La Théorie de la Régulation: Une Analyse Critique*, Paris: La Découverte, 1986.

Ruther Bregman, *Utopia for Realists: And How We Can Get There*, Bloomsbury, 2017.

Judith Butler, *Precarious Life: The Power of Mourning and Violence*, London: Verso, 2004.

William Calvin, *Global Fever: How to Treat Climate Change*, University of Chicago Press, 2008.

Neil Carter, *The Politics of the Environment: Ideas, Activism, Policy*, Cambridge: Cambridge University Press, 2007.

Manuel Castells, *The Rise of the Network Society, Vol.1, The Information Age: Economy, Society, and Culture*, Oxford: Blackwell, 2000.

Manuel Castells, *The Power of Identity, Vol.2, The Information Age: Economy, Society, and Culture*, Oxford: Blackwell, 2009.

Manuel Castells, *End of Millennium, Vol.3, The Information Age: Economy, Society, and Culture*, Oxford: Blackwell, 2010.

Manuel Castells, *Communication Power*, Oxford University Press, 2009.

Ha-Joon Chang, *Bad Samaritans: The Guilty Secrets of Rich Nations and the Threat to Global Prosperity*, London: Random House, 2008.

Ha-Joon Chang, *23 Things They Didn't Tell You About Capitalism*, London: Penguin, 2011.

Patrick Cingolani, *Révolutions précaires: essai sur l'avenir de l'emancipation*, Paris: La Découverte, 2014.

Herman E. Daly, *Beyond Growth: The Economics of Sustainable Development*, Boston: Beacon Press, 1996

Philip K. Dick, *The Man with the High Castle*, New York: Putnam, 1962.

Andrew Dobson, *Green Political Thought*, London: Routledge, 2004.

John Dryzek, *The Politics of the Earth: Environmental Discourses*, Oxford: Oxford University Press, 2005.

Barbara Ehrenreich, *Nickel and Dimed: On (Not) Getting By in America*, New York: Metropolitan, 2001.

Martin Ford, *Rise of the Robots: Technology and the Threat of a Jobless Future*, New York: Basic Books, 2015.

Alex Foti, 'Precarity and n/european identity', interview, *Metamute*, October 2004 http://www.meta-mute.org/editorial/articles/precarity-and-neuropean-identity-interview-alex-foti-chainworkers-

Alex Foti, 'Critical Dynamics of Advanced Capitalism from the Second to the Third Industrial Revolution', *Left Curve*, 31, March 2007.

Alex Foti, *Anarchy in the EU: Movimenti pink, black, green in Europa e Grande Recessione*, Milan: Agenzia X, 2009.

Alex Foti, 'Climate Anarchists vs. Green Capitalists', Reimagining Society Project, *Z Magazine*, August 2009.

Alex Foti, 'La Rivoluzione della Repubblica Continentale Europea', *Euronomade,* 20 February 2016, http://www.euronomade.info/?p=6759.

Nancy Fraser, 'A Triple Movement? Parsing the Politics of Crisis', *New Left Review*, May-June, 2013.

Paolo Gerbaudo, *The Mask and the Flag: Populism, Citizenism and Global Protest*, London: Hurst, 2017.

Robert J. Gordon, *The Rise and Fall of American Growth*, Princeton: Princeton University Pres, 2016.

Uri Gordon, *Anarchy Alive! Anti-Authoritarian Politics from Practice to Theory*, London: Pluto, 2007.

André Gorz, *Métamorphoses du travail: quête du sens, critique de la raison économique*, Paris: Galilée, 1988.

Nicholas Georgescu-Roegen, *The Entropy Law and the Economic Process*, Cambridge, Harvard University Press, 1971.

David Goodstein, *Out of Gas: The End of the Age of Oil*, New York: Norton, 2004.

David Graeber, 'The New Anarchists', *New Left Review*, 1999. https://newleftreview.org/II/13/david-graeber-the-new-anarchists

Stuart Hall, *Resistance Through Rituals: Youth Subcultures in Post-War Britain*, London: Routledge, 2006.

Marion Hamm, *Media Practices in the Trans-Urban Euromayday Movement of the Precarious*, PhD Dissertation, Luzern: University of Luzern, 2011.

Michael Hardt, 'Porto Alegre: The New Bandung?', *New Left Review*, 2002. https://newleftreview.org/II/14/michael-hardt-porto-alegre-today-s-bandung

Michael Hardt and Antonio Negri, *Empire*, Cambridge: Harvard University Press, 2001.

Michael Hardt and Antonio Negri, *Multitude: War and Democracy in the Age of Empire*, The Penguin Press, 2005.

Michael Hardt and Antonio Negri, *Commonwealth*, Cambridge: Belknap, 2009.

David Harvey, *A Brief History of Neoliberalism*, Oxford: Oxford University Press, 2005.

Paul Hawken, Amory B. Lovins, L.H. Lovins, *Natural Capitalism: The Next Industrial Revolution, Earth-scan*, 2005

Thomas F. Homer-Dixon, *The Upside of Down: Catastrophe, Creativity and the Renewal of Civilization*, Toronto: Knopf Canada, 2006.

Samuel P. Huntington, *The Crisis of Democracy: On the Governability of Democracies*, 1976.

Samuel P. Huntington, *The Clash of Civilizations and the Remaking of the World Order*, 1996.

Samuel P. Huntington, *Who Are We? The Challenges to America's National Identity.* 2004.

The Invisible Committee, *The Coming Insurrection*, Cambridge: Semiotext(e), 2009.

The Invisible Committee, *To Our Friends*, Cambridge: MIT Press, 2015.

The Invisible Committe, *Maintenant*, Paris: La Fabrique, 2017.

John Jordan, *We Are Everywhere: The Irresistible Rise of Global Anti-Capitalism*, London: Verso, 2003.

Michal Kalecki, *Theory of Economic Dynamics: An Essay on Cyclical and Long-Run Changes in the Capitalist Economy*, New York: Monthly Review Press, 2004

Michael Kalecki, *The Last Phase in the Transformation of Capitalism*, New York: Monthly Review Press, 2011.

John M. Keynes, *The End of Laissez-Faire: The Economic Consequences of Peace*, London Prometheus, 2004.

John M. Keynes, *The General Theory of Employment, Interest, and Money*, New York: Harcourt, 1964.

Paul Kingsnorth, George Monbiot, 'Is there any point in fighting to stave off industrial apocalypse?', *Guardian*, 17 August 2009, http://www.guardian.co.uk/commentisfree/cif-green/2009/aug/17/environment-climate-change.

Naomi Klein, *No Logo*, Toronto: Knopf Canada, 1999.

Naomi Klein, *The Shock Doctrine: The Rise of Disaster Capitalism*, New York: Metropolitan, 2008

Naomi Klein, *This Changes Everything: Capitalism vs. the Climate*, New York: Simon & Schuster, 2015.

Serge Latouche, 'De-growth: an electoral stake?', *Journal of Inclusive Democracy*, 3(1), January 2007, http://www.inclusivedemocracy.org/journal/vol3/vol3_no1_Latouche_degrowth.htm

Tom Levitt, 'Climate Camp: Anarchist or Saviour of the Environmental Movement?', *The Ecologist*, 6 August 2009, http://www.theecologist.org/News/news_analysis/296747/climate_camp_anarchists_or_saviours_of_the_environmental_movement.html

Assar Lindbeck and Dennis J. Snower, *The Insider-Outsider Theory of Employment and Unemployment*, Cambridge, Massachusetts: MIT Press 1988.

Alain Lipietz, *La Société en Sablier: Le Partage du Travail Contre la Déchirure Sociale*, Paris, La Découverte, 1994.

Isabell Lorie, *State of Insecurity: Governing the Precarious*, London: Verso, 2015.

James Lovelock, *The Revenge of Gaia: Earth's Climate Crisis and the Fate of Humanity*, New York: Basic Books, 2006.

Cristina Morini, 'Uno sciopero biopolitico', *Effimera*, 7 March 2017, http://effimera.org/uno-sciopero-biopolitico-cristina-morini/

McKenzie Wark, *Molecular Red: Theory for the Anthropocene*, London: Verso, 2015.

Juan Martinez-Alier, *The Environmentalism of the Poor: A Study of Ecological Conflicts and Valuation*, Cheltenham: Elgar, 2002.

Karl Marx, *Capital: Volume One*, New York: Vintage, 1977.

Karl Marx, *The Eighteenth Brumaire of Louis Bonaparte*, London: Allen & Unwin, 1926.

Michael Mann, *Sources of Social Power: Volume 1, A History of Power from the Beginning to AD 1760*, Cambridge: Cambridge University Press, 1986.

Michael Mann, *Sources of Social Power: Volume 2, The Rise of Classes and Nation States*, Cambridge: Cambridge University Press, 1986.

Michael Mann, *Sources of Social Power: Volume 3, Global Empires and Revolution, 1890-1945*, Cambridge: Cambridge University Press, 2012.

Michael Mann, *Sources of Social Power: Volume 4, Globalizations, 1945-2011*, Cambridge: Cambridge University Press, 2013.

Herbert Marcuse, *One-Dimensional Man*, Boston: Beacon Press, 1964.

David Marsh, *Knowledge and the Wealth of Nations*, New York: Norton, 2007.

Paul Mason, *Postcapitalism: A Guide to Our Future*, London: Penguin, 2012.

D.H. Meadows, Dennis L. Meadows, *The Limits to Growth: The 30-year Update*, London: Earthscan, 2004.

Frank Miller, *The Dark Night Returns*, New York: DC Comics, 2005.

George Monbiot, *Heat: How to Stop the Planet from Burning*, London: Allen Lane, 2006.

Alan Moore, *V for Vendetta*, New York: DC Comics, 2008.

Tadzio Mueller, Alexis Passadakis, '20 Theses against Green Capitalism', December 2008, http://slash.autonomedia.org/node/11656.

Arne Naess, David Rothenberg, *Ecology, Community and Lifestyle: Outline of an Ecosophy*, Cambridge: Cambridge University Press, 1993.

James O'Connor, *Natural Causes: Essays in Ecological Marxism*, New York: Guilford Press, 1997.

Claus Offe, *Europe Entrapped*, London: Wiley, 2015.

Carlota Perez, *Technological Revolutions and Financial Capital: The Dynamics of Bubbles and Golden Ages*, Cheltenham, Elgar, 2002.

Ross Perlin, *Intern Nation: How to Earn Nothing and Learn Little in the Brave New Economy*, London: Verso, 2011.

Karl Polanyi, *The Great Transformation: The Political and Economic Origins of Our Time*. Boston: Beacon Press, 1957.

Nicos Poulantzas, *Fascism and Dictatorship: The Third International and the Problem of Fascism*, London: New Left Books, 1974,

Francesco Raparelli, *La lunghezza dell'onda*, Milan: Ponte alle Grazie, 2009.

John Rawls, *A Theory of Justice*, Cambridge: Belknap Press, 1999.

Paul Romer, 'Endogenous Technical Change', *Journal of Political Economy*, 98(5), 1990.

Paul Romer, 'The Origins of Endogenous Growth', *Journal of Economic Perspectives*, 8(1), 1994.

Andrew Ross, *Nice Work If You Can Get It: Life and Labor in Precarious Times,* New York: New York University Press, 2009.

Eric Schlosser, *Fast Food Nation: The Dark Side of the All-American Meal*, Boston: Houghton Mifflin, 2001.

Trebor Scholz, *Uberworked and Underpaid: How Workers Are Disrupting the Digital Economy*, Cambridge: Polity Press, 2017.

Stephven Shukaitis, 'Recomposing precarity: Notes on the laboured politics of class composition', *Ephemera*, http://www.ephemerajournal.org/contribution/recomposing-precarity-notes-laboured-politics-class-composition

Vicki Smith and Esther Neuwirth, *The Good Temp*, Ithaca: Cornell University Press, 2008.

Rebecca Solnit, *Hope in the Dark: Untold Histories, Wild Possibilities*, New York: Nation Books, 2005.

Guy Standing, *The Precariat: The New Dangerous Class*, London: Bloomsbury, 2014.

Daniel Stedman Jones, *Masters of the Universe: Hayek, Friedman, and the Birth of Neoliberal Politics*, Princeton: Princeton University Press, 2012.

E.P. Thompson, *The Making of the English Working Class*, London: Penguin 2013.

Seth Tobocman, *Disaster and Resistance*, Oakland: AK Press, 2008.

Yanis Varoufakis, *And the Weak Suffer What They Must? Europe's Crisis and America's Economic Future*, New York: Nation Books, 2016.

Max Weber, *Economy and Society, Vol. 2*, University of California Press, 1928.

John Zerzan, *Running on Emptiness: The Pathology of Civilization*, Port Townsend: Feral House, 2008.